The Urban Economy and Housing

The Urban Economy and Housing

Edited by
Ronald E. Grieson
University of California,
Santa Cruz

LexingtonBooks
D.C. Heath and Company
Lexington, Massachusetts
Toronto

Library of Congress Cataloging in Publication Data
Main entry under title:

The Urban economy and housing.

   Based on papers presented at the Conference on
Urban Public Economics, held at University of
California, Santa Cruz, Oct. 1981.
   Includes bibliographical references.
   1. Housing policy—Congresses.   2. Urban economics
—Congresses.   3. Monetary policy—Congresses.
4. Interest and usury—Congresses.   I. Grieson,
Ronald E.   II. Conference on Urban Public Economics
(1981: University of California, Santa Cruz)
HD7287.5.U7 1982   363.5′8   81-48269
ISBN 0-669-05331-7

Published simultaneously in Canada

Printed in the United States of America

International Standard Book Number: 0-669-05331-7

Library of Congress Catalog Card Number: 81-48269

Contents

vi

Acknowledgments

This book is the end product of the Conference on Urban Public Economics held at the University of California, Santa Cruz, California, October 1981. The Conference was funded by the Seminar in Applied Economics/Public Finance of the University of California, Santa Cruz.

My thanks go out to the authors and conference participants who so willingly agreed to present and discuss papers at the conference and submit them for the volume. Acknowledgments need also be extended to the other members of the seminar, Professors Robert Adams, Sven Arndt, Jacob Michaelsen, and Peggy Musgrave, for their encouragement and assistance with financing and arrangements. Professor Edwin Mills of Princeton and Mr. Mike McCarroll of Lexington Books need also be thanked for their early encouragement of the conference and publication. Professors Robert Adams, Jacob Michaelsen, Peggy Musgrave, and Richard Musgrave helpfully agreed to chair sessions.

Perhaps most importantly, I must thank Chancellor Robert Sinsheimer and Vice-Chancellor John Marcum for encouraging and funding the conference and seminar.

Part I
Housing: Theoretical

1

The Supply of Urban Housing

Ronald E. Grieson
and *Richard J. Arnott*

In a recent article Barton Smith[1] developed a procedure for estimating the long-run supply elasticity of housing density and housing quality, and the elasticity of substitution between capital and land in the production of housing. Smith's paper significantly improves on most of the previous literature in its explicit treatment of quality. However, like most of the previous literature, it suffers from misused and imprecise terminology, which results in erroneous, or at least misleading, analysis.

The main purpose of this comment is to discuss terminological issues: the definition of quality and the importance in distinguishing between *supply* and *reduced-form* elasticities, between *partial* and *total* elasticities, and between *stock* and *flow* elasticities.

Review of Smith's Paper

The derivations in Smith are difficult to follow, owing to a lack of careful distinction between partial and total elasticities. It is therefore useful to review his results briefly.[2]

A competitive developer chooses the quality, Q, and density, D, of housing so as to maximize profits, π, per unit of land. The amount of housing per unit area of land is defined to equal QD. The cost of a unit of land, R, and the location-specific selling price, P, of housing are parametric to the developer in competition. The housing technology is represented by $K(Q, D)$, which indicates the amount of capital per unit area of land required to build at density D and quality Q. Hence, with the price of capital as *numéraire* (equal to one), the developer's profit-maximization problem is:

$$\max_{D,Q} \pi = PDG - K(Q,D) - R \qquad (1.1)$$

The first-order conditions are:

$$\frac{\partial \pi}{\partial D} = PQ - K_D = 0 \qquad K_D = \frac{\partial K}{\partial D}, \qquad (1.2a)$$

We would like to thank James MacKinnon for helpful comments and for the computational work.

and

$$\frac{\partial \pi}{\partial Q} = PD - K_Q = 0 \tag{1.2b}$$

Equations 1.2a and 1.2b relate the profit-maximizing location-specific housing quality and housing density to the location-specific housing price. These relationships may be inverted, so that the location-specific housing price may be viewed as a function of the profit-maximizing location-specific housing quality and housing density.

Performing the above analysis for all locations allows us to relate the housing prices at different locations to the corresponding profit-maximizing housing qualities and housing densities,

$$P = P(Q,D) \tag{1.3}$$

Furthermore, if, as is assumed, the urban economy is in long-run competitive equilibrium, and if there are constant returns to the production of housing,[3] then housing producers make zero profits. From equation 1.1 this implies that land values must be such that

$$R = PQD - K \tag{1.4}$$

Total differentiation of the value of housing per unit area of land, $E = PQD$, and of equation 1.4, viewing $P = P(Q,D)$, gives, respectively:

$$\frac{dE}{E} = \left(1 + \frac{1}{\varepsilon_Q}\right)\frac{dQ}{Q} + \left(1 + \frac{1}{\varepsilon_D}\right)\frac{dD}{D} \tag{1.5a}$$

and

$$\frac{dR}{R} = \frac{E}{R}\left(\frac{dQ}{\varepsilon_Q Q} + \frac{dD}{\varepsilon_D D}\right) \tag{1.5b}$$

which is derived using equations 1.2a and 1.2b where $\varepsilon_Q = (1/P_Q)(P/Q)$ and $\varepsilon_D = (1/P_D)(P/D)$ are partial elasticities. Equations 1.5a and 1.5b may be combined to eliminate the unmeasurable dQ/Q and to form an estimating equation for ε_Q and ε_D on the basis of market observables.

The Treatment of Quality

Smith gives the impression[4] that the definition of quality does not matter. In a sense this is correct since there are many consistent and general ways in which one can treat quality. However, the definition of quality ought to accord with popular usage, and if different researchers' results are to be comparable, ought to be standardized; otherwise, debates over empirical magnitudes may revolve around semantic ambiguities. Smith defines housing per unit area as QD. This formulation has the advantage of simplicity, but *the implicit definition of "quality" is at variance with popular usage of the word.*

Let us examine one of the implications of Smith's usage. Suppose that people have a taste for low buildings and open space. As a result, they are willing to pay less to live in an otherwise physically identical unit at higher density: when density doubles, the value (PQD) of a physically identical unit less than doubles. According to Smith's definition, since P is fixed at a certain location and density increased, quality has fallen, even though the physical characteristics of the unit are unaltered.

The following alternative treatment of housing quality, density, quantity, and locational attributes is suggested. Let $P(x)$ be the *average* price[5] of a unit of housing at location x of standardized quality and density, where x is an index of locational attributes which captures both accessibility and neighborhood quality; that is, $x = x(A,N)$, where A is accessibility and N is neighborhood quality. Also, define the quantity of housing[6] per unit area of land according to the function $H(\tilde{Q},D)$, where any $(\tilde{Q},D)$ such that $H(\tilde{Q},D) = \bar{H}$ has a value of $P(x)\bar{H}$ per unit area of land. As in Smith's formulation, D is density, but $\tilde{Q}$ is a measure of the *physical quality* of the housing unit, which aggregates over various attributes thereof: it is *independent of density*, and so differs from Smith's Q.

We assume that people's tastes for density are independent of housing quality in the sense that $H(\tilde{Q},D) = f(\tilde{Q})h(D)$. The specific cardinalization of $\tilde{Q}$ is analytically immaterial, but a particularly convenient one is $f(\tilde{Q}) = \tilde{Q}$, so that $H(\tilde{Q},D) = \tilde{Q}h(D)$. In this case, when the revenue obtained per unit area of land doubles, while location and density are fixed, quality doubles.

Note that $h(D)$ reflects people's tastes for density, and is unrelated to technology. A preference for low-density living in this formulation implies that $h' < 0$. In the rest of the comment, unless otherwise specified, Smith's usage of "quality" is retained.

Reduced Form and Supply Elasticities

Supply curves and supply elasticities do not depend on tastes. Unfortunately, this seems to have been forgotten in the housing supply literature. Both of Smith's *supply* elasticities depend on both tastes and technology, and should therefore be referred to as *reduced form* elasticities.[7] Since the particular cardinalization of quality adopted by Smith depends on tastes, it is evident that his *supply* elasticity of quality does also. To show that Smith's *supply* elasticity of density is dependent on tastes requires a slightly more detailed explanation. It was argued earlier that when people prefer to live at lower densities, increasing density (where quality according to Smith's definition remains fixed) must result in an improvement in the physical characteristics of housing units. How much quality must increase depends on people's tastes for density. Thus, the relationship between construction costs and density, while quantity remains fixed, $K(\bar{Q},D)$ depends on tastes, as does the *supply* elasticity of density which equals $K_D/K_{DD}D$.

The genuine supply elasticity ε_s is the elasticity of the height (number of stories) of the building with respect to marginal construction costs, the floor area per story, and the physical quality as defined herein held constant. Marginal construction costs per square foot of floor space in an apartment building, with fixed physical quality, are given in Table 1-1 as a function of height[8]. The computed local supply elasticity varies with height.

On the basis of these data and the assumption that individuals have no taste for recreational land or for building height, one may calculate what the partial stock elasticity of substitution between land and capital in the production of housing (physical quality fixed) would be if individuals had no taste for density. These elasticities are shown in Table 1-1. The difference between these elasticities of substitution and empirically estimated partial elasticities of substitution with respect to density (our definition of quality) could be attributed to individuals' tastes for density.

Grieson[9] has derived an approximate measure of the elasticity of supply, $TC/2LV$, where LV is land value and TC the total cost of the building inclusive of land, which is exact when individuals are indifferent as to density and when the marginal construction cost curve is linear. Applying this formula to another body of data,[10] he estimated elasticities of supply of various types of structures as between approximately 2 and 6, a result compatible with those presented here.

Partial and Total Elasticities

It is important to distinguish between partial and total elasticities. Although Smith does not make it explicit, the elasticity of substitution that he presents

$$Q_{KL} = \varepsilon_D \frac{R}{K} \qquad (1.6)$$

is the partial (quality fixed) stock elasticity of substitution between capital and land in the production of housing.[11,12] This differs from the *total* elasticity of substitution concept used by Muth et al.[13]—in which quantity and density vary simultaneously. This difference in the elasticity of substitution concept might account for why Smith's estimate of the elasticity

Table 1–1
Construction Cost Data and Elasticities

Height	Marginal Cost	ε_s	$\tilde{\sigma}_D{}^a$
8	26.76	6.93	0.142
12	28.35	6.01	0.416
16	29.73	4.73	0.446
20	31.16	3.29	0.488
24	32.93	3.70	0.512
28	34.37	2.66	0.527
32	36.14	2.86	0.532
36	37.66	2.11	0.542
40	39.59		

Source: Marshall Valuation Service.
Notes: The reason the elasticities are not monotonic with height is that Marshall and Swift present construction costs to the nearest cent per square foot, introducing rounding error.

The costs given in table 1–1 are costs per square foot of *floor space*. Arnott has computed the ratio of *living space* to *floor space* in a representative building as a funtion of the number of stories, and found that this ratio varies only between 0.74 and 0.76. The increased proportion of floor space allocated to elevators and stairwells as the number of stories increases is just about offset by the decreased proportion of the building floor area used for the lobby and entranceway. Hence the computed elasticities with respect to living space are very close to those given in table 1–1 for floor space. Details of the procedure for computing the ratio of living space to floor space are available from Arnott on request.
[a]$\tilde{\sigma}_D$ is the elasticity of substitution between capital and land in housing construction (physical quality fixed) when individuals are indifferent as to density.

of substitution is higher than those of other studies, which used Muth's definition.

Whether a partial or the corresponding total elasticity is of more interest depends on the model employed and the question addressed. In this context, total elasticities are probably of more interest than partial elasticities, since the profit-maximizing Q and D will vary simultaneously with P. Suppose the government wishes to ascertain the housing subsidy necessary to raise the average quality of housing in a market to $\bar{Q}$. It is not very helpful to know the partial elasticity of quality with respect to price with density fixed, since density will not remain fixed. Similarly, the total elasticity of substitution when both density and quality are variable is likely to be of more interest than the partial elasticities of substitution in which either density or quality is fixed.

Stocks or Flows

In general, there is no reason to believe that a flow elasticity equals the corresponding stock elasticity, so that it is important to distinguish between them. Muth's theoretical work is based upon flows. For instance, he uses the elasticity of substitution between land and capital services in the production of housing services. His empirical work is inconsistent in using stock value data to estimate the elasticity. Smith is consistent, however, in estimating the elasticity of substitution between land and capital stock in the production of the housing stock using value data.

Notes

1. Barton A. Smith, "The Supply of Urban Housing," *Quarterly Journal of Economics* 90 (1976): 389–405.

2. Our formulation of the problem differs inconsequentially from Smith's in that we treat capital expenditure as a function of housing quality and density, $K = K(Q,D)$, while he treats housing quality as a function of housing density and capital expenditure, $Q = Q(D,K)$.

3. If both these conditions are met, then construction at a given quality and density on two units of land is twice as expensive as on one unit of land.

4. Smith defines P^* to be the price of housing at a specific location *per unit of density*. He then sets $PQ = P^*$, justifying this as follows:

> Quality as defined here, like the concept of utility, has no measurable cardinal properties, but rather is merely an ordinal index of value. The only measurable market information is the total market price of each dwelling, P^*. It is assumed here that, given some definition of quality, a structure of market prices exists over which the entrepreneur has no control, such that $P^* = p(Q^*)$, where $p' > 0$. However, given any arbitrary ordering of quality, measured by Q^*, such that these conditions hold, another quality index, Q can always be defined through some monotonic transformation of Q^* so that P is a linear function of this new index Q. That is, $P^* = p(Q)$, and $P^*/Q = p' > 0$, for all Q. Because it simplified the analysis, such a definition of quality is used throughout the text of the paper so that the housing producer sees as given a fixed price per unit of housing quality at which he can sell each dwelling. (Barton A. Smith, "The Supply of Urban Housing," *Quarterly Journal of Economics* 90 (1976): 393. Reprinted with permission.)

5. The word *average* is inserted to reflect the fact that in a building at a specific location, the price of a unit of housing (our definition) may vary with the story. Often prices are higher for housing units on higher stories, where there is a better view and less polluted air. One could treat this explicitly by inserting F, floor, into the housing function $H(\cdot)$. It is simpler, however, not to do this.

6. $H(\tilde{Q},D)$ can be viewed as an hedonic index of housing or the quantity of housing measured in efficiency units.

7. This point is also made in R.J. Arnott, "The Reduced Form Price Elasticity of Housing," *Journal of Urban Economics* 5(1978): 293–304.

8. These costs are for reinforced concrete frame apartment buildings of average quality, with perimeters of 544 feet and floor areas of 9566 square feet, located in Toronto and built in 1976. They were computed using *Marshall Valuation Service* (Los Angeles: Marshall and Swift Publications Company, 1976).

9. R.E. Grieson, "the Economics of Property Taxes and Land Values: The Elasticity of Supply of Structures," *Journal of Urban Economics* 1(1974): 367–381.

10. R.E. Grieson, "The Supply of Rental Housing: Comment," *American Economic Review* 63 (1973): 433–436. Only density is assumed to vary.

11. The partial (quality fixed) stock elasticity of substitution in the production of housing is defined to be

$$\frac{R}{K} \left(\frac{\partial K}{\partial R} \right)_{Q=\bar{Q}} \equiv \frac{R}{KR_K}$$

where R_K is the change in land value associated with a change in construction costs, quality fixed. To prove that Smith's elasticity equals R/KR_K, it is necessary to show that $\varepsilon_D = 1/R_K$.

As previously assumed, $\pi = 0$ as K is varied. P, D and R are treated as functions of K and Q. Total differentiation of $\pi = PQD - K - R = 0$ with respect to K, Q fixed, gives the market condition:

$$P_K\bar{Q}D + (P\bar{Q}D_K - 1) - R_K = 0 \qquad (1.7)$$

The developer's problem, may be written as

$$\max_{K} = P\bar{Q}D(\bar{Q},K) - K - R \qquad (1.8)$$

Since the developer takes P and R as parametric, the first order-condition of equation 1.8 is

$$P\bar{Q}D_K = 1 \qquad (1.9)$$

Combining equations 1.7 and 1.9, and noting that $P_D = P_K K_D$, gives

$$R_K = \frac{P_D}{K_D} QD \qquad (1.10)$$

Finally, substituting $PQ = K_D$ from equation 1.2a, we obtain

$$R_K = \frac{P_D}{P} D = \frac{1}{\varepsilon_D} \qquad (1.11)$$

12. Smith argues that his data support the hypothesis that $\sigma_{KL} > 1$. He incorrectly computes the 95 percent confidence interval for σ_{KL} as (1.0, 1.4). If three- instead of two-digit accuracy is used, the 95% confidence interval is found to be (0.94, 1.36). However $\sigma_{KL} \geq 1$ at the 90 percent level.

13. R. Muth, *Cities and Housing* (Chicago: The University of Chicago Press, 1969).

2

Effects of the U.S. Tax System on Housing Prices and Consumption

Richard F. Muth

There are several features of the U.S. tax system that affect housing differently than other commodities. One of the best known is the personal-income-tax treatment of *income from owner-occupied* housing: homeowners are not required to report the *implicit* rental value of their dwelling as income. Instead, they may take deductions for mortgage interest and property taxes paid. They likewise pay no capital gains tax. Consequently the relative price of housing services to homeowners is lower than it otherwise would be. The corporate income tax also affects the relative price of owner-occupied housing. The rental rate of capital assets, gross of all taxes, must be higher in the corporate sector than in the unincorporated sector if the net return to capital after payment of taxes is to be the same for both sectors. Owner-occupied housing, of course, is one of the principal uses of capital in the unincorporated sector.

There are also several ways in which the corporate income tax impinges differentially on those corporations that produce rental housing as opposed to those which produce other goods. In addition to these taxes, the real-property tax, even if levied at uniform rates on residential and nonresidential capital, and the taxation of the capital income of persons may affect housing differently if the stock of capital assets for the economy as a whole is sensitive to the real after-tax returns to saving. This follows because the production of housing services is highly capital intensive as compared to all other commodities.

The above features of the U.S. tax system have, of course, received intensive study. Yet out current understanding of the issues raised is unsatisfactory in several important respects. At least a score of papers have been written on the partial equilibrium effects of the personal-tax treatment of owner, housing, but few have considered the effects of the tax system on the rental value of renter housing. The real-property tax has also been intensively studied, but most frequently in a partial equilibrium context. Most analyses

This chapter summarizes some of the research of a larger project entitled "Taxation and Housing." I'm happy to acknowledge the financial support of this project provided by the Hoover Institution at Stanford.

of the corporate income tax have paid no attention to its differential effects upon housing. Most important, perhaps, is the fact that most analyses of these taxes as they affect housing have ignored their general equilibrium effects. No analysis has to my knowledge, tried to access the effects of the tax system as a whole on housing in relation to all other commodities.

The first section of this chapter lays out the model upon which my assessment is based. It consists of two parts. The first develops the formulas that determine the gross rental rates of capital assets used in production as functions of the real interest rate, or the before personal-tax return to capital, and the parameters that describe the effects of the tax system. The second outlines the "two-and-a-half" sector general-equilibrium model that I used for calculating the overall real equilibrium for the economy as a whole.

The second section of this chapter also consists of two parts. The first describes how the calculations were done; the second, the results of the calculations themselves.

Two, perhaps three, major conclusions emerge from these calculations.

First, the general equilibrium effects of the tax system are indeed appreciable. Removing the personal-income-tax advantage to owner-occupied housing would result in a rise in the relative price of housing services to homeowners of approximately 15 percent at the initial real rate of interest. The resulting excess supply of capital assets would lead to a fall in the real interest rate—and in the new equilibrium the relative price of owner housing would be only about 10 percent greater than that with the tax advantage.

Second, the effects of the tax system as a whole on owner housing depend very importantly upon the elasticity of supply of capital assets to the economy as a whole. If this elasticity is zero, as many economists have long supposed it to be, then the U.S. tax system reduces the relative price of owner-occupied housing services by roughly 15 percent and increases the stock of owner-occupied housing capital by about 25 percent. If, however, this elasticity is as large as 0.4, the relative price of owner housing is only 3 percent smaller than it would be were there no taxes—while the stock is only 9 percent larger.

Finally, inflation has powerful effects upon the owner-occupied housing which arises from the nature of our tax system. With a 10 percent per year inflation and an increase of the marginal personal-income-tax rate from .2 to .3, in the real equilibrium of the economy, the relative price of owner-housing services would be 20 percent smaller than it would be in the real, noninflationary equilibrium. The rapid increase in real house prices since 1975, to say nothing of the rash of condominium conversions and the alleged crisis of the rental-housing industry, seems quite understandable for this reason.

Model

The model which serves as a basis for the calculations presented in the second section of this chapter consists of two basic elements. The first is a general formula relating the cost of capital to its users in terms of interest rates and various features of the tax system. The second is a general-equilibrium model for the production of housing services, both owner- and renter-occupied, and the production of other commodities. In this section I shall develop these two elements in turn.

Capital Rental Rates

The rental cost of capital to its users (other than homeowners) is determined by the solution of the following integral equation:

$$V(t) = cV_0\Delta + \int_t^T (R - Y - P)e^{-d(u-t)}dt + e^{-d(T-t)}[W(T) - G]$$

$$(2.1)$$

where V = value of an asset to its owner
$\quad R$ = rental cost of the asset to its owner gross of all taxes
$\quad Y$ = income taxes paid
$\quad P$ = property taxes paid
$\quad W(T)$ = sales price of the asset if sold at time T; $T \geq t$
$\quad G$ = capital-gains tax paid if the asset is sold
$\quad c$ = tax credit
$\quad \Delta = (1,0)$ for $t \geq 0$
$\quad d$ = the rate at which the owner discounts future gains and costs

Solving equation 2.1 is in general quite difficult. A particular problem is in specifying the amount offered for an asset if sold to someone else at a finite time. It is probably easiest to determine V first, first assuming that the original owner or his heir will hold it forever and, then, asking whether someone else would offer the original owner enough for the property to entice the owner to sell the asset and pay the capital gains tax. Such an investigation is beyond the scope of this paper. Here, I will merely assert that, to the degree of approximation employed below, I have yet to find an empirically plausible case in which $T \to \infty$ is not the optimal policy for the original owner. In what follows, therefore, I assume that the original owner holds the asset forever.

Even with this simplification, the solution to equation 2.1 might be rather awkward. I thus make further simplifications which essentially amount to a log-linear approximation to a more complicated reality. First, I assume income taxes are paid at a constant marginal rate, m, or that

$$Y = m(R - I - P - D) \qquad (2.2)$$

where I = interest payments on borrowed funds
  D = depreciation allowed for tax purposes

I also assume that nominal quantities such as asset rentals and values grow at a constant rate π on account of inflation, and decline at a constant real rate δ on account of depreciation and/or obsolesence. Consequently,

$$R = R_0 e^{(\pi - \delta)t} \qquad (2.3)$$

$$P = \rho V_0 e^{(\pi - \delta)t} \qquad (2.4)$$

$$I = (i + \pi) b V_0 e^{(\pi - \delta)t} \qquad (2.5)$$

where ρ = the property tax rate
  b = the constant ratio of borrowed funds to asset value

Finally, I assume that taxpayers use the declining-balance method for tax depreciation at constant rate τ or that

$$D = \tau V_0 e^{-\tau t} \qquad (2.6)$$

Taking $t = 0$ and substituting equations 2.1 through 2.6 into 2.1 yields

$$V_0 = c V_0 + [(1 - m)R_0 + mb(i + \pi)V_0 - (1 - m)\rho V_0]$$

$$\int_0^\infty e^{-(d - \pi + \delta)u} du + m\tau V_0 \int_0^\infty e^{-(d + \tau)u} du \qquad (2.7)$$

In general, d is a weighted average of the after-tax costs of equity and borrowed funds. For corporations, for whom I wish to use the solution, $d = i + \pi$, where i is the real, before-personal-tax rate of interest. Making this substitution, integrating and rearranging,

$$\frac{R_0}{V_0} = \left(\frac{i + \delta}{1 - m} \right) \left(1 - c - \frac{mb(i + \pi)}{(i + \delta)} - \frac{m\tau}{(i + \pi + \tau)} \right) + \rho$$

$$(2.8)$$

This formula is similar to many that have appeared in the literature in discussions of business investment, taxation, and related issues.

Several features of the U.S. personal-tax system suggest a separate, though similar to equation 2.1, definition of the value of an owner-occupied house. As mentioned earlier, homeowners need not include the implicit rental value of their dwelling as income. But they may deduct mortgage interest and property taxes paid. Moreover, the opportunity cost of equity funds to the homeowner is $(1 - m)$ times nominal interest earnings on taxable assets, so that $b = 1$ in equation 2.5. Finally, homeowners can effectively escape the payment of capital gains taxes. Hence, for homeowners,

$$V(t) = \int_t^T [R + mI - (1 - M)P]e^{-(i+\pi)(t-u)}du + e^{-(i+\pi)(T-t)}W(T)$$

$$(2.9)$$

Substituting equation 2.3 through 2.5 and noting that, since homeowners pay no capital gains taxes, $W(T)$ is equal to $V(T)$, solving equation 2.9 yields

$$\frac{R_0}{V_0} = (1 - m)(i + \rho) + \delta - m\pi \qquad (2.10)$$

independently of when a house is resold.

Finally, the returns to saving may be affected both by taxation and by inflation. Assuming that savers purchase financial assets denominated in nominal terms and noting that nominal interest payments are subject to tax, it follows immediately that the net after-personal-tax return to saving, r_n, is

$$r_n = (1 - m)i - m\pi \qquad (2.11)$$

General Equilibrium Model

Though space-rental consumption of housing services accounts for somewhat less than 10 percent of GNP, roughly half the U.S. economy's fixed capital stock is in the form of residential real estate. Moreover, housing services are produced using little, if any, market labor.[1] Since capital/labor ratios are so different in the production of housing services and other output, anything shifting capital into or out of the production of housing services may have important general equilibrium effects. In this section I will outline the general equilibrium model used to account for such effects.

The model outlined below is quite similar in most essential respects to the two-sector general equilibrium model first used by Arnold C. Harberger.[2] There are, however, two important differences. First, in part because differentiating equation 2.8 yields rather messy relationships, my model is stated in terms of levels of variables rather than in terms of their differential changes. Doing so means that, to the extent that the functional relationships employed approximate the correct ones, the changes I calculate are exact ones rather than first-order approximations. Second, since housing is produced in two different sectors, the owner- and renter-occupied housing sectors, and since housing uses so little market labor, I assume in my model that the output of housing services depends only on the stock of residential real estate. All market labor is assumed to be employed in the production of other commodities, which for simplicity I shall call the goods-producing sector. To allow for effects of current expenditures made for maintenance and repair, I have added .015 to the capital rental rates for both owner and renter housing.

In the model, expenditures on housing services are thus the product of the rental rate of residential fixed capital times its amount, or

$$K_j r_j = f_j \qquad j = \text{R,H} \tag{2.12}$$

where K = capital stock
$\quad\quad r$ = rental rate of the capital stock
$\quad\quad f$ = total expenditure on housing services
$\quad\quad R$ = rental-occupied housing
$\quad\quad H$ = owner-occupied housing

Knowing the f's from the national income accounts and calculating the r's from equations 2.8 and 2.10 for assumed actual values of the various variables contained therein yields initial values for residential capital stocks in the two sectors. The fraction of households who are owners is given by the following equation, which is similar to that used by Rosen and Rosen in their recent study of federal taxes and home-ownership,[3]

$$\ln g_{\text{H}} = \theta_0 + \theta_1 \frac{r_{\text{H}}}{r_{\text{R}}} \tag{2.13}$$

where g_{H} is the fraction of owner households. Equation 2.13 determines how many of the two kinds of dwellings are occupied, given their relative costs, while equation 2.14 gives the aggregate consumption of housing services and thus capital stock for each of the two tenure groups as a function of the price of housing services for that kind of housing relative to the price of goods, P_Y, namely:

$$K_j = C_j g_j \left(\frac{r_j}{P_Y} \right)^{n_j} \qquad j = \text{R,H} \tag{2.14}$$

The intercept terms, C_j, in equation 2.14 depend on the fraction of households inhabiting the particular kind of housing. They are so selected that a shift from, say, renter to owner housing affects the total stock of fixed residential capital only because of relative price effects.

The goods-production sector of my model is somewhat more complicated because both goods capital, K_Y, and market labor, L, are used in production. I assume the following production function:

$$Y = L^{1-\beta}(K_Y + \zeta L)^{\beta} \tag{2.15}$$

This function is a simple generalization of the Cobb-Douglas function, most of whose nice analytic properties it retains, while allowing for a nonunit elasticity of substitution in production, σ.[4] Indeed, σ and the factor-share ratio, s, are given by

$$\sigma = \frac{\beta w}{\beta w - \zeta r_Y} \tag{2.16}$$

$$s = \frac{rK_Y}{wL} = \frac{\beta}{1-\beta} - \frac{\zeta}{1-\beta}\frac{r_Y}{w} \tag{2.17}$$

where w is the wage rate of labor. Equations 2.16 and 2.17 can easily be solved for β and ζ, obtaining

$$\beta = \frac{\sigma s}{1 + \sigma s} \tag{2.18}$$

$$\zeta = \frac{(\sigma - 1)sw}{(1 + \sigma s)r_Y} \tag{2.19}$$

For assumed values of σ and s, one thus finds the associated production function parameters, given w and r_Y.

To solve the model, one needs relationships for capital stock demanded in the goods-production sector, and for the price of goods in terms of the wages-paid market labor and the rental value of goods-producing capital. By equating the ratio of marginal physical products of K_Y and L to the factor-price ratio, one finds

$$K_Y = \left(\frac{\beta}{1-\beta}\frac{w}{r_Y} - \frac{\zeta}{1-\beta}\right)L \tag{2.20}$$

Since L is assumed fixed and w and r_Y are known, K_Y can be determined. Because the production function in equation 2.15 is homogeneous of degree one, payments to productive factors equal total revenues, or

$$P_Y = \frac{wL}{Y} + \frac{r_Y K_Y}{Y} \qquad (2.21)$$

The average products of L and K_Y are found from equation 2.15 in terms of the capital/labor ratio in goods production; by equation 2.20, the latter are then expressed as functions of w and r_Y. Substituting the resulting expressions into equation 2.21 yields

$$P_Y = \frac{r_Y^{\beta}(w - \zeta r_Y)^{1-\beta}}{\beta^{\beta}(1 - \beta)^{1-\beta}} \qquad (2.22)$$

which, of course, is similar to the familiar Cobb-Douglas expression. Knowing w and r_Y determines P_Y. Alternatively, if P_Y and r_Y are known, equation 2.22 may be solved for w:

$$w = \beta^{\beta/(1-\beta)}(1 - \beta)P_Y^{1/(1-\beta)}r_Y^{-\beta/(1-\beta)} + \zeta r_Y \qquad (2.23)$$

Finally, I assume that the supply of capital assets to the economy as a whole is given by

$$K_s = K_0 r_n^{\varepsilon} \qquad (2.24)$$

where the returns to saving net of taxes is given by equation 2.11.

Calculations

To use the model outlined in the preceeding section in assessing the impact of the U.S. tax system, one needs to fit it to data which represent presumed current or base conditions. To do so one needs information on certain magnitudes such as the amount of output of owner and renter housing and the goods-producing sectors. One also needs information on the various tax and other parameters which affect the equilibrium capital-rental rates, as determined by equations 2.8 and 2.10. I will first describe how these values were selected and then present my calculations of the effects of various changes in tax policy.

Fitting the Model

Many units of measure are essentially arbitrary. I find it convenient to take the initial values of gross national product (GNP) and the wage rate to be unity. Using consumption expenditures on owner and renter housing, respectively, relative to GNP from the national income and product accounts for 1970,[5] the f's in equation 2.12 along with the calculated values of the r's from equations 2.8 and 2.10 determine the owner and renter capital stocks in units of GNP. It follows by definition of s_j with $w = 1_j$ that $L = f_Y/(1 + s)$, where $f_Y = 1 - f_R - f_H$. Given the capital-rental rate in the goods-producing sector, r_Y, and the parameters β and ζ inferred from equations 2.18 and 2.19, K_Y is determined by equation 2.20. From the condition that the quantity of capital assets demanded equals the quantity supplied, K_0 in equation 2.24 is then determined conditionally upon the values of ε and r_n.

The demand parameters for the housing sectors were established in a similar way. Rosen and Rosen[6] concluded from their study that the effect of the personal-income-tax treatment of income from owner housing has resulted in an increase in the fraction of dwellings which are owner-occupied of about .04, or from .60 to .64. This fraction plus values of r calculated from equations 2.8 and 2.10, using the tax parameters described later suggest a value for θ_1 of approximately $-.4$. The last parameter value plus the 1970 value of g_H, .629, was then used to determine θ_0.

The constant terms in the stock demand functions for owner and renter housing are rather more complicated since they depend upon the fraction of owner-occupied housing. Using *base-period* capital rentals and goods prices (whose calculation is described later), the assumed income elasticity of demand, and the base-period capital stock described earlier, a per-household constant term, γ_j, $j = R, H$, was calculated, as was the mean or weighted average of the two,

$$\gamma_M = g_{B,R}\gamma_R + g_{B,H}\gamma_H \qquad \text{where } g_{B,j}$$

is the base-period fraction of units of the jth tenure type. The C's in equation 2.14 were then assumed to be of the form

$$C_j = g_{B,m}\gamma_j + (g_j - g_{B,j})\gamma_M \qquad \text{where } j = R, H$$

It is easy to verify that a change in g_j affects $K_H + K_R$ only through relative price effects; for $\eta_H = \eta_R$ and $r_H = r_R$, the total is invariant to the g_j's.

The only other important value to calculate for the base period is the relative price of goods, P_Y. Substituting $w = 1$ and the base-period value of r_Y

into equation 2.22 gives this value. The general price level $P_g = f_R r_R + f_H r_H + f_Y P_Y$ may then be calculated. In subsequent computations P_g is held constant, so that changes in the $r_j, j = R,H$, determined P_Y. P_Y plus r_Y calculated from equation 2.23 then determine w from equation 2.23. At this point it is also worth noting that net national product (NNP) at any point in the calculations is determined by deducting the product of the assumed true depreciation rate multiplied by capital stock summed over the three sectors from GNP.

The behaviorial parameter values I have used for most of my calculations, which I think of as default values, are displayed in table 2-1. I have already explained the motivation for my selection of θ_1's value. Some studies have found a much greater responsiveness of the selection of home-ownership over renting so I have also made some calculations using $\theta_1 = -1$. I have long believed from a variety of comparisons that the substitution elasticity of housing demand is approximately unity, and the assumption of a unit elasticity of substitution in goods production seems as justifiable empirically as any other. I have also made calculations using numerical values of 0.75 in turn for these parameters, with little difference in the results. The factor-share ratio was calculated from data in the national income and product accounts by taking national income originating less compensation of employee divided by the latter in 1970 for all industries less real estate. Finally, regarding the elasticity of the stock of capital with respect to the returns to savings, most economists have long believed that saving is more or less a constant fraction of income in the long run, regardless of the real returns to saving. With the recent decline in the fraction of income saved and the real returns to saving, however, such beliefs are perhaps less firmly held. Therefore, as an alternative to $\varepsilon = 0$, I have also used Michael J. Boskin's recent estimate of 0.4.[7] It turns out that the only really important qualitative difference in the results occurred when I varied the value of this last parameter.

In the calculations I assumed that the real rate of interest, i, in equations 2.8, 2.10, and 2.11, is equal to .06 under the current system of taxation. I

Table 2–1
Default Behavioral Parameter Values

Parameter	Value
θ_1	−.4
η_R	−1
η_H	−1
σ	1
s	0.229
ε	0

base this judgment on the fact that conventional first-mortgage interest rate averaged just under this figure in 1965–66, following a decade or so of essentially zero inflation. Others have argued, however, that the real rate is considerably smaller, perhaps .03. Using the latter as the actual or base-period rate yielded results that are qualitatively similar to those presented below, although the quantitative effect of the U.S. tax system on owner-occupied housing was somewhat smaller.

The other parameter values used in determining base-period rental rates are displayed in table 2-2. The marginal tax rates employed were determined by comparing incremental taxes paid relative to incremental income before tax as between adjacent income classes in the *1970 Statistic on Income*. This exercise suggested that the marginal personal-income-tax rate averaged about .2. As several studies have found previously, this rate was remarkably constant over a relatively wide range of incomes. The marginal personal-tax rate is the appropriate one for evaluating both the real returns to saving and the tax advantage to homeownership. The evaluation of marginal rates for all corporations less real estate, in which rental housing is included, suggested both a relative constancy of the effective marginal rate and that the statuatory maximum rate of .48 was reached for firms with business receipts as low as a half million to a million dollars. For real estate firms, the marginal rate for firms with receipts as large or larger than the latter figure was considerably smaller, about .35, and there are relatively few such firms. For corporations producing rental housing, a marginal rate of .3 might even be appropriate, though I have used the higher one.

My estimates of the fraction of funds which are borrowed and depreciation rates for tax purposes are also calculated from data in the *1970 Statistics of Income*. For all corporations, less real-estate, depreciation and depletion divided by book value of assets less accumulated depreciation and depletion was just over 10 percent. For real-estate corporations it was about 4.4 percent. The latter value agrees quite closely with what would be expected from doubling the declining-balance depreciation with a useful life of 45

Table 2–2
Assumed Capital-Rental Parameter Values

	Sector		
	Y	*R*	*H*
m	.48	.35	.20
δ	.10	.02	.02
ρ	.02	.02	.02
b	.36	.65	na
τ	.10	.044	na

years. The former value, 10 percent, however, appears to be about the same as true depreciation implied by Department of Commerce estimates of depreciation of nonresidential fixed capital, which I also use. For residential real estate I have used 2 percent as the true depreciation rate.[8] The relative importance of debt financing was also found from the *1970 Statistice of Income* by dividing debt by debt plus equity.[9] Finally, the only good nationwide data I know of, which refer to new FHA-insured homes, suggest average property-tax rates of about 2 percent per year or slightly under. There are, of course, frequent assertions made that effective tax rates are lower, and equally frequent assertions that they are higher for nonresidential property. In the absence of any reliable data, I use the same rate for all sectors.

Results

The results of the base solution—what I take to be the actual state of the U.S. economy around 1970 in the absence of inflation—are shown in Table 2-3. They imply that about half the economy's capital stock is in residential real estate, which accords with Department of Commerce fixed capital stock estimates. The implied capital/output ratio of about 2 is rather too low, however. The primary reason for the differences in capital-rental rates between the goods-producing and housing sectors is differences in depreciation rates. Rental rates net of depreciation (and of maintenance and repair expenditures for the housing sectors) are .102 for goods producing, .084 for rental housing and .064 for owner housing. Even so, the difference in implied rates of return for goods-producing and owner-occupied-housing capital seem substantial.

Table 2-4 shows the new general equilibrium solution obtained if the personal-income-tax advantage to homeownership is eliminated, or m in equation 2.10 set equal to zero. The initial effect of so doing, of course, is to raise the rental rate of owner housing capital to .115. At this higher rate, however, there is an excess supply of capital assets for the economy as a whole. Consequently, the real before tax rate of return on capital, i, must fall. Once it has fallen to the new equilibrium level of .054, r for the H sector has fallen by about one-third of its initial increase. The fall in the real rate of interest also reduces the rental rate for goods producing capital by about one percentage point, or about halfway from its base solution to its no-tax solution level (to be discussed later). Associated with the change is a fall in owner-housing capital of about 16 percent and an increase of goods-producing capital of about 6 percent. These results suggest that the general equilibrium effects of the homeowner tax advantage are indeed substantial. With the increase in goods-producing capital, the real wage rises by about 1

Table 2–3
Base Solution

Variable	Value	
i	.06	
g_H	.629	
w	1.0	
NNP	.898	

Sector	r	K
Y	.202	0.838
R	.119	0.227
H	.099	0.658
S	.048	1.723

percent. Moreover, national income rises by about two-thirds of 1 percent with the greater equalization of net of depreciation capital-rental rates.

Table 2-5 shows the impact of removing all the important taxes that differentially affect housing services as opposed to the production of other commodities. Since removal of corporate income and property taxes as well as the homeowner tax advantage leads to an excess demand for capital assets, the real rate of interest rises to .083. At this higher rate, the rental rates of capital assets net of depreciation are equalized among the three sectors. The calculated result suggests that the tax system as a whole reduces the relative price of owner-occupied housing by about 16 percent and increases the stock of owner-housing capital by about 26 percent. Real wages are about 2 percent higher in the no-tax as opposed to the base solution, while NNP is about 1.2 percent greater—small in percentage terms but of the order or $30 billion. Note also that, for the default parameters used in the

Table 2–4
Removal of Homeowner Tax Advantage

Variable	Value	
i	.054	
g_H	.595	
w	1.01	
NNP	.904	

Sector	r	K
Y	.193	0.886
R	.112	0.269
H	.109	0.568
S	.043	1.723

Table 2–5
Removal of All Taxes

Variable	Value	
i	.083	
g_H	.588	
w	1.021	
NNP	.909	

Sector	r	K
Y	.183	0.944
R	.118	0.260
H	.118	0.519
S	.083	1.723

calculations discussed to this point, specifically for $\varepsilon = 0$, these differences are due wholly to the personal-income-tax treatment of income from owner-occupied housing and the corporate-income tax. For, if the stock of capital to the economy as a whole is perfectly inelastic with respect to the after-tax returns to saving, a real property tax at uniform rates on all capital and taxing returns to saving have no effect at all on the allocation of capital and its gross rental rates as among the different sectors.

As I have indicated previously, I have calculated solutions of the type just described for a variety of different parameter values. With a few notable expections, the results of these calculations were remarkably similar and the conclusions from them quite robust. This was especially the case in regard to the homeowner tax advantage itself. In virtually every calculation J made, it reduced the relative price of owner-occupied housing services by about 10 percent and increased the stock of owner-occupied housing on the order of 15 percent. Moreover, the results were virtually the same whether the personal-tax treatment was introduced with all other taxes present or no other ones. The only exception to this result was the case where $\theta_1 = -1$ rather than $-.4$. Here the homeowner tax treatment increased the fraction of home-owners from about 55 to 63 percent in the presence of all other taxes and increased the stock of homeowner capital by about 25 percent.

The results also suggest that the corporation income tax by itself has an important effect upon owner-occupied housing. The introduction of such a tax, given that the homeowner tax advantage, real-property tax, and tax on savings already exist, reduces the relative price of housing to homeowners by 5 to 8 percent depending upon the specific parameter values used. Similarly, the stock of owner-occupied residential capital rises from 60 to 10 percent.

These calculations are all somewhat larger numerically if the corporate-income tax is introduced where no other taxes are present. The relative price of housing services to homeowners falls by around 10 percent and the stock of owner-housing capital rises by about 12 percent—somewhat more if homeownership is more responsive to relative owner/renter prices. Finally, the effects of the corporate-income tax are only about half as large if $\varepsilon = .4$ rather than if $\varepsilon = 0$.

Indeed, several notably different results occur when the elasticity of the supply of capital to the economy as a whole is positive. Most important, perhaps, is the effect of the real-property tax. As is now well known, if $\varepsilon = 0$, a uniform real-property tax has no effect upon the allocation of capital among sectors or on capital-rental rates gross of taxes. For $\varepsilon = .4$, however, a real-property tax of .02 for all sectors increases the relative price of housing services by about 8 percent if no other taxes exist, and reduces the stock of owner- and renter-housing capital by a similar amount with unit substitution elasticities of demand. It does so because the economy's total capital stock is reduced by about 7 percent. The effect upon housing is differentially strong because housing is capital intensive relative to goods production. Partly for this reason and partly because the effects of the corporate-income tax on housing are weaker when $\varepsilon = .4$, the overall impact of the tax system on owner-occupied housing is considerably smaller. When $\varepsilon = 0$, the tax system as a whole tends to reduce the relative price of homeowner housing services by about 15 percent and to increase the stock of owner-occupied housing by about 25 percent. For $\varepsilon = .4$ and all other parameters as shown in table 2-1, these changes are only about 3 and 9 percent, respectively. Any judgment, then, of the effect of our tax system on owner-occupied housing depends critically on one's judgment about the responsiveness of savings to its real return.

The calculations also reveal one interesting finding—a genuine "second-best" effect. With $\varepsilon = 0$, eliminating the real property tax in the presence of the homeowner tax advantage and the corporate income tax actually reduces NNP slightly. The reason is as follows. The other two taxes make the returns to capital lower for owner-occupied housing than for goods production. Since capital costs are relatively more important for housing, eliminating the real property tax not only widens the disparity, but also withdraws more capital into the owner-occupied housing sector. The capital stock in the owner-occupied housing was too large relative to other uses before the elimination of the real-property tax. For $\varepsilon = .4$, however, eliminating the real property tax in the presence of other taxes increases the total capital stock by about 6 percent. The effect of a larger capital stock more than offsets its increased misallocation and produces a slight rise in NNP.

Finally, I would like to comment upon my model's implication for the effect of inflation on our tax system. Many writers have noted that inflation increases the distortions caused by our tax system. This is the case partly because we tax nominal rather than real interest payments, the capital costs are relatively more important for housing. The distortions are also increased to the extent marginal tax rates rise because surtax brackets are defined in nominal rather than real terms. What my calculations reveal, however, is the surprising strength of such effects. With an inflation rate of 10 percent per year and a marginal personal tax rate of .3, the real before-tax depreciation return to goods-producing capital rises only slightly—from .202 to .204. For goods producers, the effect of larger nominal-interest deductions almost counterbalances smaller real deductions for depreciation. Interest payments are relatively more important for housing producers, however. Consequently, at $i = .06$, the capital rental rate for producers of rental housing falls to .093, for owners to .061, and there is an excess demand of amost 30 percent of the existing capital stock. As table 2-6 shows, the new equilibrium real-interest rate is .087 is almost 50 percent greater than without inflation. Even at the higher real-interest rate, the relative price of owner-occupied housing services falls by almost 20 percent. Moreover, real wages fall by about 4 percent and NNP by about 2.5 percent from the base solution, where a zero rate of inflation is assumed. The real wage and NNP effects are roughly twice as large as produced by out tax system alone.

Now, of course, my calculations refer to long-run equilibrium position in which the capital stock has adjusted fully to inflation. Because of the long life of residential capital, it seems unlikely to me that the U.S. economy would as yet have fully adjusted to a 10 percent inflation rate. Still, these calculations make the rise in real house prices in the U.S. in the late 1970s more understandable. They also suggest that inflation, given our current tax system, may have substantial real costs over and above those associated with the tax that inflation imposes upon the holding of cash balances.

Table 2–6
Effect of Inflation Plus "Bracket Creep"

Variable	Value	
i	.087	
g_H	.677	
w	.961	
NNP	.876	

Sector	r	K
Y	.242	0.671
R	.124	0.183
H	.080	0.868
S	.031	1.723

Note: Assuming a marginal personal-income-tax rate = .3

Notes

1. According to National Income and Product Account Data for 1970, the real estate industry—which includes the production of housing services—accounted for almost three-tenths of national income less compensation of employees but only about 1 percent of full-time equivalent employment.

2. "The Incidence of the Corporation Income Tax," *Journal of Political Economy* 70 (June 1962): 215–40.

3. Harvey S. Rosen and Kenneth T. Rosen, "Federal Taxes and Homeownership: Evidence from Time Series," *Journal of Political Economy* 88 (February 1980): 59–75.

4. Equation 2.15 is sometimes called a VES (variable elasticity of substitution) function because the value of σ depends not only on the capital/labor ratio but also on β and ζ.

5. I allocated farm-housing expenditures among owner and renter housing in proportion to the respective fractions of the two tenures for rural farm dwellings shown in the 1970 census. Though this probably involves some error since farm-owner units probably contain more capital per dwelling than farm-renter units, the total space-rental value for farm housing is small relative to that for nonfarm housing.

6. Rosen and Rosen, "Federal Taxes."

7. Michael J. Boskin, "Taxation, Saving, and the Rate of Interest," *Journal of Political Economy* 86 (April 1978): S3–S27.

8. This is the value estimated and used by Leo Grebler, David M. Blank, and Louis Winnick, *Capital Formation in Residential Real Estate: Trends and Prospects* (Princeton, N.J.: Princeton University Press, 1956), esp. App. E, pp. 377–382.

9. Specifically, debt is defined as the sum of mortgages, notes, bonds, and loans from stockholders, while equity is capital stock, surplus and retained earnings less the cost of treasury stock.

3

Housing Investment, Housing Consumption, and Tenure Choice

Jerome Rothenberg

Most of the standard theoretical treatments of urban housing markets have focused on housing as a consumption good, whether or not they have emphasized the durability of the capital that provides the service.[1] My own work, of which the present chapter is a part, while strongly emphasizing very important consequences of durability, has until quite recently also concentrated on a decision calculus exclusively dependent on the consumption of housing services as part of a consumption-mix question. But the present strong long-lasting general inflation in the United States, and the higher inflation of housing prices that has accompanied it in many places, have raised persistent questions about the use of the ownership of housing property as a hedge against inflation. The issue of housing assets in optimal portfolio management has become timely and important.

This chapter attempts to raise the question of housing ownership in the context of protfolio management, but to integrate it with the theory of the household consumption-mix. In the course of doing so, I shall concentrate on only one type of housing ownership. Let us distinguish between the owning of housing property as a landloard and as an owner-occupant. I am chiefly concerned with owner-occupancy, although some comparison will be given between the evaluations of the two roles in delineating the market equilibrium process.

I've divided this chapter into five parts. The first presents the model of portfolio: consumption choice for the individual household. The second relates the portfolio decision aspect of choice with that of current consumption. The third uses these materials to explicate a theory of household tenure choice. The fourth aggregates the analysis to the level of market equilibrium. Finally, the last indicates how the model can be applied to phenomena like inflationary processes.

Model of Portfolio: Consumption Choice for an Individual Household

Housing Choice for Consumption and Investment

The household can obtain current housing services either by renting them from a landlord or by occupying a dwelling unit owned by itself. While the

29

larger housing-market model of which this is a part emphasizes the multi-dimensional heterogeneity of housing, in the present work I drastically simplify to a single dimension of a *quality/quantity*, or *amount, size,* or *level* (*H*). Owner-occupiers (S) and renters (R) consume an identical range of housing service levels; that is, each level *H* consumed by renters is identical to level *H* consumed by owner-occupiers. But there is one difference in the nature of the consumption: an owner-occupier of *H* obtains a set of consumption experiences, opportunities, and responsibilities not equally open to a renter. An S has the right to modify, adapt, repair the premises with more flexibility than an R. S has more security of tenure, more privacy than an R in similar premises; also, both the responsibility for maintenance and the opportunity to employ a wider variety of inputs and technologies (including own labor) than is open to a tenant.

We summarize this by defining a variable called *D*, the consumption elements in owner-occupancy. *D* is a fixed, all-or-nothing variable, being present in constant size for owner-occupancy, and entirely absent for rental tenancy. The size of *D* does not vary with *H*.

We assume the market is perfect, so a rental-dwelling unit costs a price per unit of service, P_H, which can be realized as well by an owner-occupier who decides to rent its erstwhile owner-occupied unit. In the U.S. owner-occupancy also carries with it substantial tax advantages over rental status. The *tax incentive* influence on tenure choice is a very important topic in its own right. In further elaborations of the present model, I intend to examine this influence systematically. The present analysis largely omits explicit consideration of the tax system. Therefore I simplify its effect by collapsing all tax advantages into *D*, the *consumption* elements in owner-occupancy. Moreover, I neglect tax advantages on property owned for rental purposes. So P_H is the price of both a rental unit providing *H* level of services *and* of an owner-occupancy unit providing the same *H* level as well as *D*.[2]

The explicit-implicit rental parity plus the existence of *D* as a so-called free byproduct of owner-occupancy imply that a household making its first investment in purchasing a housing asset for its portfolio will find it advantageous to intend the unit for owner-occupancy (or at least one unit of a multiple-unit structure). Instead of paying $P_H H$ for *H* housing services by continuing to be a tenant, the household would be implicitly paying $P_H H$ for both *H* and *D*, which gives higher utility. For this reason we assume in the model that all households owning at least one dwelling property will be owner-occupiers. Tenants are assumed to hold no housing assets in their portfolio.

On the consumption side owner-occupancy brings a level of housing services, *H* and certain other consumption elements, *D* (including our simplified package of tax advantages from owner-occupancy). On the portfolio side, it brings the usual two benefit ingredients: an annual income flow (implicitly PH) and the prospects for capital gain (α, rate of appreciation in the price of the property). The implicit income flow is the elimination of the need to make an annual outlay of PH if the household were a tenant. So this asset has a rate of return in which the benefits are an explicit financial opportunity (α) and a joint-product "free" consumption (incorporating stylized tax advantages).

Housing investment embodies two kinds of cost. Rarely is a house bought outright. Generally a mortgage loan is obtained to joint-finance the investment. The paid-up equity, a sum less than—usually much less than—the total value of the investment, represents for the investor a decreased availability of purchasing power for other consumer goods and financial investments in the present period. In addition, the mortgage interest payable in the next period represents a decrease in purchase power in that period.

Housing investment competes with other portfolio opportunities. Its overall net returns must compare favorably with those of other portfolio assets for owner-occupancy to be sought. Moreover, the amount of housing bought as an investment must be balanced against both the claims of alternative portfolio investments and of other forms of current consumption—since housing investment determines a specific level of housing consumption and influences the size of alternative consumption. So two kinds of tradeoff are involved: current housing versus other current consumption, and present versus future consumption. Both must be included in the model.

In selecting an optimal budgetary allocation across these dimensions, the household is faced with a distinctive institutional constraint in its decision about investment in housing property. In U.S. cities, the combination of government zoning and code regulations results in an effective minimum character of housing property. We reflect this in *a minimum permissible level of investment in housing to secure owner-occupancy* (I^*). So investment in housing is a lumpy investment. Any I less than I^* gains no legal dwelling, so is a financial waste. Thus, the calculation as to whether to shift from rental to ownership status involves the decision whether an investment of at least I^* is more attractive overall than zero investment.

Context and Dimensions of the Model

The model addresses itself to the budgetary allocation problem facing a given household in the first (present) period. It must allocate its outlay resources now over two forms of current consumption and two forms of portfolio asset that embody opportunities for additional future consumption. In each period the two consumption goods are housing services with or without the consumption elements of owner-occupancy, that is, H or (H,D), and a residual composite nonhousing commodity, Z. The two portfolio assets are housing property, I, and a composite nonhousing financial asset. The two assets are *durable*: they continue to generate an annual flow of returns (explicit or implicit) into the indefinite future. They may differ in riskiness. If so, the differences are priced in the market. Rates of return as discussed here are expressed *net of risk premia*, or discounts.

The approach assumes that the household's allocation decisions today between present and future consumption, and between holdings of the two assets for defined consumption, are based upon a period-by-period allocation for maximum advantage. The tradeoff between present and future consumption depends on a personal time-preference structure, which explicitly evaluates one against the other; but the evaluation of any specific consumption *mix* for one period is assumed not to be affected by the consumption mix for another period (quasiseparability). Each depends on the structure of relative prices in each (including expected price changes in the future). This simplifies the household's utility function to throw into relief the major issues being addressed.

The household's desired tradeoffs from present to future requires that future utility be calculated for alternative allocations to today's portfolio. This requires knowing the money value of the assets in the future and what combinations of consumer goods this money value can buy. These derive from expectations about future asset and consumer-good prices. Application of preferences to this feasible future consumption set indicates a maximum future utility gain from each present allocation to today's portfolio. Balance between this maximum future income and the minimum utility that must be sacrificed today provides the basis for the equilibrium choice.

To contend with the durability of assets so as to give the household a continuing incentive to hold a portfolio in the next period, I have divided the temporal decision space into three periods. Period 1 is the present, when the allocation decision focused on in this paper must be made. No actual decisions for any future times are made in the present other than what assets will be carried over beyond the present. The future is divided into two periods, periods 2 and 3. These two are unequal in length. Period 2 is similar to period 1 in duration, but period 3 is everything thereafter. As indicated above, the period-1–period-2 tradeoff depends on knowledge about asset and commodity prices in the future. We assume that the household has grounds for discriminating predictions about these prices for period 2, but the uncertainty connected with period 3 is so great that no such discriminations are possible between period 2 and 3: that is, the household simply projects a common-price trend for all commodities into period 3. Since *relative* prices will thereby be equal in periods 2 and 3, the reference optimal mixes necessary for utility maximization that hold for the former will hold as well for the latter. Our chief interest is in the present-future interchange, so this flattening of the dimensionality of the future does little damage.

The model is formulated for an individual household. When we aggregate to the market level, we shall allow households to differ with respect to utility function, income and wealth, and price expectations.

Specification of the Model

Utility Function. Each household has a utility function which, under our assumption of quasi separability for intertemporal preferences, can be expressed as a set of identical one-period consumption evaluations:

$$T = T[U_1(H_1, D_1, Z_1), U_2(H_2, D_2, Z_2), U_3(H_3, D_3, Z_3)] \quad (3.1)$$

where T = the welfare index for the household
$\quad U_i$ = the direct one-period consumption evaluation function, such that U_1, U_2 and U_3 are the same function for consumption-mix preferences but $(\partial T/\partial U_1) > (\partial T/\partial U_2) > (\partial T/\partial U_3)$ because of discounting (time preference)
$\quad H_i$ = consumption of housing services at level H in period i
$\quad D_i$ = the consumption component of owner occupancy in period i
$\quad Z_i$ = the consumption of the composite good at level Z in period i

Our interest in integrating financial investment and consumption aspects of housing throws into relief the effect of this period's portfolio holdings (of housing and the nonhousing asset) on next period's consumption opportunities. Moreover, since the effect of this period's housing-tenure choice on *this* period's consumption behavior is our main concern, the influence of the former on next period's consumption is important primarily in affecting this year's consumption via the intertemporal tradeoff between present and future consumption. For these reasons it is more illuminating to specify the utility function in a way that directly expresses the effect of portfolio holdings on future budgetary opportunities. We therefore convert the periods-2 and -3 evaluation functions into a composite indirect evaluation function:

$$W = W[U(H_1, D_1, Z_1), V(B_1, P_{H_2}, P_{Z_2}, r, \gamma)] \quad (3.2)$$

where $V(\cdot)$ = an indirect valuation (utility) function for periods 2 and 3
$\quad B$ = the size of budgetary opportunities available in period 2 (the money value of the investment portfolio carried over from

period 1 plus period 2's noninvestment annual income flow—
to be explicitly defined later)

P_{H_2} = the price per unit of housing services in period 2

P_{Z_2} = the price per unit of composite-good consumption in period 2

r = the annual income yield for each dollar's worth of nonhousing
assets (the interest rate)

γ = the common expected rate of price appreciation of housing
and nonhousing assets between periods 2 and 3

The utility function is to be interpreted as follows. Given a period-1 budget constraint—which includes annual noninvestment income plus the value of initial portfolio holdings of nonhousing assets (and assuming zero housing assets carried over from a period earlier than the present, period 1)[3]—consider some feasible mix of H_1, Z_1 and holdings of A_1 (end of period-1 holding of nonhousing assets) and I_1 (end of period-1 holding of ownership in owner-occupied housing with capital value I_1).[4]

Since next period's annual noninvestment income is given, along with the interest rate on A and the expected price appreciation of A and I, this period-1 allocation determines the budget opportunity for period 2. We are given also the period-2 prices of H and Z and the portfolio returns available between periods 2 and 3, along with consumer-good prices in period 3. Function V collapses all this information by indicating the maximum *one-period* utility level derivable by allocating period 2's budget over H_2 and Z_2 as well as added consumption purchasing power in period 3 via carryover portfolio holdings. The U_2 and U_3 functions, and the discounting of period-3 utility with respect to period 2 as given by the T function, enable the periods-2–3 maximization to take in terms of an optimal (H_2, Z_2, I_2, A_2)—implying also an optimal H_3, Z_3. So for some (H_1, Z_1, I_1, A_1), we pair optimal mix (H_2, Z_2, I_2, A_2), and this gives (via the original T function) a value of W. Each period-1 allocation thus generates, by optimal pairing with a periods-2–3 mix, an overall utility value, W. This process generates the overall utility function. In it, function U gives period-1 evaluations, function V gives optimal compatible periods-2–3 evaluations, and $(\partial W/\partial V)/(\partial W/\partial U)$ gives the intertemporal tradeoff between present and future consumption—the marginal rate of time preference. This formulation makes it possible to see directly the effect of present investments on future consumption opportunities via $\partial B/\partial I_1$ and $\partial B/\partial A_1$.

For

$$W_U > 0 < W_V$$

$$U_{H_1}, U_{D_1}, U_{Z_1} > 0$$

$$V_B > 0$$

$$V_{P_{H_2}} < 0 > V_{P_{Z_2}}$$

$$W: W_{UU} < 0 W_{VV}$$

$$U_{HH}, U_{DD}, U_{ZZ} < 0$$

Future Budgetary Opportunities. The size of budgetary opportunities in period 2, B, is an important mechanism by which housing investment decisions influence and are influenced by both the balance of present and future consumption and the balance between housing and nonhousing portfolio holdings.

Period-2 budget opportunity is the sum of period 2's regular income flow (which is assumed constant over time) and the money value of the portfolio and its associated income flow at the beginning of period 2.

$$B \equiv Y + A_1(1 + \beta + r) + I_1(1 + \alpha) - M_1(1 + i) \quad (3.3)$$

where B = period-2 budget opportunities
$\quad Y$ = the regular periodic-income flow (constant over time)
$\quad A_1$ = the total money value of nonhousing assets carried over from period 1 to period 2
$\quad I_1$ = the total money value of housing assets carried over from period 1 to period 2
$\quad M_1$ = the size of the mortgage loan borrowed in period 1
$\quad \beta$ = the expected value appreciation of A_1 between periods 1 and 2
$\quad \alpha$ = the expected value appreciation of I_1 between periods 1 and 2
$\quad r$ = the rate of interest earned on A_1 net of tax
$\quad i$ = the rate of interest paid on M_1 net of tax

This initial period-2 budget is assumed to be spent during period 2 on period-2 consumption and portfolio holdings designed to be carried over into period 3. It is given as follows:

$$B = \delta_1(I_2 - M_2) + A_2 + \delta_2 P_{H_2} H_2 + P_{Z_2} Z_2 \quad (3.4)$$

$$\delta_1 = \begin{matrix} 1 & \text{if } I_2 \geq I* \\ 0 & \text{if } I_2 < I* \end{matrix}$$

$$\delta_2 = \begin{matrix} 0 & \text{if } I_2 \geq I* \\ 1 & \text{if } I_2 < I* \end{matrix}$$

where

and

Period-2 budget opportunities come from the ability to cash in both one's periodic income and one's whole initial portfolio plus net accrued asset income. (I assume interest is paid on both A and M at the beginning of period 2.) One's total income at the beginning of period 2 is Y plus interest return on A_1, rA_1, less interest owed on the mortgage loan, iM_1. The market value of assets is $A_1(1 + \beta)$ plus the value of one's equity in housing property, $I_1(1 + \alpha) - M_1$. Period-1 value of equity is $(I_1 - M_1)$.

Equation 3.4 shows the disposition of B during period 2 into consumption and portfolio holdings $(I_2 - M_2)$ and A_2. Term $(I_2 - M_2)$ drops out if the household is a renter (R); term $P_{H_2}H_2$ drops out if the household is an owner-occupier (S).

Budget Constraint for Period-1 Choice. The household's equilibrium in period is the choice that maximizes welfare, (1), subject to the budget constraint operative in period 1. This constraint is as follows:

$$Y + A_0(1 + r) = A_1 + \delta_3(I_1 - M_1) + \delta_4 P_{H_1}H_1 + P_{Z_1}Z_1 \qquad (3.5)$$

where

$$\delta_3 = \begin{array}{ll} 1 & \text{if } I_1 \geq I^* \\ 0 & \text{if } I_1 < I^* \end{array}$$

and

$$\delta_4 = \begin{array}{ll} 0 & \text{if } I_1 \geq I^* \\ 1 & \text{if } I_1 < I^* \end{array}$$

where A_0 is the value of nonhousing asset holdings at the beginning of period 1—before period-1 allocation occurs.

Budget opportunities at the start of period are the regular income flow Y and the interest income on A_0. These must be allocated during the period over H and Z, as well as A and, if any, $I - M$. Again, if the household is R, term $(I_1 - M_1)$ drops out; if S, the term $P_{H_1}H_1$ drops out. This last means that owner-occupancy earns an implicit rental of $P_{H_1}H_1$ (part of its rate of return and part of period 1's income), and that this must be paid, implicitly, if not explicitly, so long as H_1 is consumed.

Prices, Expected Prices, Appreciation of Value. In period 1, three prices are assumed to be given: P_{H_1}, P_{Z_1}, and r. In addition, the household must predict period-2 and -3 prices in order to determine an optimal period-1 allocation: P_{H_2}, P_{Z_2}, r, γ. Since B, an argument of period-2 utility-function V, is determined by α and β, the rate of appreciation of asset prices, between 1 and 2, these must be predicted too. We assume that each household can make these predictions. But different households make different predictions. We assume that predictions of α and β differ randomly over the population, with a normal distribution $N(\alpha, \sigma_\alpha)$, $N(\beta, \sigma_\beta)$. Predictions of P_{H_2} and P_{Z_2} have the same kind of distributions. Moreover, predictions of α and a are related because they refer to entities that are linked by flow-capitalized value relationships.

Ownership of housing capital confers on the owner a stream of housing services over time. This stream has two components: H and D. The value of H (as given in the rental market) is P_{H_1} in period 1 and rises by $\underline{a}$ in period 2 by $\underline{\gamma}$ thereafter. We may assume that the value of the D component follows the same growth path. This stream is discounted to present value capitalization at the discount rate $1 + r$. I in the market is the capitalized value of this stream of future benefits. The value of this flow is given as follows (assuming that period 3 is actually a very long duration of time):

$$I_1 = \text{PDV}(D) + P_1 H_1 + \frac{P_1 H_1 (1 + a)}{1 + r} \left(1 + \frac{1 + \gamma}{r - \alpha} \right) \quad (3.6)$$

where $\text{PDV}(D) =$ the present discounted value of the flow of D services over the house's lifetime

Thus, given some amount of I_1 and its associated annual housing services (H_1, D), $\underline{a}$ and α can be expressed as functions of one another.

More central to our work than the relationship between a and α is the relationship between I and H. We shall explicitly examine the effect of the difference between $I_1 = 0$ and $I_1 > I^*$ on the level of H_1. For this we make use of equation 3.6 in a more general form:

$$I = I(H, P_H, D, P_D, r, a, \gamma) \quad (3.7)$$

or

$$H = I^{-1}(I, P_H, D, P_D, r, a, \gamma) \quad (3.8)$$

where $P_D =$ the price of D

All partial derivatives of I are positive except that for r, which is negative.

Mortgage Borrowing Constraint. If the mortgage rate of interest is favorable, so that it falls short of the opportunity cost of nonhousing assets, r, we assume the household will want to finance as much of I as possible though a mortgage loan. If $i > r$, the household will attempt to finance as much of I as possible by shifting out of A, as well as through some saving out of current income. The household will do most by exhausting A, since in practical terms I^* will tend to be a multiple of annual income, so current saving will be a small part. For a household with little or no A in its portfolio, financing I almost exclusively out of borrowing must be worthwhile even if $i > r$, if $I > I^*$ is to be attractive.

Thus, the amount of borrowing is likely to be determined by its availability instead of by household demand, since i is typically, although not always, less than r, (because, chiefly, a mortgage loan is backed by substantial collateral). Its availability is assumed here to be limited by institutional practices of mortgage lenders, in their down-payment requirements. We assume a down payment that is responsive both to the total value of the house and the nonhousing collateral possessed by the borrower—that is, the household's wealth (G). A required percentage of the value of the house as down payment is one example of such an institutional policy, but not the only one. The borrowing constraint is as follows:

$$M(I, G) \qquad \text{if } i < r$$

$$M = I - A_0 \qquad \text{if } i > r,\ I \ge A_0$$

$$M = 0 \qquad \text{if } i > r,\ I < A_0$$

$$1 \ge M_I > 0 < M_G$$

$$M = 0 = M(I = 0,\ G) \qquad (3.9)$$

where G is wealth, defined as $A_0 + (y/r)$. We simplify the $i > r$ case, so that $i > r$ leads to desired disinvestment of A to the extent of the housing investment, with no attempt to finance I at the expense of Z.

Optimization Conditions and Household Equilibrium

Lagrangian Maximization. We form the Lagrangian expression to be maximized for overall welfare maximization—the household's desired equilibrium:

$$\max L = W(U,V) + \mu[Y + A_0(1 + r) - A_1 - \delta_3(I_1 - M_1)$$
$$- \delta_4 P_{H_1} H_1 - P_{Z_1} Z_1] + \lambda[B - \delta_1(I_2 - M_2) - A_2$$
$$- \delta_2 P_2 H_2 - PZ_2 Z_2] \tag{3.10}$$

First-Order Conditions

$$\frac{\partial L}{\partial \mu} = 0 = Y + A_0(1 + r) - A_1 - \delta_2 P_{H_1} H_1 - P_{Z_1} Z_1 \tag{3.11}$$

$$\frac{\partial L}{\partial \lambda} = 0 = B - \delta_1(I_2 - M_2) - A_2 - \delta_2 P_{H_2} H_2 - P_{Z_2} Z_2 \tag{3.12}$$

$$\frac{\partial L}{\partial Z_1} = 0 = W_u U_{Z_1} - \mu P_{Z_1} \tag{3.13}$$

For $I_1 = 0$:

$$\frac{\partial L}{\partial H_i^0} = 0 = W_U U_{H_1} - \mu P_{H_1} \tag{3.14a}$$

For $I_i > I^*$:

$$\frac{\partial L}{\partial H_1^*} = 0 = W_U U_{H_1} + W_V V_B B_{I_1} I_{1_{H_1}} - (I_{1_{H_1}} - M_{1_{I_1}} I_{1_{H_1}})\mu$$
$$+ [(1 + \alpha)I_{1_{H_1}} - (1 + i)M_{1_{I_1}} I_{1_{H_1}}]\lambda \tag{3.14b}$$

where H^0 refers to rental housing and H^* to owner-occupancy housing.

$$\frac{\partial L}{\partial A_1} = 0$$
$$= W_V V_B(+ \beta + r) - \mu + \lambda(1 + \beta + r) \tag{3.15}$$

For $I_2 = 0$:

$$\frac{\partial L}{\partial H_2} = 0$$
$$= W_V V_{H_2} - \lambda P_{H_2} \tag{3.16a}$$

For $I_2 > I^*$:

$$\frac{\partial L}{\partial H_2} = 0$$

$$= W_V V_{H_2} - \lambda(I_{2_{H_2}} - M_{2_{I_2}} I_{2_{H_2}}) \tag{3.16b}$$

$$\frac{\partial L}{\partial Z_2} = 0$$

$$= W_V V_{Z_2} - \lambda P_{Z_2} \tag{3.17}$$

$$\frac{\partial L}{\partial A_2} = 0$$

$$= W_V V_{A_2} - \lambda \tag{3.18}$$

In addition to these, the tenure-choice decision depends on whether optimal $(\hat{H}_1, I_1 = 0)$ or optimal $(\hat{H}\text{*}, I_1 \geq I^*)$ gives a higher W_i. That is:

If $\hat{W}(I_i = 0) > \hat{W}(I \geq I^*)$ then $\hat{I}_1 = 0(P_3 = 0, \delta_4 = 1)$
$\hat{W}(I_i = 0) < \hat{W}(I \geq I^*)$ then $\hat{I}_1 \geq I^*(\delta_3 = 1, \delta_4 = 0)$
$\hat{W}(I_i = 0) = \hat{W}(I \geq I^*)$ then $\hat{I}_1$ either 0 or $\geq I^*$ (3.19)

A similar formulation holds for I_2 and (δ_1, δ_2).

In this model the following are unknowns to be solved:

> (1) H_1 (2) I_1 (3) Z_1 (4) A_1
> (5) M_1 (6) H_2 (7) I_2 (8) Z_2
> (9) A_2 (10) M_2 (11) μ (12) λ
> (13) each δ pair

The following variables are assumed "given":

> (1) D (2) r (3) i (4) a
> (5) γ (6) P_{H_1} (7) P_{Z_1} (8) α
> (9) β (10) Y (11) A_0

To solve for the thirteen unknowns we have thirteen equations: the utility functions (equations 3.1 and 3.2), the housing investment-housing-service relationship (equation 3.17), the mortgage-borrowing equation (equation 3.9) the eight first-order conditions for maximization (equations 3.11–3.18) (one of each pair for $\partial L/\partial H_1$ for each tenure choice), and the tenure choice (equation 3.19).

The model is closed and, assuming satisfaction of the usual Jacobian conditions, the thirteen equations suffice to determine the thirteen unknowns.

In the present chapter I am less interested in establishing the exact expressions for each unknown through solution of the system than in examining the relationships among the variables under different tenure choices. It will be convenient, therefore, to focus the analysis on the implications of some of the first-order conditions themselves. In each case it should, of course, be understood that only a partial analysis is being used, since the full general equilibrium is determined only by the simultaneous solution of the whole equation system.

Portfolio Investment and Consumption

Significance of Portfolio Options for Period-1 Consumption of Housing Services

We shall now indicate how the existence of owner-occupancy as an alternative to rental status in consuming housing services affects the amount of housing services so consumed. We begin with equations 3.13, 3.14a, and 3.14b.

From equation 3.13

$$\mu = \frac{W_u U_Z}{P_Z} \tag{3.20}$$

From equation 3.14a,

$$\mu = \frac{W_u U_{H_1}}{P_H} \quad \text{for } I_1 = 0 \tag{3.21}$$

From equation 3.14b,

$$W_u U_{H_1} + W_V V_B[(1 + \alpha) - (1 + i)M_{1_{I_1}}]I_{1_{H_1}} = (I_{1_{H_1}} - M_{1_{I_1}} I_{1_{H_1}})\mu$$
$$- [(1 + \alpha)I_{i_{H_1}} - (1 + i)M_{1_{I_i}} I_{1_{H_1}}]\lambda \tag{3.22}$$

λ can be taken from equation 3.18:

$$\lambda = W_V V_{A_2} \qquad (3.23)$$

$$\mu = \frac{W_U U_{H_1}}{E_H} + \frac{W_V R_I I_H (V_B + V_{A_2})}{E_H} \qquad (3.24)$$

where $R_I \equiv (1 + \alpha) - (1 + i) M_{1_{I_1}}$

$E_H \equiv I_{1_{H_1}} - M_{1_{I_1}} I_H \qquad$ since $E \equiv I - M$

$R_I =$ the marginal net return from equity in an owned house

$E_H =$ marginal change of equity for an increment of owner-occupied housing services

Suppose a household faces only an opportunity to rent housing. Then, by equations 3.20 and 3.21, the amounts of Z_1 and H_i chosen will be related by the following:

$$\frac{W_U U_{Z_1}}{P_{Z_1}} = \frac{W_U U_{H_1^0}}{P_{H_1}} \quad \text{or} \quad \frac{U_{Z_1}}{P_{Z_1}} = \frac{U_{H_i^0}}{P_{H_1}} \qquad (3.25)$$

The LHS (left-hand side of the equation) is the marginal utility of composite commodity consumption per dollar of expenditure on Z. The RHS (right-hand side of the equation) is the comparable marginal utility of housing services consumed per dollar of expenditures on rental housing. The *absolute* equilibrium magnitudes of Z_1 and H_i depend, of course, on solution of the whole system, but their relationship to one another depends only on equation 3.25.

Now let the household be given the alternative opportunity to consume housing by purchasing a home for owner-occupancy, and let the optimum choice under this option dominate the rental option by equation 3.19. The new relationship between Z_1 and H_i^* will be given by:

$$\frac{W_U U_{Z_1}}{P_{Z_1}} = \frac{W_U U_{H_1^*}}{E_{H^*}} + \frac{W_V (V_B + V_{A_2}) R_I I_H}{E_{H^*}} \qquad (3.26)$$

The first term of the RHS is the marginal utility of housing services consumed via each dollar of equity in owner-occupancy. The second term is the marginal utility of the increased net-investment return resulting from the additional housing investment necessitated by one extra unit of housing-service consumption. Together they thus represent both the consumption and investment benefits resulting from housing investment.

W_U, W_V, $U_{Z_1} U_{H_1^*}$, V_B, V_{A_2}, P_{Z_1}, I_H are all obviously positive. I shall argue that E_{H^*} is also positive. E_{H^*} the change in value of equity as total housing is increased. It seems quite plausible for mortgagees to wish borrowers to hold additional financial interest in each increment of housing investment, so that there is genuine collateral associated with each portion of the mortgage loan. This implies that $E_{H^*} > 0$.

The situation is different for R_I. R_I is the financial gain from an extra unit of housing investment (via price appreciation) less the financial cost of that unit (via interest payment on the extra mortgage borrowed). If housing were an ordinary investment good or an ordinary consumption good, one would not observe owner-occupancy status being undertaken unless R_I were positive. In fact, its mixed consumption-investment character, and the existence of D_1 benefits associated with the consumption of housing services via owner-occupancy but not via rental status, makes it possible for R_I to be negative as well as, more normally, positive. The impact on housing consumption aspects of owner-occupancy very highly, this is possible for two markedly different scenarios.

In a situation where α (and β) > 0, it would be especially rare for R_I to be negative. It is most likely to be negative where prices are expected to remain stable: $\alpha = 0 = \beta$. Our two scenarios will accordingly be a stable price and a significant inflation ($\alpha > \beta$) situation.

Stable Prices

$$\alpha = 0 = \beta \tag{3.27}$$

so

$$R_I \equiv 1 - (1 + I)M_{1_{I_1}} \quad \text{and} \quad R_I < 0 \quad \text{where} \quad M_{1_{I_1}} > \frac{1}{1 + i}$$

If i is approximately 10 percent, R_I will be negative if at least 91 percent of each additional investment value is mortgaged—unlikely but not impossible. Assume R_I is negative. Will any household be willing to invest in owner-occupancy in such a situation? Two questions have to be answered: (1) Can owner-occupancy be preferable to rental status? (2) Can it be attractive to invest in housing instead of nonhousing assets?

Owner-Occupancy Consumption versus Rental Consumption. From the partial derivatives $\partial L/\partial H_1^0$ and $\partial l/\partial H_1^*$ in equations 3.14a and 3.14b, the utility gains from consuming the same amount of housing via owner-occupancy rather than via rental status is given by:

$$G_{H^* H^0} = \mu(P_{H_1}H_1 - E_{H_1}H_1) + W_V I_H (V_B + V_{A_2})H_1 R_I + W_U U_D$$

(3.28)

The first RHS term is the difference between the two tenure states in first-period diversion of purchasing power. The second term is the effect of owner-occupancy on second-period purchasing power. The third term is the consumption aspects of owner-occupancy. If R_I is negative, then

$$G_{H^* H^0} > 0 \qquad \text{if and only if } \mu(P_{H_1}H_1 - E_{H_1}H_1)$$

$$+ W_U U_D > W_V I_{H_1}(V_B + V_{A_2})H_1 R_I$$

While R_I may be only slightly negative, the whole term may be substantial. The inequality is reasonably possible if

$$P_{H_1}H_1 > E_{H_1}H_1$$

For this to be true, mortgage borrowing must be a very high proportion of the value of the house. We have seen that such a high borrowing proportion is also required for R_I to be negative. Where

$$P_{H_1}H_1 < E_{H_1}H_1$$

nevertheless, $G_{H^* H^0} > 0$ only if $W_U U_D$ alone is large enough (positive) to exceed the negative sum of the other two terms. For households that rate the consumption aspects of owner-occupancy very highly, this is possibel for various values of the variables. Thus, negative R_I is compatible with owner-occupancy especially where commodity D is very highly valued.

Owner-Occupancy Investment versus Nonhousing Investment. From equations 3.15 and 3.23 we obtain:

$$\mu = W_V(1 + \beta + r)(V_B + V_{A_2}) \qquad (3.29)$$

From equations 3.10 and 3.23 we obtain a first-order condition in terms of $\partial L/\partial I_1$:

$$\frac{\partial L}{\partial I_1} = 0 = W_U U_{H_{1_I}} + W_V V_B R_I - \mu E_I + \lambda R_I \qquad (3.30)$$

which leads to

$$\mu = \frac{W_U U_{H_1} H_{1I}}{E_I} + \frac{W_V R_I(V_B + V_{A_2})}{E_I} \qquad (3.31)$$

So, in optimizing budget allocation, A_1 and I_1 fulfill the following relation:

$$(1 + \beta + r) = \frac{W_U U_{H_1} H_{1I}}{W_V(V_B + V_{A_2})E_I} + \frac{R_I}{E_I} \qquad (3.32)$$

Since the first term of RHS is positive, $1 + \beta + r$, the rate of return on nonhousing assets, will exceed the marginal net rate of financial return of housing investment. With $\alpha = \beta = 0$, equation 3.32 becomes:

$$1 + r > \frac{1 - (1 + i)M_{1_{I_1}}}{1 - M_{1_I}} \qquad (3.33)$$

which always holds, since $i > 0 < r$.

If, in addition, $R_I < 0$, the first term of RHS must be greater to equal the sum of $1 + r$ and $- R_I/E_I$. This is not, however, impossible. The first term is the utility valuation of the housing-service consumption that comes with investment in housing. Moreover, for the all-or-nothing choice of owner-occupancy versus rental status, the benefits from D are added. So negative R_I is compatible with investment in housing so long as the housing consumption linked with it is sufficiently valued.

What, then, are the consequences for housing consumption under owner-occupancy if R_I is negative? Repeating equation 3.26,

$$\frac{W_U U_{Z_1}}{P_{Z_1}} = \frac{W_U U_{H_1^*}}{E_{H^*}} + \frac{W_V(V_B + V_{A_2})R_I I_H}{E_{H^*}}$$

since the last term is negative, $W_u U_{Z_1}/P_{Z_1} < W_u U_{H^*}/E_{H^*}$. Since, by equation 3.25 $W_U U_{Z_1}/P_{Z_1} = W_U U_{H^0_1}/P_{H_1}$, then regardless how E_{H^*} is financed (that is, out of Z_1, which would *raise* $W_U U_{Z_1}/P_{Z_1}$, or mostly out of A_0, which would leave $W_U U_{Z_1}/P_{Z_1}$ largely unchanged),$(W_U U_{H^0}/P_{H_1}) < (W_U U_{H^*}/E_{H^*})$. This essentially implies that $H > H^*$, that is, that a financially unattractive $(R < 0)$ housing investment is partly financed by *decreasing* the level of housing consumption, the attractive fixed D benefits being attained simply so long as $I_1 > I^*$.[5]

Significant Inflation. For this scenario, $\alpha > 0 < \beta$. To appreciate the recent inflationary experience, assume $\alpha > \beta$. Here a high α strongly suggests that $R_I \equiv (1 + \alpha) - (1 + i)M_{1_{I_1}} > 0$. Now, by equation 3.26, (W_U/P_{Z_1}) $> (W_U U_{H*}/E_H^*)$. It is not possible to make inferences about $U_{H_i^0}$ relative to U_{H*} from this without information about the financing of $I_1 - M_1$. If most of $I_1 - M_1$ comes out of Z_1, then $W_U U_{Z_1}/P_{Z_1}$ may rise enough relative to $W_U U_{H_i^0}/P_{H_1}$ so $H_i^0 \geq H*$. But $I_1 - M_1$ is typically a large number, large relative to the whole of $P_{Z_1} Z_1$. Most typically, $I_1 - M_1$ is predominately financed out of A_0, leaving Z_1 not very diminished. In this usual situation, an essentially unchanged $W_U U_{Z_1}/P_{Z_1} = W_U U_{H_i}/P_{H_1}$. So

$$\frac{W_U U_{H_i^0}}{P_{H_1}} > \frac{W_U U_{H*}}{E_{H*}} \tag{3.34}$$

This comes about chiefly if $H* > H_i^0$: that is, attractive financial housing investment leads to an increase in housing consumption above the level that would be chosen under rental tenure. Moreover, the greater the portfolio gain via housing investment, the greater will be the tendency to increase current housing consumption.

In both the stable price and inflation cases, the linkage between investment and consumption elements for housing does influence the tradeoff between housing and nonhousing consumption in the present period. Where the financial returns are, in the normal case, positive, the effect is to augment housing at the expense of other consumption; where the financial returns are negative, housing investment is accompanied by an offsetting shrinkage of housing consumption relative to other consumption. The size of the effects varies directly with the size of the financial returns.

The Relation between Housing and Nonhousing Investment

Consider the tradeoff between housing and nonhousing investment given in equation 3.32:

$$\rho = \frac{W_U U_{H_1} H_{1_I}}{W_V(V_B + V_{A_2})E_I} + \frac{R_I}{E_I} \quad \text{where } \rho \equiv (1 + \beta + r) \tag{3.35}$$

In our discussion of the stable price case, we noted that a utility maximizing allocation between A_1 and I_1 would require a financial rate of return on A_1 exceeding the purely financial rate of return on I_1, the difference balancing the linked consumption component of I_1.

This result must be put into perspective. In this model, we have fully abstracted from the riskiness of different types of investment, and partially abstracted from their differential tax advantages. If we consider riskiness and differences in the risk inherent in different types of investment, the rates of return in this model are to be interpreted as those which offset differences in risk: that is, they are *net* of risk differences. So the $\rho > R_I/E_I$ result means a difference between returns in A and I *over and above* differences necessary to equalize risk. Similiarly, since an explicit treatment of tax advantages on I would establish these as a positive function of I (not as the simplifying constant which we are here including in D), we are in effect treating R as net of tax advantages.

An increase in ρ (via β or r) calls for an increase in the overall marginal return on I_1. This could conceivably come about without much altering of I_1, and thus H_1, by so much enhancing future-relative-to-present-consumption opportunities that total current relative to future consumption falls sufficiently to raise W_U/W_V enough to reestablish personal equilibrium without decreasing H_1 much. But this involves heavy sacrifice of Z_1 relative to H_1. It is highly likely that A and I are closer substitutes than H and Z. If so, any scaling down of Z_1 will be significantly accompanied by a decrease in H_1 (and thus in I_1). More directly, the rise in A (via an increase in ρ *relative* to R_I/E_I) is very likely to come mostly at the expense of I_1. So, while some intertemporal shift toward future consumption may occur, the preponderant shift will be away from I_1 into A_1, and will thereby have a larger negative impact on H_1 than on Z_1.

An increase of α, or a decrease in i, relative to ρ, increases R_I/E_I relative to ρ and thereby enhances the attractiveness of I_1, relative to A_1. Then I_1 should rise significantly relatively to A_1, with a collateral rise of H_1 relative to Z_1, both because of the *period-price* effect (via the overall opportunity cost of H_1 relative to Z_1) and the *intertemporal-price* effect (via the greater attractiveness of future consumption relative to present consumption).

The effect of M_{1_I} is more complex. M_I represents a leverage factor in housing investment. As such, it increases the profitability of an already profitable investment prospect, and increases the rate of loss in a losing prospect. The basic relationship is:

$$\frac{\partial}{\partial M_U} \frac{R_I}{E_I} > 0 \qquad \text{if } \alpha > i$$

$$\frac{\partial}{\partial M_U} \frac{R_I}{E_I} = 0 \qquad \text{if } \alpha = i \qquad\qquad (3.36)$$

$$\frac{\partial}{\partial M_U} \frac{R_I}{E_I} = 0 \qquad \text{if } \alpha < i$$

Thus, the effect of an increase in M_I in I is positive where $\alpha > i$, negative where $\alpha < i$, and zero where $\alpha = i$.

For all of these qualitative results, the possible negativity of R_I has no effect. It does, of course, effect the size of the impact.

The equilibrium financial-rate differential between A and I in this analysis refers to a single household. But it can be reflected in market equilibrium as well. Insofar as households like this are marginal to the market equilibrium, the market equilibrium will also show a differential in financial rates of return between the two kinds of assets (actually three, because *net* returns for I involves mortgage assets as well).

The Tradeoff between I_1 *and* Z_1

Previous sections have established the basic results of this tradeoff, but they did so indirectly, primarily in terms of housing consumption. It is useful to establish the direct interaction between housing investment and what, in consumption models, is taken as the *numéraire* commodity—"general spending." The presence of other spending options decreases somewhat the *generality* of Z_1, but it still remains a fair approximation to the "general usefulness of purchasing power."

The basic relationship, from equations 3.11 and 3.31, is:

$$\frac{W_U U_{Z_1}}{P_{Z_1}} = \mu$$

$$= \frac{W_U U_{H_1} H_{1_I}}{E_I} + \frac{W_V R_I (V_B + V_{A_2})}{E_I} \quad (3.37)$$

For our present purposes, the key variable is R_I, and within R_I, α. An increase in α will increase the attractiveness both of future-relative-to-present consumption via investment in housing (in the second RHS term), and of housing services as present consumption via linkage with I_1 (in the first RHS term) relative to Z_1. The size of the tradeoff between I and Z_1 thus again depends on the relative substitutabilities between present and future consumption (W_V/W_U), different portolio assets (ρ and R_I/E_I), and between housing and nonhousing consumption (U_H/U_Z).

Summary of Determinants of H_I–Z_I *Impacts*

Now we are able to summarize the effects of an owner-occupancy option on current housing consumption as follows:

The following inferences can be made about the determinants of H_I:

α

Increasing α will raise H_I via owner-occupancy: it increases R_I. If S status is already attractive, rising α will raise H_1 by raising the optimal $I(>I^*)$; if S status is not yet attractive, rising α will raise the probability that optimal I exceeds I^* and so raise H_I via lumpy jump into S status.

i

Increasing i lowers H_1 by lowering the net rate of return on I, R_I, thereby decreasing $\hat{I}$: H_1 falls gradually if I is still above I^*, falls more abruptly if I_1, hitherto above I^*, falls below I^* and the household reverts to R status. It also operates indirectly, by affecting the direction in which changes in M_I influence I. The higher is i, the more likely it is that an increase in M_I will discourage I_1, and therefore H_1.

$M_{1_{I_1}}$

An increase in $M_{1_{I_1}}$ can have positive, negative, or zero effect on H_1, depending on the relative size of i versus α. A high i relative to α causes increasing $M_{1_{I_1}}$ to have a negative effect on H_1. Whereas a low i relative to α yields a potitive effect on H_1, and equal values if i and α causes increasing $M_{1_{I_1}}$ to have a neutral effect on H_1.

W_V

If $R_I > 0$, the higher is W_V, the valuation of period-2 prospects relative to period-1 prospects (that is, the lower is time preference), the more attractive is I, relative to Z_1 and so H_1, but the less attractive I_1 is relative to A_1, since part of its real payoff is via *present* consumption. The net effect depends on the specific degrees of substitutability among H_1 relative to Z_1, I_1 and H_1, present and future consumption, and A_1 and I_1 in the detailed model.

If $R_1 > 0$, the higher W_V *decreases* the attractiveness of H_1 relative to Z_1, since it directly worsens the attractiveness of I-linked H_1 relative to Z_1, and indirectly hurts H_1 by lowering the attractiveness of I relative to A_1.

V_B

Increasing V_B raises the utility payoff to the income effect of B on future consumption prospects, thus to portfolio investment generally; it tends to increase I_1 and A_1 together, and thus H_1, at the expense of Z_1. If $R_I < 0$, increasing V_β increases the attractiveness of future-relative-to-present consumption but makes A_1 more attractive relative to I_1. The overall effect is likely to be higher A_1, at the expense both of lower Z_1 and lower I_1—so H_1 falls.

The conclusion of this section is that portfolio opportunities do influence the present consumption of housing. Empirically, investment in housing is financed largely out of mortgage borrowing, and the sizable residual-equity investment is, in turn, largely financed out of nonhousing portfolio assets rather than out of current consumption. The result is that the sheer availability of the owner-occupancy option results typically in an increase in current consumption of housing over rental-status owner-occupancy. The

size *and direction of change of this effect depends* on the variables of the
system. For some of these, the direction of change is invariant. For others, it
depends on solution of the entire system.

The Choice between Renting and Owner Occupancy: A Theory of Tenure Choice

Individual Tenure Choice

We are now able to put together elements of the analysis to delineate the
determinants of tenure choice. We have established that I unambiguously rises
relative to Z_1 with α and falls with i. It rises relative to A_1 with α, W_U, and
U_{H_1}, and inversely with β, r, W_V, and i. The effects of W_V, V_B, and $M_{1_{I_1}}$ are
ambiguous, conditional on the context: the first two indicate the valuation of
future gains relative to present gains; so they enhance the pull of I_1 relative to
Z_1 but not necessarily relative to A_1. Indeed, W_V enhances the pull of A_1
more than that of I_1, because all of A_1's benefits are future benefits, whereas
I_1's benefits are divided between present and future.

From the point of view of the present model, a theory of tenure choice
consists in spelling out configurations of parameter values for which the
model would predict that utility is maximized by one tenure choice or the
other (equation 3.19). Since so many of the parameters have ambiguous net
impacts on I_1, this can be fully accomplished only by solving the system
explicitly. Three kinds of information are required for this: the specifics of the
utility function, the initial endowment and nonproperty income, and price
expectations. An important feature of our approach is that aggregation of
housing choice to a market level is accomplished by assuming the existence
of a population that differs with respect to tastes (the utility function), budget
size, and price expectations. Thus, at any one moment the population will
make a variety of choices about both level of housing H_1 and tenure status.
The aggregate model is designed to predict the distribution of levels of
housing and the tenure mix.

To illustrate the method, it is not necessary to delineate the complete set
of parameter configurations that determines the tenure split. It will be
instructive simply to let variables with unambiguous tenure effect vary
systematically and track their consequences. Accordingly, let us hypo-
thetically vary this set of variables in the direction to make optimal I_1, $\hat{I}_1$ rise
systematically. We can start from $\hat{I}_1 = 0$, induce $\hat{I}_1$ to rise above 0 but below
I^*—so I_1 rises only "implicitly", since an optimal $0 < \hat{I}_1 < I^*$ will, in fact,
result in $I_1 = 0$ (since $I_1 < I^*$ buys no valid housing services, yet costs I_1, so
is wasteful). Continuing the process, $\hat{I}$ is induced to rise until it equals I^*. Up

to this point the household has remained a renter. Now actual I_1 leaps abruptly from 0 to I^*, and the household becomes an owner-occupier. Further changes in the determinants of I_1 in the same direction keep the household in S status, but with higher and higher actual housing property investment.

Comparison of the intrinsic characteristics of the two tenures can be schematized as follows:

Rental Tenure (R):

$$H^0, Z_1^0, A_0 < A_1, I_1 = 0, D = 0, M_1 = 0$$

Owner-Occupier Tenure (S):

$$H_1^*, Z_1^*, A_1 < A_0, \hat{I}_1 \geq I^*, D = 1, M_1$$

The differences are:
  (a) S brings $D = 1$, R brings $D = 0$.
  (b) Under S that part of $I_1 - M_1$ financed out of A_0 decreases B because I investment has a lower net financial rate of return than A; but it is offset via the linkage with cost-free present housing services resulting from I_1.
  (c) That part of $I_1 - M_1$ financed out of Z_1 increases B_1 and H_1 at the expense of Z_1.

In general, these differences do not have an unambiguous net effect on W. So in general, the sign of $W(S) - W(R)$ is indeterminate. The specifics of parameters and situations are required to predict which is superior.

The contrary effects of I's tradeoffs with A and Z_1 are continuous; the unambiguous effect of the switch-on– switch-off D and the min I^* require-ment are discontinuous. The discontinuity is important at the aggregate level because it predicts that there are ranges within which modest changes in "conditions" (the determinants of I_1) can lead to large, abrupt changes in tenure choice. At the aggregate market level, households differ in the parameters of tastes, budget size, and price expectations, but it is not a uniform distribution. Quantum changes in the situation may simultaneously push over the threshold households which began at different distances from the threshold. The number of households so pushed can jump widely up and down for similarly modest changes in conditions. So *bunching* in tenure choice is a distinct possibility.

Besides aggregate discontinuities, the differences among households in tastes and expectations will give rise at the market level to distinctive *sequences* of tenure changes with households arrayed successively in terms of the attractiveness of I_1 under given conditions. As conditions overall favor I, households shift to S status sequentially along this array.

Proportion of Home Ownership

We now deal explicitly with the market level, where many participants interact competitively. How will household intentions be translated into market outcomes?

Start with some set of initial conditions, resulting in a given percentage of the population being owner-occupiers, the rest renters. Now let the determinants of I improve so that I rises for all. So a number of households at the head of the S-proneness queue will now want to shift to ownership tenure. Will they succeed in doing so? We examine two cases: (1) no new production of dwelling, (2) additional dwellings produced.

Case I: No New Production of Dwellings. The issue here hinges on whether the landlords of existing rental units will be willing to sell their houses to erstwhile renters. Will changes in conditions make these landlords comparably more determined to retain ownership of their properties, so that competition simply results, for the most part, in inflation of property values with little redistribution of ownership to renter households?

The market will, in fact, see a nontrivial shift in ownership. Previous renters in the S-proneness queue will be willing to assume S status at a net rate of *financial* return on housing investment below that of A assets because they gain D and H *consumption* returns as well. They bid up prices of houses to levels generating such lower rates of return on I; but at those prices landlords, whose interest in the property is only financial, can gain by selling their "excess" houses and buying A. So the proportion of owner-occupiership will rise under these circumstances.

Case II: Additional Dwellings Produced. Renters at the top of the queue bid up the prices of existing houses above the offer-prices of landlords, and higher than before the strengthening of I determinants. So prospective profitability rises for new construction and additional units are produced. But these compete with existing houses. The same competitive bidding process ensues, with R households high on the queue, outbidding existing landlords— the larger number of houses serving mainly to moderate the absolute rise in dwelling prices, not changing the relative valuations of renters and landlords. So the percentage of owner-occuipership will rise nontrivially.

Market Equilibrium

The market equilibrium in terms of tenure choice depends importantly on differences among market participants. Let us classify these as consuming households and landlords. Consuming households differ in several especially important respects: (1) tastes for housing services, (2) tastes for the consumption element in owner-occuperiship, (3) time preference, (4) expectations about housing price appreciation, (5) expectations about price appreciation of other consumer goods, (6) expectations about price appreciation of nonhousing assets, (7) the sum of income and initial holdings of nonhousing assets.

Market participants in their role of landlords also differ in terms of their various price expectations.

For formal analysis of market equilibrium, we can make explicit distributional assumptions about these differences. For our present purposes, it is enough to give a practical sense of what these differences signify for equilibrium.

With some given starting situation, specifying housing supplies and ownership as well as the value of the determinants of household equilibrium, there will be an ordering of eagerness for ownership of houses for owner-occupier or landlord status. For similar expectations and nonhousing-asset purchasing power, a household consumer will have a higher bid price than that of a landlord. But expectations will differ: a landlord with a higher expected α can outbid a household consumer with a lower expected α.

Thus, the market price and the allocation of owner-occupier status is determined by a competitive bidding among participants until the market clears. In terms of implicit (fictional) sequence, those most eager to own at least one dwelling will outbid those less eager. If the supply of units exceeds the number of this group, less eager groups are required to own units in order to clear the market; so the price of ownership continues to fall (rate of financial return on I rises) until the marginally most eager are induced to own the last remaining units, at prices which equate their marginal evaluations. Intramarginal owners receive surplus returns in financial and consumption terms.

Not all owners will be pure owner-occupiers; some will be landlords with higher-than-average relative-price expectations favoring housing assets. Households that remain renters will tend to have lower-than-average such expectations, or be generally poorer households. Poorer households are likely to remain renters for a number of reasons: (1) an inability to borrow as much as wealthier households, and an absence of significant nonhousing assets to finance dwelling purchase; (2) a probability of lower-than-average U_D/U_Z because of the low absolute level of Z affordable; (3) a low W_V/W_U

and hence low W_B/W_Z because of the same low level of current consumption as a whole, with a resulting greater "impatience."

Finally, the dispersed presence of pure owner-occupiers in the ordering of eagerness to own property suggest that some of them will be marginal at market equilibrium, and will therefore project their own equilibrium conditions onto the market. As such, equilibrium prices will generate lower expected net rates of financial return on housing than on nonhousing assets for those who hold similar expectations. Of course, the same present prices can suggest different absolute and relative expected returns for those who hold different price expectations.

Inflation and Tenure Choice

Let us make a brief mention of the applicability of the present analysis to behavior during inflation.

Suppose there is general inflation. Then expected a,b (appreciation P_{H_1} and P_{Z_1}) and α,β will be high. If there is no special reason for a and α to exceed b and β, housing will be essentially neutral and no special application of the model is very illuminating. But housing inflation can exceed general inflation for a number of reasons. First, demographic trends and industrial sector changes may suggest more stringent demand-and-supply pressure in this sector in the future (for demographic, migrational or financial, materials reasons) than for average industrial sectors. Second, the combination of physical durability of the asset and solidity of trends making for strong future-excess demands may give prospective investors the perception of housing investment as safer than many other kinds of investment (thus, lower risk). Both grounds mean that in terms of our model, from an initial situation resulting in given appropriate household and landlord equilibrium, the determinants of I change—namely, mean α rises in the population relative to mean β (and mean $\underline{a}$ relative to mean $\underline{b}$). (A decrease in risk, for a given expected mean return, implies a higher real risk-adjusted return.) Then the analysis of our model comes into play, predicting a higher proportion of owner-occupiership within an increasing stock of houses (unless the increase in stock is deterred by devastating rises in mortgage interest rates). Detailed predictions of change require, of course, spelling out parameter distributions and specific initial conditions. It is hoped that the outline of the model presented here suggests how a detailed analysis would proceed.

Notes

1. Richard Muth, *Cities & Housing* (Chicago: University of Chicago Press, 1969); Edwin Mills, "An Aggregative Model of Resource Allocation in a Metropolitan Area," *American Economic Review* 57 (May 1967);

James Sweeney, "Quality Commodity Hierarchies and Housing Markets," *Econometrica* 42, no. 1 (January 1974); Frank de Leeuw and Raymond Struyk, *The Web of Urban Housing*, The Urban Institute, 1975.

2. The assumed constancy of D makes this an awkward treatment, since absolute tax advantages are a rising function of the absolute size of housing investment, mortgage interest paid—which is here treated as a rising function of housing investment—and capital appreciation. Though awkward, I am refraining from making tax advantages variable because I wish to show the extent to which portfolio considerations per se—independent of tax considerations—can influence consumption behavior. To make this emphasis clear, I, in effect, assume away existence of the kinds of tax advantage operating in the U.S. context. Later work will bring in the two influences explicitly together.

3. This is a simplification to highlight the conditions under which owner-occupancy will be chosen. Little of substance is thereby excluded.

4. The mortgage in I as well as *its* interest rate are also given.

5. Real-world tax advantages from owner occupancy are a positive function of I. Explicit treatment of them would not lump them into D, but rather make them explicit ingredients of R_I. As such, they would further decrease the probability of real-world situations involving a negative R.

**Part II
Housing: Empirical**

4

On the Determinants of the Probability of First-Home Acquisition and Its Relation to Credit Stringency

Phoebus J. Dhrymes

The purpose of this study is to investigate the determinants of the probability of first-home acquisition and its relationships to the stringency in financial markets. The chief motivation was the concern often expressed in policy circles that in the recent past the exigencies of monetary policies and other factors have made it increasingly difficult for households to make a first-home purchase.

The nature of the financial stringency is twofold: first, an increase in the market rate of interest (specifically the mortgage rate) makes it more costly to support homeownership. Second, financial stringency is often manifested by nonprice restrictions such as the variation of the percent down payment. This generally excludes some households from the housing market owing to their inability to accumulate the requisite down payment. In principle, this latter aspect would not affect households that are currently homeowners, since upon their moving, the sale of their previous residence would ordinarily provide sufficient reserves to enable a subsequent purchase, if so desired.

For this reason, we have confirmed our attention to first-homeowners. Although a fair number of homeownership studies are available in the literature (David, 1962; Kain and Quigley, 1975; Lee, 1963, Maisel, 1966, and Orcutt et al., 1961), to my knowledge there is no previous study of first-homeownership. The nonavailability of such studies is not accidental, it is due to lack of data, a gross deficiency in our information set regarding this topic. In recent years, this gap was filled by the Annual Housing Surveys (AHS), which since 1977 records first-homeownership.

Theoretical Underpinnings of the Study

When we speak of homeownership, we shall invariably refer to ownership of owner-occupied dwellings (homes, as distinct from cooperative apartments

The research on which this work is based was in part supported by funding from a cooperative agreement between the U.S. Department of Housing and Urban Development and the Center for the Social Sciences, Columbia University (HA-5289-CA). The views expressed herein are those of the author and do not necessarily reflect the views of the DHUD or any other branch of the U.S. Government.

59

or condominiums). Homeownership serves a dual function: first, it provides housing-shelter services (though this household also has the option of obtaining such services through the rental market). Second, homeownership performs the function of an income-yielding asset: the income it yields is the *value* of home-shelter services it provides the owner-occupant household. Further, the income it yields is *not* taxable, while the costs of acquisition or holding of this asset *are*, where appropriate, tax-deductible. This aspect is almost unique; take, for example, an investment in tax-exempt municpal bonds: if debt is incurred in their acquisition, *both* the cost *and* the return are treated symmetrically, from a tax-liability viewpoint.

It is a commonly held view that treating homeownership in this light should lead to the conclusion that the household contemplating buying shelter services for itself will consider the comparative costs of home-ownership versus renting and will make a decision based on these considerations, *inter alia*. It is quite trivial to write down the standard apparatus of utility-function maximization in the present case. In fact, this is done for the generic case in Dhrymes (1978), Chapter 7. The questions of real importance are (1) how to define the variables that enter into this decision and (2) how to select the sample on which the analysis is to be carried out.

Let us deal with the second aspect first, basing our study on data obtained from the 1977 AHS. (For a detailed description of the method of sampling and the nature of the AHS survey, see appendix B of *Current Housing Reports*, Series H150-78, published by the Bureau of the Census.) The survey involves around 80,000 housing units and their occupants nationwide about which information is solicited annually. Since this sample reflects the nature not only of the housing stock in the country but also of the households that move in and out of the sampled dwellings randomly, it is reasonable to conclude that if we look at the set of households who are in the first year of occupancy of dwellings in the sample in any given year, we shall have a random sample of all "movers" in the country. These facts are easily ascertained from AHS, and yield the basic sample with which we can operate. Systematic biases should not arise.)

Even though, upon moving, a household may have an option between renting a new dwelling or buying one, what makes our study possible (in the sense that we are able to employ the standard econometric formulation based on the independent identically distributed aspect of the relevant random variables) is our assertion that moving is independent of the choice of tenure between "rentership" and homeownership.

We are mindful of the fact that our assertion may not be entirely true, since one may well think of circumstances in which home acquisition is the primary factor and the moving is incidental to the process, the opposite of the underlying conceptual framework of this study, which asserts that (1) moving is the primary factor, (2) moving is determined by considerations other than the desire to acquire a home, and (3) the decision to acquire a home or not is made conditional on having to *move*.

It is my view that in the overwhelming majority of cases under consideration our assertion corresponds to the truth. One possibility of checking on the validity of this proposition is to examine the distance between the previous and current residence of new home buyers, as well as the *size* of the two residential units. This is not possible however, with our sample as now constituted. In subsequent work we shall attempt to obtain the distance between two successive loci of a mover's (first-homeowner's) residence, as well as the size of the two residences and examine the data.

One may assume that various socioeconomic factors affect first-home purchase, such as the age of the head and possibly other members of the household, race, urban/nonurban location, region of the country, number of household members, as well as the relevant costs and household income and wealth.

Unfortunately, information on wealth is not available in AHS files. We may, however, in subsequent work be able to exploit the longitudinal character of the AHS files in order to define a proxy for wealth or "permanent income" by simply looking at the time series of income subsequent to first-home purchase for the households in question.

It is really not possible to define satisfactorily the comparative costs of homeownership versus *rentership* for all movers. In principle, we could look at the flow of costs associated with homeownership, both actual and imputed, net of expected capital gains and/or losses, and compare this with a proper rental-cost index. Alternatively, we can look at the present discounted value of housing services rendered by a housing unit (net of costs of maintaining the unit and servicing the debt involved and net of capital gains) and compare it with the price of the unit. Both of these approaches, however, are operationally impractical at the moment. As more data become available, and again exploiting the longitudinal nature of the AHS, we hope to gain some information on actual capital gains realized for individual housing units, and then an interesting question to ask would be: would we add appreciably to the explanatory power of the relationship if we assumed that the household in question correctly anticipated the capital gains involved?

Given the nature of the sample, which will be discussed more extensively at a later stage, what we are able to obtain is the cost associated with previous and current tenure. These data are reasonably unambiguous and generally founded on the actual experience of the households involved. We are also able to construct the cost of homeownership and the percent down payment for first-homeowners from information provided in the AHS files. For recurring renters, we have unambiguous data only on their current rental costs. We impute to them the homeownership costs associated with first-home buyers by region and urban status. In this fashion, we have constructed a series of cost of homeownership and percent down payment for all observations in our sample.

The equation actually estimated thus renders the probability of homeownership as a function of the household's current income, the ratio of current to previous housing costs, the percent down payment, and various sociolocational variables alluded to above, and the cost of homeownership. The ratio of current to previous housing expenses is meant to account for the fact that housing mobility is associated with either the acquisition of better housing amenities or housing-cost inflation, while specific homeownership-cost variables are meant to reflect the effect of the costs specifically associated with homeownership on the probability of first-home acquisition.

The theoretical underpinnings of this specification are not entirely impeccable, since many expectations and the role of wealth are not, and cannot be, taken into account given the nature of our data set. Abstracting from these difficulties—some of which will be dealt with in later studies utilizing the longitudinal nature of the sample—the specification is certainly admissible and the results obtained therefrom can be expected to provide a unique and hitherto unavailable insight into the determinants of first-homeownership, and to provide some quantification of the effect exerted by the stringencies, or tightness, of financial markets on this important aspect of household experience.

Finally, there is another aspect that requires comment. Choice of residential location determines certain other consumption patterns associated with the bundle of public goods made available to a household through its choice of residential location. Indeed, there is a view that holds that the constant ebb and flow of households between central city and suburbs is due, in part, to the fact that the education of many households' children through primary and secondary schools is de facto tax-deductible in suburbs but not in central cities. If this is the primary factor dictating moving, then it is conceivable that some part of the sample is induced to move *because* it must acquire a home; this would be so when rental accommodations are not available in a given jurisdiction.

The Nature of the Data

The sample on which this analysis is based derives, as mentioned earlier, from the 1977 AHS, and we obtained the sample as follows (more detail is given in appendix 4A):

In broad terms we *began with all movers*: all movers were identified by a coded entry in the XTENURE file. The entry indicates that the housing unit in question has changed occupants between the previous (1976) and the current (1977) surveys.

The next step consisted of fixing on those dwelling units whose occupants were previously renters. Within this class, we selected only the data for first-homeowners and (recurring) renters.

This left us with a final sample consisting of 1,293 observations, of which 172 were first-homeowners and 1,121 were recurring renters.

Although we have a tendency to speak of households in this context, it is important to appreciate the fact that the basic AHS files refer to dwelling units. Thus, if one desires, one may think of the probabilistic problem as one involving the placing of balls (households) into boxes (dwelling units). Since every household is, at any moment in time, associated with a given dwelling unit, in order to study the process of moving and tenure change, it was sufficient to concentrate our attention on the dwelling units (boxes); the latter constituted a random probabilistic sample of all dwelling units in the United States. Consequently, it is immaterial whether we obtained a random sample of households and asked what sort of dwellings they inhabited, or whether we selected a certain number of dwelling units (as the AHS does) and asked what sort of households inhabited them. The difference in the two approaches consists only in the treatment of migrating households.

What was required was that the process of moving be independent of the process of tenure choice. As we have indicated in the introduction, this assumption was not, in all likelihood, absolutely correct. On the other hand, we still do not have the resources to pursue this line of inquiry and, moreover, it is not clear whether the AHS files contain sufficient information to take this facet into account.

In subsequent analyses we assumed that we had a random sample of households that changed their residences between 1976 and 1977. We modelled their choice of tenure between first homeownership and recurring renter status, *given that they have moved.* It is our view that this conceptualization of the problem does not do serious violence to the nature of the phenomenon we wish to study.

Definitions of the Variables Used in the Analysis

Given the sample as just set forth, we have modelled the phenomenon as a logit analytic problem. Thus, the dependent variable DV was coded as zero if the household in question was in recurring renter status in 1977, and one, if in first homeownership status.

Income of the households was defined as the total income of all related members of the households as given in the AHS files.

The cost of homeownership was defined in a rather complex way, which bears explaining in some detail here. First, from monthly mortgage payments and the total amount of mortgage debt, it is possible to find various combinations of interest rates and maturity corresponding to the mortgage in question. Bearing in mind that mortgages are usually for a term, in months, divisible by 12, we are nearly always able to determine the pair uniquely. In some instances, where this was not possible, we were able to determine a limited range of the mortgage interest rate corresponding to the published data of the Federal Home Loan Bank Board, which are given annually by SMSA. This generally narrowed the range of possibilities to one combination. Once the mortgage interest rate was determined, the cost of ownership was defined as the implicit interest on the *total purchase price of the house* plus the real estate taxes (both on a monthly basis) times one minus the effective personal-income-tax rate given in the *Statistics of Income, 1977* (table 2.9) for the appropriate number of exemptions and income size, plus the monthly insurance and utility costs. This determined rather accurately[1] the homeownership cost faced by households that opted for first-homeownership.

For those households in recurring renter status, the homeownership cost was computed as the mean costs of first-homeowners in the four census regions by center city/noncenter city classification for each SMSA.

The other variables are generally dummy variables reflecting the socio-locational characteristics of the households involved. As such they are generally self-explanatory.

Characteristics of First-Homeowners and Recurring Renters

Insofar as the question of first-homeownership has not received much attention in the literature, we display in appendix 4C a number of tables giving tabulations of characteristics of homeowners versus recurring renters. Generally, tables 4C-1 through 4C-18 refer to homeowners, while tables 4C-19 through 4C-29 refer to recurring renters.

In these tables, the age of an overwhelming number of first-homeowners is under 40, while an appreciable proportion (about 10 percent) are over 40. Recurring renters tend to be somewhat older, approximately 21 percent of them being over 40. Incidentally, the age referred to above is the age of the head of the household.

First-homeowners tend to be overwhelmingly male; whereas about 31 percent of recurring renters are female. Blacks are somewhat underrepresented in the first-homeownership group, while both "Others" and "White" are somewhat overrepresented. The obverse is true for recurring renters, although the "Others" category seems to correspond closely to the results of the 1980 U.S. Census.

On the average, first-homeownership households are somewhat larger than recurring renter households, while the Northeast seems to be underrepresented in the first-homeownership group, and the North Central region seems to be overrepresented. As is to be expected, homeownership is underrepresented in central cities and overrepresented in noncentral cities vis-à-vis recurring renters.

By far the most striking difference between the two groups, however, lies in their income distribution (tables 4C-8 and 4C-26). Mean first-homeowner income is almost twice mean recurring-renter income (about $21,000 versus $12,000). The same is generally true of the costs of homeownership versus the rental costs of recurring renters[2] ($400 versus $230). Similarly, the current to previous cost of shelter is appreciably higher among first-homeowners than among recurring renters (1.9 versus 1.1).

The mean value of a house purchased by first-homeowners is about $45,000, while the mean mortgage taken is about $34,500, with the mean percent down payment being about 24 percent.

The mean house value–to–household-income ratio is about 2.3, somewhat less than the conventional wisdom would have it; an appreciable component, however, about 20 percent, display a ratio of 3.0 or higher.

The mean educational level attained by first-homeowners is two years of college, while for recurring renters it lies between high school graduation and one year of college.

In general, the tables show that first-homeowners are somewhat younger, wealthier, and better educated than recurring renters, although an appreciable proportion of them (about 10 percent) are over 40, earn less than $15,000 a year (21.5 percent), and have only completed high school (34.9 percent).

Fewer of the first-homeowners are black and they tend to be less concentrated in the Northeast than the distribution of the U.S. population would suggest.

Finally, even after adjusting for fiscal aspects, first-homeowners spend more on housing (on an average per capita basis) than do recurring renters. Recall that the mean household size for first-homeowners is 3.0, while for recurring renters it is 2.4; mean homeownership costs are about $400 per month, while mean rental costs are about $230 per month. Whether this reflects a higher "quantity" and/or "quality" of shelter services in the case of first-homeowners, or whether this is due to other characteristics of homeownership such as the expectation of capital gains, is a question that cannot be answered without further analysis.

Econometric Analysis of the Data

As we indicated in previous sections, we hypothesized that the probability of making a first-home purchase upon moving is given by the logistic distribution with argument, say, t. The latter may be specified to be a function of the economic and sociolocational characteristics of the household in question. The variables involved were discussed briefly earlier, and are more completely in appendix 4B.

The basic fundamental assumption is that the observations are mutually independent, so that their log-likelihood function may be written as

$$L(\beta; y, X) = \sum_{s=1}^{T} \ln F(x_s \beta)$$

where x_s is the vector of characteristics applicable to the sth household and β is the vector of parameters to be estimated; $F(.)$ denotes the usual logistic distribution function.

The basic results are given in table 4-1, where the column *Beta* gives the estimated coefficients and the column *Chi-square* gives the square of the usual t-ratio. This statistic, by asymptotic theory, is distributed as chi-square with one degree of freedom. The critical points are: at 5 percent level of significance, 3.84; at the 2.5 percent level of significance, 5.02; and at the 1 percent level of significance, 6.63.

In table 4-2 we give the means, minimum, maximum, and range of the independent variables. The entries in the Classification Table, appearing at the bottom of table 4-1, are meant to convey some information about goodness of fit, since a statistic like the coefficient of determination of multiple regression (the R^2 of the general linear model) is lacking in the current context. I have argued elsewhere (Dhrymes, 1981) that if one wishes to define a statistic that is similar in certain respects to the R^2 of the general linear model, one should define it by

$$R^{*2} = 1 - [L^*(\tilde{\beta})/L^*(\hat{\beta})]$$

where L^* is the likelihood function (*not* the log-likelihood function). In the expression above, $L^*(\tilde{\beta})$ is thus the likelihood function evaluated at its maximum, when the maintained hypothesis is that no socioeconomic-locational variables enter the model, that is, $\tilde{\beta}$ corresponds solely to the "constant" term. On the other hand, $L^*(\hat{\beta})$ is the likelihood function evaluated at its maximum, corresponding to the model as specified. Roughly speaking, this summary statistic tells us how much of the maximized value of the likelihood function is *due* to the bona fide explanatory variables as distinct from the constant term. Such a computation for the current case will yield:

$$R^* = 1 - e^{-207.68} \approx 1$$

Table 4-1
Explanation of the Probability of a Mover Becoming a First-Homeowner

Independent Variables	Beta	Standard Error	Chi-Square	P	D
INTERCEPT	-4.39965339	1.25229843	12.34	0.0004	0.031
Total household income, TINC	0.00008265	0.00001290	41.02	0.0000	0.082
Ratio of current to previously monthly costs, RMHCOR	2.24814434	0.21008477	114.51		0.020
Monthly home ownership costs, AVGOC	-0.00807192	0.00157989	26.10	0.0000	0.015
Percent down payment, PDP	-0.05393090	0.01205917	20.00	0.0000	0.010
Sex dummy, DSM	2.03173194	0.57086452	12.67	0.0004	0.001
Dummy race white, DRW	-0.050287003	0.60540887	0.70	0.4025	0.0001
Dummy race black, DRB	-0.86830502	0.72638635	1.43	0.2319	0.004
Center city of SMSA dummy, DCC	-0.53270991	0.22943888	5.39	0.0202	0.000
Regional dummy, Dwelling Northeast, DNE	-0.27668616	0.37752052	0.54	0.4636	0.001
Regional dummy, Dwelling North Central, DNC	0.27031928	0.28967089	0.87	0.3507	0.004
Regional dummy, Dwelling South, DS	-0.70335621	0.31657507	4.94	0.0263	0.007
Age of head of household, ZAGE	-0.21397261	0.07045237	9.22	0.0024	0.005
Number of household members, PER	0.20154945	0.07918293	6.48	0.0109	0.005
Highest grade of school completed by head, GRADE	0.10856582	0.04429412	6.01	0.0142	

Logistic Regression Procedure: Classification Table
(Dependent Variable: DV)

	Predicted		
	Negative	Positive	Total
True Negative	1084	37	1121
Positive	91	81	172
Total	1175	118	1293

Sensitivity: 47.1%
Specificity: 96.7%
Correct: 90.1%
False positive rate: 31.4%
False negative rate: 7.7%

Table 4-2
Logistic Regression Procedure
(Dependent Variable: DV)

Independent Variables	Mean	Minimum	Maximum	Range
TINC	14162.7	1060	63100	62040
RMHCOR	1.24834	0.1634	5.2857	6.1223
AVGOC	399.621	118	1015	897
PDP	24.3308	0	69.62	69.62
DSM	0.731632	0	1	1
DRW	0.82908	0	1	1
DRB	0.136118	0	1	1
DCC	0.489559	0	1	1
DNE	0.178654	0	1	1
DNC	0.25522	0	1	1
DS	0.228152	0	1	1
ZAGE	4.58314	1	17	16
PER	2.48105	1	12	11
GRADE	13.6767	0	19	19

Notes: -2 Log-likelihood for model containing intercept only $= 1013.96$
$-2 \text{Log } L = 598.60$

1293 Observations
172 Positives
1121 Negatives
0 Observations deleted due to missing values

so that *nearly all* of the maximized value of the likelihood function is *due* to the bona fide explanatory variables and relatively little is due to the constant term. We recognize, of course, that this is an overstatement of the goodness-of-fit characteristics of this model as applied to the case under consideration.

In the Classification Table, the term *Sensitivity* refers to the number of correct positive predictions divided by the total number of positive observations, where a positive prediction is made if the predicted probability is .5 or more. *Specificity* refers to the ratio of correct negative predictions to the total number of negative observations. The term *Correct* refers to the sum of correct positive and negative predictions divided by the total number of observations. *False positive rate* and *False negative rate* are perhaps self-explanatory and are evidently the ratios of incorrectly predicted positive and negative cases to the total number of positive and negative predictions, respectively.

Thus, by most goodness-of-fit accounts, the model is reasonably well suited for the purposes intended, although it tends to predict relatively much better the recurrence of rental status.

The coefficients of the variables have the expected signs and, in general, we have no compelling reason for doubting the usefulness of this representation of the phenomenon we wish to study.

In table 4-1, the specification of the argument of the logistic distribution is linear. In tables 4-3 and 4-4, we give an alternative set of results where the nondummy variables are stated in logarithmic terms, except for the percent down payment, which continues to be stated in linear terms. The statistic R^{*2} corresponding to this formulation is

$$R^{*2} = 1 - e^{-240.45} \approx 1$$

so that it is not appreciably different from that attained by the previous formulation. On the other hand, the Classification Table of table 4-3 corresponding to this formulation gives an indication of a somewhat better fit in that it predicts somewhat better positive observations (that is, it gives the same predicting performance when predicting recurring renters (1084 versus 1084, out of a total of 1121) but gives a better performance when predictive first-homeownership (92 versus 81, out of a total of 172). Thus, in discussing the empirical implications for substantive issues, we shall give the results from both formulations.

We note, before we continue with the substantive findings, that income is stated in dollars, and so is cost of homeownership.[3] Percent down payment is stated in percentage terms, that is, 20 percent enters the calculations as 20.0 AGE is stated in intervals, and so is GRADE, which refers to the highest educational level attained; both these variables were coded in AHS in exactly the same fashion as they appear in the tabulations of appendix 4B. The number of persons in the household are stated in the natural way, as is the ratio of current to previous housing costs.

What substantive implications can we derive from our study? Let us begin with the obvious ones. First, although from the results of tables 4C-3 and 4C-21 it would appear that blacks are underrepresented among first-homeowners, and overrepresented among recurring renters, *there is no econometric evidence to support the proposition that being black per se lowers the probability of acquiring a home; nor is there evidence to suggest that being white per se increases the probability of homeownership*. This is indicated by the coefficients of the variables DRW and DRB in tables 4-1 and 4-2. These are dummy variables and their coefficients are to be interpreted as the difference in the constant term of the equation as between "whites" and "others," and "blacks," and "others," respectively. In the language of the analysis of variance they are *contrasts* and the hypothesis of zero contrasts is easily accepted in both cases. *Being a central city resident significantly lessens the probability of first-homeownership*. This is in-

Table 4–3
Alternate Set of Results

Independent Variables	Beta	Standard Error	Chi-Square	P	D
INTERCEPT	3.11568282	4.23787394	0.54		0.034
LTINC	1.94627770	0.29170258	44.52	0.0000	0.089
LRMHCOR	4.31407761	0.38717038	124.16	0.0000	0.038
LAVGOC	-4.77481920	0.67318587	50.31	0.0000	0.008
PDP	-0.04027115	0.01226905	10.77	0.0010	0.009
DSM	1.94780520	0.57567378	11.45	0.0007	0.001
DRW	-0.79215869	0.63873301	1.54	0.2149	0.002
DRB	-1.04875208	0.75580715	1.93	0.1653	0.002
DCC	-0.61747957	0.24387013	6.14	0.0113	0.005
DNE	-0.61407499	0.40097991	2.35	0.1257	0.002
DNC	0.04777465	0.30194920	0.03	0.8743	0.000
DS	-1.00742648	0.33305520	9.15	0.0025	0.007
LZAGE	-0.63041569	0.28487532	4.90	0.0269	0.004
LPEP	0.56202879	0.24788456	5.14	0.0234	0.004
LGRADE	1.45849483	0.69560592	4.40	0.0360	0.003

Logistic Regression Procedure: Classification Table
(Dependent Variable: DV)

	Predicted		
	Negative	Positive	Total
True Negative	1084	37	1121
Positive	80	92	172
Total	1164	129	1293

Sensitivity: 53.5%
Specificity: 96.7%
Correct: 91.0%
False positive rate: 28.7%
False negative rate: 6.9%

Table 4–4
Logistic Regression Procedure, With Some Logarithmic Variables
(Dependent Variable: DV)

Independent Variables	Mean	Minimum	Maximum	Range
LTINC	9.37174	6.96602	11.0525	4.08645
LRMHCOR	0.134151	−1.81155	1.665	3.47656
LAVGOC	5.97653	4.77068	6.92264	2.15196
PDP	24.3308	0	69.62	69.62
DSM	0.731632	0	1	1
DRW	0.82908	0	1	1
DRB	0.136118	0	1	1
DCC	0.489559	0	1	1
DNE	0.178654	0	1	1
DNC	0.25522	0	1	1
DS	0.228152	0	1	1
LZAGE	1.35218	0	2.83321	2.83321
LPER	0.748659	0	2.48491	2.48491
LGRADE	2.65101	0	2.99573	2.99573

Notes: −2 Log-likelihood for model containing intercept only = 1013.96
$-2 \text{ Log } L = 533.05$

1293 Observations
172 Positives
1121 Negatives
0 Observations deleted due to missing values

dicated by the coefficient of the variable *DCC*, which estimates the "contrast" between central city and noncentral city residents of a metropolitan area.

Being in the South lessens the probability of first-homeownership; this is indicated by the negative coefficient of the variable *DS*, which represents the contrast between being a resident of the southern region vis-à-vis the western region of the country. Just why this should be so is not entirely clear.

Contrary to the impressions left by tables 4C-5 and 4C-23, there is no econometric evidence to suggest that being in the northeastern or the north-central region of the country reduces the probability of first-homeownership.

The larger the household and the higher the educational level attained by the head, the higher the probability of first-homeownership.

Most of the preceding results are more or less what one would expect, or at least are readily acceptable and occasion no consternation.

Looking at the coefficient of the variable *ZAGE*, that is, the age of the head of the household, we encounter the first result that is, at first glance, counterintuitive. Upon reflection, however, the surprise evaporates and it appears to tell us that if a household with certain characteristics did not acquire a home when younger, it is less likely that, maintaining these characteristics, it would be led to buy a home at a later age.

Turning now to the economic variables and their impact on homeownership, it would be convenient to explore these issues for the linear and nonlinear specifications separately.

From table 4-1, we easily determine that the probability of first-homeownership evaluated at the mean of the sample is given (where $\bar{x}$ is the vector of sample means of the explanatory variables) by

$$F(\bar{x}\hat{\beta}) = .03201$$

while the logistic density evaluated at the same point yields

$$f(\bar{x}\hat{\beta}) = .03098$$

To evaluate the impact of changes in income, interest rates, percent down payment, etc., on the probability of first-homeownership, it will suffice to change the corresponding element of $\bar{x}$ by the desired amount. Thus, consider an increase in mean income by $10,000; this corresponds to about a 70 percent increase in mean income. How does this impact the probability of first-homeownership? Well, define the vector $\bar{x}^{(1)}$, which is in every respect the same as $\bar{x}$, except that the component corresponding to income has been increased by $10,000. We easily determine that

$$F(\bar{x}^{(1)}\hat{\beta}) = .07035$$

which indicates a change in the probability by

$$\Delta F = .03835$$

in other words, a change by about 120 percent; hence the corresponding elasticity (arc) is about 1.7.

Next consider an increase in interest rates that leads to an increase in mean housing costs from $399.6 to $500.0 per month. Defining the vector $\bar{x}^{(2)}$ appropriately, we see that in this case

$$F(\bar{x}^{(2)}\hat{\beta}) = .01449$$

which indicates a change in the probability by

$$\Delta F = -.01751$$

or by approximately 55 percent; hence, the corresponding arc elasticity is $(-)$ 2.2.

Finally, considering an increase in the percent down payment from 24 to 30 percent—an increase of approximately 25 percent—leads to

$$F(\bar{x}^{(3)}\beta) = .02378$$

which indicates a change in the probability of first-homeownership by

$$\Delta F = -.00823$$

or by approximately 26 percent; hence, the appropriate arc elasticity is approximately of the order of $(-)$ 1.

We now explore exactly the same issues in the context of the nonlinear formulation.

The probability of first-home purchase, estimated by this formulation and evaluated (where appropriate) at the logarithms of the mean of the sample is given by

$$F(\ln \bar{x}\dot{\gamma}) = .02804$$

while the logistic density function evaluated at the same point is

$$f(\ln \bar{x}\dot{\gamma}) = .02725$$

If, in this context, we wish to find out what is the consequence of increasing mean income by, say, $10,000, the proper way of proceeding is to find the means of the explanatory variables in their natural form and increase mean income by $10,000. Then, where appropriate, take the logarithms of the elements of this vector, and denote it by $\ln \bar{x}^{(1)}$. The mean probability at this new vector is

$$F(\ln \bar{x}^{(1)}\dot{\gamma}) = .07542$$

Thus, the change in probability entailed by this 70 percent increase in mean income is

$$\Delta F = .04738$$

or approximately 169 percent. Hence, the arc elasticity of the probability of first-home purchase with respect to income is about 2.4.

Next, we consider an increase of $100 in monthly costs associated with first-homeownership of owner-occupied dwellings. Again, redefining the basic mean vector $\bar{x}$ by changing the mean housing costs from $399.6 to $500.0, yields a new vector, say, $\bar{x}^{(2)}$. The probability at this new vector is

$$F(\ln \bar{x}^{(2)}\dot{\gamma}) = .00980$$

Consequently, the change in probability is

$$\Delta F = -.01824$$

or a change of approximately 65 percent. Here the elasticity is about 2.6.

Finally, an increase in the mean percent down payment to 30 percent (from 24 percent), that is, a 25 percent increase, yields the result

$$F(\ln \bar{x}^{(3)}\hat{\gamma}) = .02244$$

which implies the change in probability

$$\Delta F = -.00560$$

or a change by approximately 20 percent. Hence, the arc elasticity implied with respect to percent down payment is approximately $(-)$ .8.

Comparing the implications of the two formulations in terms of the arc elasticities for these three economic variables, we see that the nonlinear formulation yields somewhat higher income and housing-cost elasticities, and somewhat lower percent-down payment elasticities; the magnitude of the differences are such that, confining our attention to the financial stringency variables, we are likely to get very similar results for typical configurations of interest rate rises and changes in percent down payment.

Conclusions

We have explored, in this chapter, using the abundant information conveyed by the AHS files, the question of the determinants of the probability of first-home purchase and the impact thereon of stringency in the financial markets.

We have used logit analytic procedures and experimented with two formulations, one in which the argument of the logistic is a linear function of all variables, and another in which the nondummy variables were expressed in logarithmic terms, with the exception of the percent-down-playment variable, which was expressed linearly. Generally, the logarithmic formulation may fit somewhat better than the linear formulation, although extensive experimentation was not carried out.

The general substantive findings supported by both formulations are the following: *despite the apparent underrepresentation of black households in the first-homeownership sample, there is no econometric evidence that race is an appreciable determinant of homeownership, once characteristics like income, costs, age, and education are taken into account. Residents of central cities (at the time of the survey) are less likely to have become first-*

homeowners upon moving, and there is also some evidence that the same is true of the region defined as "South" by the Census.

Financial market stringency exerts a very powerful impact on the probability of first-homeownership. *First, we note that both formulations support the view that the income elasticity of the probability of first-homeownership is higher than unity.* In fact, the first formulation implies 1.7 and the second implies 2.4. *Both formulations imply a homeownership-cost elasticity less than −2.* In fact, the first formulation yields −2.2, while the second yields −2.6. Finally, the percent-down-payment elasticity is −1 and −.8, respectively.

We should note certain caveats at the end of our investigation. First, it would be highly desirable to convert this investigation from a dichotomous to a polytomous problem, since we are overlooking the intermittent home-buyer. Second, the longitudinal character of the AHS files has not been exploited, and the integration of cross-section and time-series information may be highly informative on a number of issues on which the current formulation is inevitably deficient. Third, more investigation is required on the consequences of misspecification analysis for the properties of the resulting estimators in logit and probit formulations. Not enough is known regarding the consequences of fitting a logit when a probit formulation is more appropriate, or of having too many variables in the argument of the logistic, or too few, or regarding the use of proxies.

Notes

1. One may argue, of course, that the interest cost as computed may overstate the issue, since in 1977 (or at other times) the household may not have had an alternative of investing its funds at a rate of return equal to the mortgage rate it was forced to pay, while in subsequent years, as interest rates moved up, our computation would represent an understatement of the true opportunity costs.

2. It may be argued that the homeownership costs are overstated due to the inclusion of insurance costs, and their exclusion from the rental cost of recurring renters. Some insurance costs are incidental to the mortgage indebtedness, and this is a proper component of the cost of homeownership. Another component, however, the personal effects component, ought not to be included for comparability with renters' costs. It is impossible, from the data, to eliminate this discrepancy. The differences, however, would be rather small even if we were to make the correction, and in no way could we attribute the differences in mean costs substantially to this item.

3. It should be noted that in a completely specified model, in which homeownership other than first is properly taken into account, this is the correct formulation.

References

David, Martin. *Family Composition and Consumption.* Amsterdam: North Holland Publishing Co., 1962.

Dhrymes, P.J. 1978. *Introductory Econometrics.* New York: Springer-Verlag New York: Inc.

———. 1981. "Limited Dependent Variables," mimeographed.

Kain, J., and Quigley, J. *Housing Markets and Racial Discrimination.* New York: National Bureau of Economic Research, 1975.

Lee, T.H. "Demand for Housing: A Cross Section Analysis." *Review of Economics and Statistics* 45 (1963):190–196.

Maisel, S.J. "Rates of Ownership, Mobility and Purchase." In *Essays in Urban Land Economics,* Los Angeles: UCLA Real Estate Research Program, 1966.

Orcutt, G.H., et al. *Microanalysis of Socioeconomic Systems.* New York: Harper & Row, 1961.

U.S. Bureau of the Census, *Current Housing Reports,* Series H150-78, Appendix B. Describes the method of sampling and the nature of the Annual Housing Surveys (AHS).

Appendix 4A:
Selection of the Data

Selection of Dhrymes Master File

The master file which we are working with is a subfile of the National Housing Survey Data Base. The Dhrymes file was selected by the following rule:

when

$XTENURE = 1$ the mover owned a house
         2   the mover owned a coop
         3   the mover owned a condo
         4   the mover rented
         5   the mover paid no rent

and

$TENURE = 1$ the mover now owns a house
         2   the mover now owns a coop
         3   the mover now owns a condo
         4   the mover now rents
         5   the mover now pays no rent

This rule in effect selects all data on observations where there has been a move since the last survey, that is, all movers. This data is in five files by year (1973–1977).

After units, for which no cash rent was previously paid, were deleted, the sample contained 5204 cases.

Selection of the First-Homeownership Study Data

Data for the actual analysis were selected by identifying those observations representing first-homeowners and recurring renters.

Rule 1

Selected if

$XTENURE = 4$ the mover rented

and

$TENURE = 1$ the mover now owns a house
          2   the mover now owns a coop
          3   the mover now owns a condo

and

$FRSTHO = 1$ the mover has not owned a home previously

or

$XTENURE = 4$ the mover rented

and

$TENURE = 4$ the mover now rents.

Rule 1 reduces the number of cases to 4759. Exactly 445 cases were dropped due to a nonfirst-time homeownership for those cases where there had been a move from renter status to ownership status since the last survey. This rule deletes cases where $FRSTHO$ was coded as 2, 3, and 9.

$FRSTHO = 2$ the mover has owned a home previously
          3   the head of household is not the owner
          9   data is not available

In addition to Rule 1, the following conditions were imposed:

Rule 2

Selected if METRO $= 1$ or 2
(rule 2 reduces the sample by 2362 to 2397 cases).

Rule 3

Selected if previous monthly rent + utility cost for current renters and owners was not missing
(Rule 3 reduces the sample by 154 to 2243 cases.)

Rule 13

Selected if annual real-estate taxes for owners was not missing.
(Rule 13 reduces the sample by 31 to 1844 cases.)

Rule 14

For recurring renter data the following *SMSA* coded observations were
deleted: 80, 160, 360, 1000, 1280, 1640, 2800, 2960, 3640, 5560, 5640,
5720, 5880, 6040, 6480, 6920, 7280, 7400, 8400
(Rule 14 reduces the sample by 450 to 1293.)

Rule 15

Restoring omitted zeros (000) as follows:

IF *AMMORT* =   270, THEN *AMMORT* = 27000.
IF *AMMORT* =   474, THEN *AMMORT* = 47400.
IF *AMMORT* =   307, THEN *AMMORT* = 30700.
IF *AMMORT* = 2300, THEN *AMMORT* = 23000.

Rule 16

After all the conditions on the data were imposed the sample consisted of
1293 cases, out of which 172 were first-time-homeowners and 1121 were
recurring renters.

**Explanation as to Why Condo/Coop Units Were
Excluded in 1977 Data**

From the total sample of all movers (5204), 60 cases represented moves
from rental status to condo/coop ownership status, 39 cases indicated first-
time-ownership, 20 cases pertained to non-first-time-home-ownership, and 1
case did not indicate either condition.

None of the 60 cases contained any value for the dollar amount of the
mortgage.

Changes Made to the Data Values from Housing
Survey Data Base

Table 4A–1
Changes in AMMORT

AMMORT	AMMORT*	HVALUE	PDP	RMHCO	ZXRENT	RMHCOR	TINC
270	27000	55480	51.3	516	320	1.61	14600
474	47400	88000	46.1	722	330	2.19	20000
307	30700	32000	4.7	370	307	1.21	11800
2300	23000	36400	49.4	471	312	1.51	14200

When it appeared obvious that adding zeros to *AMMORT* would bring the monthly costs into line with the corrected amount of the mortgage the values were edited.

Table 4A–2
Definitions of Variables Used in Table 4A–1

Variables	Definitions	Source[a]
AMMORT	Dollar Amount of the Mortgage	AHSDB
AMMORT[b]	Corrected amount of the mortgage	
HVALUE	House Value $= (ZVI)(ZINC) 1$	AHSDB
PDP	Percent down payment $= (1 - AMMORT/HVALUE)(100)$	AHSDB
RMHCO	Monthly homeownership costs	
ZXRENT	Previous selected monthly housing costs	AHSDB
RMHCOR	Current to previous monthly housing costs	
TINC	Total household income $= ZINC + YIWS$	AHSDB

[a]AHSDB = Annual Housing Survey Data Base.
[b]Corrected data.

When the amount of the mortgage was greater than the computed value of the house (*HVALUE*), *HVALUE* was set equal to *AMMORT*. The resulting changes in *ZVI* and *HVALUE* are shown in table 4A–3.

Table 4A-3
Changes in House Value

AMMORT	HVALUE	HVALUE[a]	PDP	ZVI	ZVI*	RMHCO	ZXRENT	RMHCOR	TINC
27511	26620	27511	0	10	10.3	273	227	1.2	26620
39900	37728	39900	0	24	25.4	392	307	1.3	15720
38000	27750	38000	0	25	25.2	329	151	2.2	15100
32950	31622	32950	0	13	13.5	303	189	1.6	24325
49999	46340	49999	0	14	15.1	468	375	1.2	60600
46500	44154	46500	0	22	23.2	396	425	.9	12007
38950	38400	38950	0	16	16.2	342	182	1.9	24000
29000	27153	29000		18	19.2	335	221	1.5	15085
29000	27524	29000		27	28.4	229	280	1.4	10194
29900	27360	29900		19	20.8	339	190	1.8	14400

[a]Corrected data.

Table 4A–4
Definitions of Variables Used in Table 4A–3

Variable	Definitions	Source[a]
AMMORT	Dollar amount of the mortgage	AHSDB
HVALUE	Dollar value of house $= (ZVI)(ZINC)(.1)$	AHSDB
HVALUE[b]	Corrected house value $= AMMORT$	AHSDB
PDP	Percent down payment $=$ $(1 - AMMORT/HVALUE)(100)$	
ZVI	House value to income (relatives) ratio	AHSDB
RMHCO	Monthly homeownership costs	AHSDB
ZXRENT	Previous selected monthly housing costs	AHSDB
RMHCOR	Current to previous monthly housing cost	AHSDB
TINC	Total household income $= ZINC + YIWS$	AHSDB

[a]AHSDB = Annual Housing Survey Data Base.
[b]Corrected data.

Changes in Monthly Mortgage Payment

For one observation, the implicit maximum annual interest rate on a mortgage of $40,000, given monthly payments of $121, was 3.66%. At 3.25% the life of the mortgage would be 69 years; at 3% it would be 58 years. Due to this obvious error in either *AMMORT* or *PMT*, we assumed *PMT* = $321 and *AMMORT* was correct. Using *PMT* = $321, we then assigned to this observation mortgage rate of 8.75% and a mortgage life of 25 years.

Appendix 4B:
Explanation of
Variables and
Underlying Data

Dependent Variable (DV)

The dependent variable takes on the value 1 when there has been a move from rental to first-homeownership status ($TENURE = 1$ and $XTENURE = 4$, and $FRSTHO = 1$). $DV = 0$ when there has been a move from rental to rental status ($TENURE = 4$ and $XTENURE = 4$). (*Source*: Annual Housing Survey Data Base.)

Independent Variables

Total Household Income (*TINC*). *TINC* was computed by combining total income from related household members:

$$ZINC = \text{Salaries} + \text{Pensions} + \text{Interest} + \text{etc.}$$

With total income from unrelated household members (YIWS). (*Source*: Annual Housing Survey Data Base.)

Dummy on *TINC* (*DTINC*). $DTINC = (DNSAL)(TINC)$

where $DNSAL = 1$ two or more salaries
                0   one salary

An additional salary is registered only if that salary is greater than 40 percent of the maximum salary. (*Source*: Annual Housing Survey Data Base.)

Percent Down Payment (PDP)

For $DV = 1$ $PDP = [1-(AMMORT/HVALUE)] *100$
For $DV = 0$ $PDP = $ (Average percent down payment by SMSA)

House value $= \text{HVALUE} = (ZVI)(ZINC)(.1)$. Computed house value lies within the intervals of the *VALUE* variable in the survey data base. (*Source*:

Annual Housing Survey Data Base and the Federal Home Loan Bank Board.)

Monthly Homeownership Costs (AVGOC). For $DV = 1$ the cost of home ownership is defined to be

$$(HVALUE)(RM + AMTX/12)(1 - AITR) + AMTI/12 + UT$$

where

$HVALUE$ = Computed house value in dollars
$AMTX$ = Annual real estate taxes in dollars
$AMTI$ = Annual insurance payments in dollars
UT = Monthly utility costs in dollars
$AITR$ = Average income tax rate computed on the basis of the number of dependents
RM = Monthly interest rate on individual sample mortgages

For $DV = 0$, the cost of homeownership was defined to be the average of housing costs of the actual first-time homeowners in the sample. These averages were computed for each region of the country (Northeast, North-Central, Southwest) and reflected whether or not the renter, to which the average was applied, was in the center city of a SMSA or noncenter city of a SMSA. (*Source*: Annual Housing Survey Data Base and the U.S. Treasury Annual Statistics. Mortgage rates were deduced from data on the amount of individual mortgages and monthly payments.)

Average Rental Costs (AVGR). For $DV = 1$, the cost of home rental was defined to be the average of housing costs of the actual renters in the sample. These averages were computed for each region of the country (Northeast, North-Central, Southwest) and reflected whether or not the owner, to which the average was applied, was in the center city of a SMSA or noncenter city of a SMSA.

For $DV = 0$ the cost of home rental was taken from the Annual Housing Survey Data Base

$$ZRENT = \text{RENT} + \text{UTILITIES} + \text{ETC.}$$

(*Source*: Annual Housing Survey Data Base.)

Ratio of Current to Previous Monthly Costs (RMHCOR).

$$\text{FOR } DV = 1, RMHCOR = (RMHCO/ZXRENT)$$
$$\text{FOR } DV = 0, RMHCOR = (ZRENT/ZXRENT)$$

where

$$ZXRENT = \text{PREVIOUS RENT} + \text{UTILITIES} + \text{ETC.}$$
$$ZRENT = \text{CURRENT RENT} + \text{UTILITIES} + \text{ETC.}$$
$$RMHCO = (HVALUE)(RM + AMTX/12)(1 - AITR) + AMTI/12 +$$
$$UT \text{ (defined as in homeownership cost variable)}$$

(*Source*: Annual Housing Survey Data Base and the U.S. Treasury Publication Annual Statistics.)

Sex Dummy (*DSM*)

$$DSM = \text{If male}$$
$$= \text{If female}$$

(*Source*: Annual Housing Survey Data Base.)

Race Dummies (*DRW, DRB*)

$$DRW \quad 1 \qquad \text{If white}$$
$$= 0 \qquad \text{If black or other}$$
$$DRB = 1 \qquad \text{If black}$$
$$= 0 \qquad \text{If white or other}$$

(*Source*: Annual Housing Survey Data Base.)

Center City of SMSA Dummy (*DCC*)

$$DCC \quad 1 \qquad \text{If Dwelling in center city of SMSA}$$
$$= 0 \qquad \text{If Dwelling not in center city of SMSA}$$

(*Source*: Annual Housing Survey Data Base.)

Regional Dummies (*DNE, DNC, DW, DS*)

$$DNE = 1 \qquad \text{If Dwelling in Northeast}$$
$$= 0 \qquad \text{Other}$$
$$DNC = 1 \qquad \text{If Dwelling in North-Central}$$
$$= 0 \qquad \text{Other}$$
$$DW = 1 \qquad \text{If dwelling in West}$$
$$= 0 \qquad \text{Other}$$
$$DS = 1 \qquad \text{If dwelling in South}$$
$$= 0 \qquad \text{Other}$$

(*Source*: Annual Housing Survey Data Base.)

Number of Household Members (*PER*)

(*Source*: Annual Housing Survey Data Base.)

Highest Grade of School Completed by Head (*GRADE*)

(*Source*: Annual Housing Survey Data Base.)

Appendix 4C:
Frequency
Distributions of the
Data Used

Table 4C–1
1977 First-Homeowners by Age of Head

ZAGE	Frequency	Cumulative Frequency	Percent	Cumulative Percent
20–24	30	30	17.442	17.442
25–29	68	98	39.535	56.977
30–34	42	140	24.419	81.395
35–39	16	156	9.302	90.698
40–44	9	165	5.233	95.930
45–49	3	168	1.744	97.674
50–54	4	172	2.326	100.000

	Mean	Median
ZAGE	25–34	25–29

Table 4C–2
1977 First-Homeowners by Sex of Head

Sex	Frequency	Cumulative Frequency	Percent	Cumulative Percent
Male	168	168	97.674	97.674
Female	4	172	2.326	100.000

Table 4C–3
1977 First-Homeowners by Race of Head

Race	Frequency	Cumulative Frequency	Percent	Cumulative Percent
White	154	154	89.535	89.535
Black	11	165	6.395	95.930
Other	7	172	4.070	100.000

Table 4C–4
1977 First-Homeowners by Number of Persons

PER	Frequency	Cumulative Frequency	Percent	Cumulative Percent
1	13	13	7.558	7.558
2	64	77	37.209	44.767
3	48	125	27.907	72.674
4	24	149	13.953	86.628
5	11	160	6.395	93.023
6	8	168	4.651	97.674
7	1	169	0.581	98.256
8	2	171	1.163	99.419
9	1	172	0.581	100.000
		Mean		Median
PER		3		3

Table 4C–5
1977 First-Homeowners by Region of House

Region	Frequency	Cumulative Frequency	Percent	Cumulative Percent
Northeast	21	21	12.209	12.209
North-Central	54	75	31.395	43.605
South	39	114	22.674	66.279
West	58	172	33.721	100.000

Table 4C–6
1977 First-Homeowners by Metropolitan Region of House

Metropolitan Region	Frequency	Cumulative Frequency	Percent	Cumulative Percent
Center City	57	57	33.140	33.140
Noncenter City	115	172	66.860	100.000

Table 4C–7
1977 First-Homeowners by Total Income of Household
(Relative's and Nonrelative's Income)
(Dollars)

TINC	Frequency	Cumulative Frequency	Percent	Cumulative Percent
5,000– 9,999	5	5	2.907	2.907
10,000–14,999	31	36	18.023	20.930
15,000–19,999	53	89	30.814	51.744
20,000–24,999	37	126	21.512	73.256
25,000–29,999	23	149	13.372	86.628
30,000–34,999	8	157	4.651	91.279
35,000–39,999	7	164	4.070	95.349
40,000–44,999	4	168	2.326	97.674
45,000–49,999	3	171	1.744	99.419
60,000–64,999	1	172	0.581	100.000

	Mean	Median
TINC	21,308	19,420

Table 4C–8
1977 First-Homeowners by Income of Household
(Relative's Income Only)
(Dollars)

ZINC	Frequency	Cumulative Frequency	Percent	Cumulative Percent
5,000– 9,999	6	6	3.488	3.488
10,000–14,999	31	37	18.023	21.512
15,000–19,999	54	91	31.395	52.907
20,000–24,999	37	128	21.512	74.419
25,000–29,999	23	151	13.372	87.791
30,000–34,999	8	159	4.651	92.442
35,000–39,999	7	166	4.070	96.512
40,000–44,999	4	170	2.326	98.837
45,000–49,999	2	172	1.163	100.000

	Mean

	Mean	Median
ZINC	20,818	19,200

Table 4C–9
1977 First-Homeowners by Monthly Home-Ownership Cost
(Dollars)

SMHCO	Frequency	Cumulative Frequency	Percent	Cumulative Percent
100– 119	1	1	0.581	0.581
120– 139	1	2	0.581	1.163
140– 159	1	3	0.581	1.744
160– 179	2	5	1.163	2.907
180– 199	4	9	2.236	5.233
200– 219	3	12	1.744	6.977
220– 239	2	14	1.163	8.140
240– 259	7	21	4.070	12.209
260– 279	12	33	6.977	19.186
280– 299	10	43	5.814	25.000
300– 319	11	54	6.395	31.395
320– 339	11	65	6.395	37.791
340– 359	12	77	6.977	44.767
360– 379	10	87	5.814	50.581
380– 399	10	97	5.814	56.395
400– 419	10	107	5.814	62.209
420– 439	8	115	4.651	66.860
440– 459	7	122	4.070	70.930
460– 479	7	129	4.070	75.000
480– 499	5	134	2.907	77.907
500– 519	5	139	2.907	80.814
520– 539	7	146	4.070	84.884
540– 559	5	151	2.907	87.791
560– 579	5	156	2.907	90.698
580– 599	4	160	2.326	93.023
600– 619	3	163	1.744	94.767
640– 659	1	164	0.581	95.349
680– 699	2	166	1.163	96.512
700– 719	1	167	0.581	97.093
720– 739	2	169	1.163	98.256
740– 759	1	170	0.581	98.837
900– 919	1	171	0.581	99.419
1000–1019	1	172	0.581	100.000

	Mean	Median
RMHCO	399	378

Table 4C–10
1977 First-Homeowners by Current to Previous Monthly Cost Ratio

RMHCOR	Frequency	Cumulative Frequency	Percent	Cumulative Percent
0.60–0.69	1	1	0.581	0.581
0.80–0.89	2	3	1.163	1.744
0.90–0.99	3	6	1.744	3.488
1.00–1.09	8	14	4.651	8.140
1.10–1.19	7	21	4.070	12.209
1.20–1.29	12	33	6.977	19.186
1.30–1.39	6	39	3.488	22.674
1.40–1.49	11	50	6.395	29.070
1.50–1.59	14	64	8.140	37.209
1.60–1.69	17	81	9.884	47.093
1.70–1.79	11	92	6.395	53.488
1.80–1.89	16	108	9.302	62.791
1.90–1.99	7	115	4.070	66.860
2.00				
2.00–2.09	10	125	5.814	72.674
2.10–2.19	6	131	3.488	76.163
2.20–2.29	4	135	2.326	78.488
2.30–2.39	5	140	2.907	81.395
2.40–2.49	2	142	1.163	82.558
2.50–2.59	2	144	1.163	83.721
2.60–2.69	4	148	2.326	86.047
2.70–2.79	3	151	1.744	87.791
2.80–2.89	5	156	2.907	90.698
2.90–2.99	1	157	0.581	91.279
3.00–3.09	2	159	1.163	92.442
3.10–3.19	2	161	1.163	93.605
3.20–3.29	1	162	0.581	94.186
3.30–3.39	2	164	1.163	95.349
3.40–3.49	1	165	0.581	95.930
3.60–3.69	2	167	1.163	97.093
3.80–3.89	1	168	0.581	97.674
3.90–3.99	1	169	0.581	98.256
4.00–4.09	1	170	0.581	98.837
4.90–4.99	1	171	0.581	99.419
5.20–5.29	1	172	0.581	100.000

	Mean	Median
RMHCOR	1.9	1.7

Table 4C–11
1977 First-Homeowners by Highest Grade Completed by Head

GRADE	Frequency	Cumulative Frequency	Percent	Cumulative Percent
Grade 4	2	2	1.163	1.163
Grade 8	3	5	1.744	2.907
Grade 9	1	6	0.581	3.488
Grade 10	2	3	1.163	4.651
Grade 11	6	14	3.488	8.140
Grade 12 high school graduate	46	60	26.744	34.884
1 year college	10	70	5.814	40.698
2 years college	28	98	16.279	56.977
3 years college	12	110	6.977	63.953
4 years college	34	144	19.767	83.721
5 years college	5	149	2.907	86.628
6+ years college	23	172	13.372	100.000

	Mean	Median
GRADE	2 years college	2 years college

Table 4C–12
1977 First-Homeowners by Reported Value of House
(Dollars)

Value	Frequency	Cumulative Frequency	Percent	Cumulative Percent
10,999–12,499	2	2	1.163	1.163
12,500– 14,999	1	3	0.581	1.744
15,000– 17,499	3	6	1.744	3.488
17,500– 19,999	2	8	1.163	4.651
20,000– 24,999	13	21	7.558	12.209
25,000– 29,999	18	39	10.465	22.674
30,000– 34,999	25	64	14.535	37.209
35,000– 39,999	15	79	8.721	45.930
40,000– 49,999	36	115	20.930	66.860
50,000– 59,999	26	141	15.116	81.977
60,000– 74,999	21	162	12.209	94.186
75,000–124,999	8	170	4.651	98.837
125,000 ++	2	172	1.163	100.000

	Mean	Median
Value	35,000–49,000	40,000–49,000

Table 4C–13
1977 First-Homeowners by Calculated Value of House
(Dollars)

HVALUE	Frequency	Cumulative Frequency	Percent	Cumulative Percent
10,000– 14,999	3	3	1.744	1.744
15,000– 19,999	5	8	2.907	4.651
20,000– 24,999	13	21	7.558	12.209
25,000– 29,999	18	39	10.465	22.674
30,000– 34,999	25	64	14.535	37.209
35,000– 39,999	15	79	8.721	45.930
40,000– 44,999	16	95	9.302	55.233
35,000– 49,999	20	115	11.628	66.860
50,000– 54,999	11	126	6.395	73.256
55,000– 59,999	15	141	8.721	81.977
65,000– 69,999	21	162	12.209	94.186
85,000– 89,999	8	170	4.651	98.837
135,000–139,999	2	172	1.163	100.000

	Mean	Median
HVALUE	45,063	44,384

Table 4C–14
1977 First-Homeowners by Amount of Home Mortgage
(Dollars)

AMMORT	Frequency	Cumulative Frequency	Percent	Cumulative Percent
5,000– 9,999	1	1	0.581	0.581
10,000– 14,999	7	8	4.070	4.651
15,000– 19,999	15	23	8.721	13.372
20,000– 24,999	18	41	10.465	23,837
25,000– 29,999	32	73	18.605	42.442
30,000– 34,999	23	96	13.372	55.814
35,000– 39,999	25	121	14.535	70.349
40,000– 44,999	15	136	8.721	79.070
45,000– 49,999	16	152	9.302	88.372
50,000– 54,999	7	159	4.070	92.442
55,000– 59,999	3	162	1.744	94.186
60,000– 64,999	5	167	2.907	97.093
65,000– 69,999	1	168	0.581	97.674
70,000– 74,999	1	169	0.581	98.256
75,000– 79,999	1	170	0.581	98.837
95,000– 99,999	1	171	0.581	99.419
100,000–104,999	1	172	0.581	100.000

	Mean	Median
AMMORT	34,502	32,125

Table 4C–15
1977 First-Homeowners by Percent-Down Payment
(Computed House Value)
(Percent-Down Payment Rounded to Nearest One)

PDP	Frequency	Cumulative Frequency	Percent	Cumulative Percent
0.0	12	12	6.977	6.977
0.5– 1.4	2	14	1.163	8.140
1.5– 2.4	1	15	0.581	8.721
3.5– 4.4	4	19	2.326	11.047
4.5– 5.4	5	24	2.907	13.953
5.5– 6.4	1	25	0.581	14.535
6.5– 7.4	3	28	1.744	16.279
7.5– 8.4	4	32	2.326	18.605
8.5– 9.4	7	39	4.070	22.674
9.5–10.4	4	43	2.326	25.000
10.5–11.4	9	52	5.233	30.233
11.5–12.4	5	57	2.907	33.140
12.5–13.4	2	59	1.163	34.302
13.5–14.4	4	63	2.326	36.628
14.5–15.4	5	68	2.907	39.535
15.5–16.4	6	74	3.488	43.023
16.5–17.4	7	81	4.070	47.093
17.5–18.4	4	85	2.326	49.419
18.5–19.4	1	86	0.581	50.000
19.5–20.4	3	89	1.744	51.744
20.5–21.4	3	92	1.744	53.488
21.5–22.4	5	97	2.907	56.395
22.5–23.4	6	103	3.488	59.884
23.5–24.4	4	107	2.326	62.209
24.5–25.4	5	112	2.907	65.116
25.5–26.4	5	117	2.907	68.023
26.5–27.4	4	121	2.326	70.349
27.5–28.4	4	125	2.326	72.674
28.5–29.4	3	128	1.744	74.419
30.5–31.4	5	133	2.907	77.326
31.5–32.4	2	135	1.163	78.488
32.5–33.4	2	137	1.163	79.651
33.5–34.4	5	142	2.907	82.558
34.5–35.4	1	143	0.581	83.140
35.5–36.4	3	146	1.744	84.884
36.5–37.4	1	147	0.581	85.465
37.5–38.4	1	148	0.581	86.047
38.5–39.4	2	150	1.163	87.209
40.5–41.4	1	151	0.581	87.791
41.5–42.4	2	153	1.163	88.953
42.5–43.4	1	154	0.581	89.535
43.5–44.4	2	156	1.163	90.698
45.5–46.4	4	160	2.326	93.023
46.5–47.4	1	161	0.581	93.605
48.5–49.4	2	163	1.163	94.767
50.5–51.4	2	165	1.163	95.930
54.5–55.4	2	167	1.163	97.093
55.5–56.4	1	168	0.581	97.674
58.5–59.4	1	169	0.581	98.256
61.5–62.4	2	171	1.163	99.419
69.5–70.4	1	172	0.581	100.000

	Mean	Median
PDP	21.6	19.6

Table 4C–16
1977 First-Homeowners by House Value-Income Ratio
(Computed House Value, Relative's Income Only)

HVZI	Frequency	Cumulative Frequency	Percent	Cumulative Percent
0.60–0.69	2	2	1.163	1.163
0.70–0.79	2	4	1.163	2.326
0.80–0.89	1	5	0.581	2.907
0.90–0.99	2	7	1.163	4.070
1.00–1.09	5	12	2.907	6.977
1.10–1.19	2	14	1.163	8.140
1.20–1.29	1	15	0.581	8.721
1.30–1.39	4	19	2.326	11.047
1.40–1.49	5	24	2.907	13.953
1.50–1.59	8	32	4.651	18.605
1.60–1.69	12	44	6.977	25.581
1.70–1.79	10	54	5.814	31.395
1.80–1.89	5	59	2.907	34.302
1.90–1.99	9	68	5.233	39.535
2.00–2.09	8	76	4.651	44.186
2.10–2.19	11	87	6.395	50.581
2.20–2.29	10	97	5.814	56.395
2.30–2.39	7	104	4.070	60.465
2.40–2.49	1	105	0.581	61.047
2.50–2.59	12	117	6.977	68.023
2.60–2.69	5	122	2.907	70.930
2.70–2.79	4	126	2.326	73.256
2.80–2.89	6	132	3.488	76.744
2.90–2.99	7	139	4.070	80.814
3.00–3.09	4	143	2.326	83.140
3.20–3.29	3	146	1.744	84.884
3.40–3.49	5	151	2.907	87.791
3.50–3.59	5	156	2.907	90.698
3.70–3.79	2	158	1.163	91.860
3.80–3.89	3	161	1.744	93.605
3.90–3.99	1	162	0.581	94.186
4.00–4.09	1	163	0.581	94.767
4.20–4.29	2	165	1.163	95.930
4.40–4.49	1	166	0.581	96.512
4.50–4.59	1	167	0.581	97.093
4.60–4.69	2	169	1.163	98.256
4.70–4.79	1	170	0.581	98.837
5.00–5.09	1	171	0.581	99.419
5.10–5.19	1	172	0.581	100.000

	Mean	Median
HVZI	2.3	2.1

Table 4C–17
1977 First-Homeowners by House Value-Income Ratio
(Computed House Value, Relative's and Nonrelative's Income)

HVTI	Frequency	Cumulative Frequency	Percent	Cumulative Percent
0.60–0.69	2	2	1.163	1.163
0.70–0.79	2	4	1.163	2.326
0.80–0.89	2	6	1.163	3.488
0.90–0.99	2	8	1.163	4.651
1.00–1.09	5	13	2.907	7.558
1.10–1.19	2	15	1.163	8.721
1.20–1.29	2	17	1.163	9.884
1.30–1.39	4	21	2.326	12.209
1.40–1.49	5	26	2.907	15.116
1.50–1.59	7	33	4.070	19.186
1.60–1.69	12	45	6.977	26.163
1.70–1.79	11	56	6.395	32.558
1.80–1.89	5	61	2.907	35.465
1.90–.99	9	70	5.233	40.698
2.00–2.09	8	78	4.651	45.349
2.10–2.19	11	89	6.395	51.744
2.20–2.29	9	98	5.233	56.977
2.30–2.39	7	105	4.070	61.047
2.40–2.49	1	106	0.581	61.628
2.50–2.59	13	119	7.558	69.186
2.60–2.69	5	124	2.907	72.093
2.70–2.79	5	129	2.907	75.000
2.80–2.89	6	135	3.488	78.488
2.90–2.99	7	142	4.070	82.558
3.00–3.09	4	146	2.326	84.884
3.20–3.29	3	149	1.744	86.628
3.40–3.49	5	154	2.907	89.535
3.50–3.59	4	158	2.326	91.860
3.70–3.79	2	160	1.163	93.023
3.80–3.89	3	163	1.744	94.767
3.90–3.99	1	164	0.581	95.349
4.00–4.09	1	165	0.581	95.930
4.20–4.29	2	167	1.163	97.0933
4.40–4.49	1	168	0.581	97.674
4.50–4.59	1	169	0.581	98.256
4.60–4.69	1	170	0.581	98.837
5.00–5.09	1	171	0.581	99.419
5.10–5.19	1	172	0.581	100.000

	Mean	Median
HVTI	2.3	2.1

Table 4C–18
1977 First-Homeowners by Reported House Value-Income Ratio

ZVI	Frequency	Cumulative Frequency	Percent	Cumulative Percent
0.60–0.69	2	2	1.163	1.163
0.70–0.79	2	4	1.163	2.326
0.80–0.89	1	5	0.581	2.907
0.90–0.99	2	7	1.163	4.070
1.00–1.09	5	12	2.907	6.977
1.10–1.19	2	14	1.163	8.140
1.20–1.29	1	15	0.581	8.721
1.30–1.39	4	19	2.326	11.047
0.40–1.49	5	24	2.907	13.953
1.50–1.59	8	32	4.651	18.605
1.60–1.69	12	44	6.977	25.581
1.70–1.79	10	54	5.814	31.395
1.80–1.89	5	59	2.907	34.302
1.90–1.99	9	68	5.233	39.535
2.00–2.09	8	76	4.651	44.186
2.10–2.19	11	87	6.395	50.581
2.20–2.29	10	97	5.814	56.395
2.30–2.39	7	104	4.070	60.465
2.40–2.49	1	105	0.581	61.047
2.50–2.59	12	117	6.977	68.023
2.60–2.69	5	122	2.907	70.930
2.70–2.79	4	126	2.326	73.256
2.80–2.89	6	132	3.488	76.744
2.90–2.99	7	139	4.070	80.814
3.00–3.09	4	143	2.326	83.140
3.20–3.29	3	146	1.744	84.884
3.40–3.49	5	151	2.907	87.791
3.50–3.59	5	156	2.907	90.698
3.70–3.79	2	158	1.163	91.860
3.80–3.89	3	161	1.744	93.605
3.90–3.99	1	162	0.581	94.186
4.00–4.09	1	163	0.581	94.767
4.20–4.29	2	165	1.163	95.930
4.40–4.49	1	166	0.581	96.512
4.50–4.59	1	167	0.581	97.093
4.60–4.69	2	169	1.163	98.256
4.70–4.79	1	170	0.581	98.837
5.00–5.09	1	171	0.581	99.419
5.10–5.19	1	172	0.581	100.000

	Mean	Median
ZVI	2.3	2.1

Table 4C–19
1977 Recurring Renters by Age of Head

ZAGE	Frequency	Cumulative Frequency	Percent	Cumulative Percent
14–19	18	18	1.606	1.606
20–24	229	247	20.428	22.034
25–29	295	542	26.316	48.350
30–34	180	722	16.057	64.407
35–39	108	830	9.634	74.041
40–44	59	889	5.263	79.304
45–49	50	939	4.460	83.764
50–54	43	982	3.836	87.600
55–59	45	1027	4.014	91.615
60–61	4	1031	0.357	91.971
62–64	18	1049	1.606	93.577
65–67	16	1065	1.427	95.004
68–69	10	1075	0.892	95.897
70–74	25	1100	2.230	98.127
75–79	14	1114	1.249	99.376
80–84	6	1120	0.535	99.911
85–89	1	1121	0.089	100.000

	Mean	Median
ZAGE	30–39	30–34

Table 4C–20
1977 Recurring Renters by Sex of Head

Sex	Frequency	Cumulative Frequency	Percent	Cumulative Percent
Male	778	778	69.402	69.402
Female	343	1121	30.598	100.000

Table 4C–21
1977 Recurring Renters by Race of Head

Race	Frequency	Cumulative Frequency	Percent	Cumulative Percent
White	918	918	81.881	81.891
Black	165	1083	14.719	96.610
Other	38	1121	3.390	100.000

Table 4C–22
1977 Recurring Renters by Number of Persons

PER	Frequency	Cumulative Frequency	Percent	Cumulative Percent
1	348	348	31.044	31.044
2	365	713	32.560	63.604
3	194	907	17.306	80.910
4	120	1027	10.705	91.615
5	46	1073	4.103	95.718
6	29	1102	2.587	98.305
7	9	1111	0.803	99.108
8	8	1119	0.714	99.822
9	1	1120	0.089	99.911
12	1	1121	0.089	100.000

	Mean	Median
PER	2.4	2

Table 4C–23
1977 Recurring Renters by Region of Dwelling

Region	Frequency	Cumulative Frequency	Percent	Cumulative Percent
Northeast	210	210	18.733	18.733
North-Central	276	486	24.621	43.354
South	256	742	22.837	66.191
West	379	1121	33.809	100.000

Table 4C–24
1977 Recurring Renters by Metropolitan Region of Dwelling

Metropolitan Region	Frequency	Cumulative Frequency	Percent	Cumulative Percent
Center city	576	576	51.383	51.383
Noncenter city	545	1121	48.617	100.000

Table 4C–25
1977 Recurring Renters by Total Income of Household
(Relative's and Nonrelative's Income)
(Dollars)

TINC	Frequency	Cumulative Frequency	Percent	Cumulative Percent
0– 4,999	133	133	11.864	11.864
5,000– 9,999	309	442	27.564	39.429
10,000–14,999	298	740	26.583	66.012
15,000–19,999	187	927	16.682	82.694
20,000–24,999	104	1031	9.277	91.971
25,000–29,999	39	1070	3.479	95.450
30,000–34,999	27	1097	2,409	97.859
35,000–39,999	15	1112	1.338	99.197
40,000–44,999	5	1117	0.446	99.643
45,000–49,999	3	1120	0.268	99.911
60,000–64,999	1	1121	0.089	100.000

	Mean	Median
TINC	13,066	12,000

Table 4C–26
1977 Recurring Renters by Income of Household
(Relative's Income Only)
(Dollars)

ZINC	Frequency	Cumulative Frequency	Percent	Cumulative Percent
0– 4,999	147	147	13,113	13.113
5,000– 9,999	329	476	29,349	42.462
10,000–14,999	306	782	27.297	69.759
15,000–19,999	173	955	15.433	85.192
20,000–24,999	95	1050	8.475	93.666
25,000–29,999	33	1083	2.944	96.610
30,000–34,999	20	1103	1.784	98.394
35,000–39,999	12	1115	1.070	99.465
40,000–44,999	4	1119	0.357	99.822
45,000–49,999	2	1121	0.178	100.000

	Mean	Median
ZINC	12,297	11,000

Table 4C–27
1977 Recurring Renters by Monthly Home Rental Cost
(Dollars)

ZRENT	Frequency	Cumulative Frequency	Percent	Cumulative Percent
20– 39	2	2	0.178	0.178
40– 59	16	18	1.427	1.606
60– 79	13	31	1.160	2.765
80– 89	15	46	1.338	4.103
100–119	44	90	3.925	8.029
120–139	52	142	4.639	12.667
140–159	66	208	5.888	18.555
160–179	101	309	9.010	27.565
180–199	119	428	10.616	38.180
200–219	126	554	11.240	49.420
220–239	113	667	10.080	59.500
240–259	97	764	8.653	68.153
260–279	98	862	9.742	76.896
280–299	68	930	6.066	82.962
300–319	46	976	4.103	87.065
320–339	38	1014	3.390	90.455
340–359	28	1042	2.498	92.953
360–379	21	1063	1.873	94.826
380–399	4	1067	0.357	95.183
400–419	14	1081	1.249	96.432
420–439	10	1091	0.892	97.324
440–459	8	1099	0.714	98.037
460–479	3	1102	0.268	98.305
480–499	7	1109	0.624	98.930
500–519	4	1113	0.357	99.286
520–539	1	1114	0.089	99.376
540–559	2	1116	0.178	99.554
560–579	2	1118	0.178	99.732
600–619	1	1119	0.089	99.822
640–659	1	1120	0.089	99.911
800–819	1	1121	0.089	100.000

	Mean	Median
ZRENT	229	220

Table 4C–28
1977 Recurring Renters by Current-Previous Monthly Cost Ratio

IRMHCOR	Frequency	Cumulative Frequency	Percent	Cumulative Percent
0.10–0.19	1	1	0.089	0.089
0.20–0.29	5	6	0.446	0.535
0.30–0.39	5	11	0.446	0.981
0.40–0.49	25	36	2.230	3.211
0.50–0.59	42	78	3.747	6.958
0.60–0.69	59	137	5.263	12.221
0.70–0.79	73	210	6.512	18.733
0.80–0.89	100	310	8.921	27.654
0.90–0.99	99	409	8.831	36.485
1.00–1.09	152	561	13.559	50.045
1.10–1.19	152	713	13.559	63.604
1.20–1.29	120	833	10.703	74.309
1.30–1.39	63	896	5.620	79.929
1.40–1.49	47	943	4.193	84.121
1.50–1.59	50	993	4.460	88.582
1.60–1.69	38	1031	3.390	91.971
1.70–1.79	13	1044	1.160	93.131
1.80–1.89	19	1063	1.695	94.826
1.90–1.99	9	1072	0.803	95.629
2.00–2.09	11	1083	0.981	96.610
2.10–2.19	7	1090	0.624	97.235
2.20–2.29	7	1097	0.624	97.859
2.30–2.39	3	1100	0.268	98.127
2.40–2.49	1	1101	0.089	98.216
2.50–2.59	6	1107	0.535	98.751
2.60–2.69	3	1110	0.268	99.019
2.70–2.79	2	1112	0.178	99.197
2.80–2.89	1	1113	0.089	99.286
3.10–3.19	2	1115	0.178	99.465
3.30–3.39	2	1117	.178	99.643
4.20–4.29	1	1118	.089	99.732
4.30–4.39	2	1120	0.178	99.911
5.20–5.29	1	1121	0.089	100.000

	Mean	Median
RMHCOR	1.1	1.1

Table 4C-29
1977 Recurring Renters by Highest Grade Completed by Head

GRADE	Frequency	Cumulative Frequency	Percent	Cumulative Percent
No School	5	5	0.446	0.446
Grade 1	1	6	0.089	0.535
Grade 2	4	10	0.357	0.892
Grade 3	10	20	0.892	1.784
Grade 4	9	29	0.803	2.587
Grade 5	13	42	1.160	3.747
Grade 6	19	61	1.695	5.442
Grade 7	19	80	1.695	7.136
Grade 8	43	123	3.836	10.972
Grade 9	46	159	4.103	15.076
Grade 10	49	218	4.371	19.447
Grade 11	74	292	6.601	26.048
Grade 12 High School Graduate	368	660	32.828	58.876
1 year college	82	742	7.315	66.191
2 years college	87	829	7.761	73.952
3 years college	50	879	4.460	78.412
4 years college	129	1008	11.508	89.920
5 years college	25	1033	2.230	92.150
6+ years college	88	1121	7.850	100.000

	Mean	Median
GRADE	High school graduate 1 year college	High school graduate

5 A Microeconometric Analysis of Vacant Housing Units

Robert F. Engle and *Robert C. Marshall*

The objectives of this research are to determine the causes of vacancies in rental-housing units and learn how landlords set and adjust rents in response to their own experience with vacancies. The literature on urban housing has rarely paid any attention to vacant units. There are passing references in Simon (1955), Gordon and Hynes (1970), and Stull (1978) which set the problem within the search theoretic models of matching units and tenants. Empirically, Bradbury et al. (1977) incorporated vacancy rates as a determinant of aggregate housing supply in an area and then sought to determine these rates as a quantity response to sticky price changes. More recently, in the analysis of the Housing Allowance Supply Experiment, Rydell (1979) has attempted to determine how changes in demand, caused by experimental design, would be split between price and quantity adjustments of the occupied housing stock. To the authors' knowledge there have been no studies using microeconomic data to analyze the behavior of vacant units.

In contrast, there is a vast and very technical literature on the dynamic behavior of unemployed workers. In general, these models assume some form of search behavior of workers, although usually not firms, and derive stochastic time paths of the status of the workers. Consequently, probability distributions of various characteristics of a class of workers can be derived. For example, the probability of the occurrence of various states, the distribution of durations of completed or interrupted spells of a state, and the probabilities of transition from one state to another which are possibly dependent upon the length of stay in the state, can all be derived theoretically from the underlying stochastic process. Although the theoretical model is usually based upon a structural model of reservation wages and a distribution of job opportunities as measured by wage offers, the outcome is usually viewed simply as a dichotomous variable which indicates the state at each point in time. Data on the accepted wage rate or quality of the job or reservation wages are rarely analyzed. An exception to this is a pair of papers by Kiefer and Neumann (1979a, 1979b), whose work is closest in spirit to that employed here. The structural underpinning of the stochastic process generating unemployment is the search model. Thus to understand the causes of unemployment or vacancy, it is essential to estimate the parameters of this process directly, not merely the reduced-form state equations.

The analysis employed in this chapter differs from that of Kiefer and Neumann in several respects which reflect the particulars of the data set and the questions of interest in housing. The data set used for this study is the Annual Housing Survey, which follows 75,000 housing units over a four-year period. It includes rents for occupied units as well as asking rents for vacant units. When a unit is rented, the measured rent is reasonably assumed to be the asking rent; thus the reservation rents of landlords are observable in all cases. However, because the data are annual, there may be many spells of vacancy which are not observed in this survey.

The vacancy of a housing unit is often assumed to be simply a result of frictions in the transition from one tenant to another. Because both searchers and landlords are imperfectly informed and searching is costly, there is an optimal nonzero equilibrium vacancy rate. This would presumably generate equal probabilities of vacancy for all units of a particular type. The equilibrium rate would be the same for units of all types if the costs of search by both tenants and landlords were invariant to the types of units. This might be a first simplifying assumption. Vacancies would then be randomly distributed over the housing units.

Conversely, most stories about neighborhood change generate particular nonuniform patterns of vacancies. For example, a center-city neighborhood with a decline in population will initially have an excess supply of housing units. Which units become vacant will depend upon the response of landlords to this excess supply: if all the landlords rapidly lower rents to the new equilibium level, some of the units will reach their opportunity cost in a next-best use. These units will disappear from the housing market, and an equilibrium with an optimal vacancy rate again random across units will be restored. However, this may not be the way landlords respond. They may instead attempt to hold up rents, either looking for the few prospective tenants who would pay these rents or perhaps hoping to maintain capital value of the unit through high asking-rents, even though the units are vacant. Eventually, as durations of vacancy become long, the landlords must adapt their policies and lower rents. The same story would be told if landlords did not know about the decline in population and merely learned about it from their own rising vacancy rates.

An important comcept in neighborhood transition is the idea of *filtering*. Here the stock disequilibrium is caused by an increase in the quantity of high-quality housing. Eventually, the rents on existing units fall sufficiently that the lowest-quality units remain vacant and exit from the housing stock to some alternative use. The result is, of course, the upgrading of the housing package for each income class. The transitions that are postulated to occur in filtering will generate vacancies that depend upon landlord behavior in response to this perhaps slowly perceived excess supply. Eventually, one would expect the vacancies to be concentrated in the low-quality units, but this might perphaps not be the case along the way.

Throughout this chapter, the analysis must be viewed as a preliminary investigation of a single location to determine whether future investigation along these lines is warranted. In the next section, the model is derived.

Model

Any given housing unit is described by a vector of observable characteristics X which will be indexed by i for the unit and t for the year. These include structural information such as size and age, location, neighborhood characteristics such as adequacy of schooling and existence of rundown buildings, and past values of these variables plus rent and vacancy status. There may also be unobservable characteristics, which will be described by a random variable, α_i, which is constant over time. The characteristic of prospective tenants for unit i includes both those currently looking and those currently occupying a unit. Each tenant has an implicit offer for unit i based upon his or her offer-rent schedule. In a nonstochastic equilibrium, only the maximum of these offers is relevant to the occupancy of the unit. In a world of imperfectly informed agents, however, the entire distribution may be relevant, since the maximum bidder may not discover the unit either before it is rented to someone else or before the bidding period is over. At any point in time, this distribution may be defined by $f(R_{it}^\circ | X_{it}, \alpha_i)$, where R_{it}° is the random variable which is the offer for unit i at time t. It should also be pointed out that a low offer need not actually occur only after a family has had a chance to inspect the unit and decide it is inappropriate. They could have decided that it was not likely that they would rent it anyway, given what they already knew—and thus inspection by them was unnecessary. In short, there may appear to be little or no search occurring.

The probability that a unit will be vacant after one draw from the offer distribution is

$$P(V_{it} | X_{it}) = P(R_{it}^a > R_{it}^\circ)$$

The probability of a vacancy after M independent searches is simply

$$P_M(V_{it} | X_{it}) = P_1(V_{it} | X_{it})^M$$

In this paper we assume $M = 1$, although we expect to investigate the possibility that larger values would better fit the data by maximizing the likelihood function over M.

The key to understanding why a unit is vacant conditional only on its characteristics is the behavior of landlords. To observe that a unit is vacant because the asking rent is too high is merely to pose the question, why is it so high? The solution to this question is empirical in the sense that it is estimated from the data rather than derived from theory. However, in marshall and Guasch (1982) a theoretical model of optimal behavior under uncertainty does suggest a variety of explanations for such landlord behavior.

Here it is simply assumed that landlords set asking rents based upon the same measured and unmeasured variables, including past performance, described earlier. Thus the density of R_{it}^a is given by $g(R_{it}^a | X_{it}, \alpha_i)$. Particular interest focuses on how asking rents adjust to lagged vacancy status.

To make the offer and asking-rent distributions precise, the following structure is assumed.

$$\log R_{it}^\circ = X_{it}\beta^\circ + \alpha_i + \varepsilon_{it}^\circ$$
$$= X_{it}\beta^\circ + u_{it}^\circ \tag{5.1}$$

$$\log R_{it}^a = X_{it}\beta^a + \alpha_i + \varepsilon_{it}^a$$
$$= X_{it}\beta^a + u_{it}^a \tag{5.2}$$

where the ε's are normal and independent over t and i
the α's are normal and independent over i
the ε's are independent of the α's over t and i

The probability of a vacancy can be derived as follows:

$$P(V_{it}) = P(R_{it}^a > R_{it}^\circ) = P[X_{it}(\beta^a - \beta^\circ) + \varepsilon_{it}^a - \varepsilon_{it}^\circ > 0] \tag{5.3}$$
$$= P[\varepsilon_{it}^\circ - \varepsilon_{it}^a < X_{it}(\beta^a - \beta^\circ)]$$
$$= \phi \frac{X_{it}(\beta^a - \beta^\circ)}{\sigma}$$

where $\sigma = \sqrt{\sigma_{\varepsilon_{it}^\circ}^2 + \sigma_{\varepsilon_{it}^a}^2 - 2\sigma_{\varepsilon_{it}^\circ \varepsilon_{it}^a}}$

ϕ = the cumulative normal distribution function.

Without any exclusion restrictions on the β's, the above formulation allows probit estimates of the parameter $(\beta^a - \beta^\circ)/\sigma$. Since asking-rents are always observed, the β^a can be estimated directly.

In the next section the data are discussed and in section 4 simple correlations are presented to discern any pattern to vacancies. Finally, sections 5 and 6 present maximum likelihood estimates of the rent ask equation and the vacancy equation respectively along with economic interpretations of the results.

The Data

In the Annual Housing Survey, units are revisited annually from 1974 to 1977 and data on 500 variables are coded for each year. Since we are interested in studying the behavior of agents within a single housing market, we chose a single SMSA (Standard Metropolitan Statistical Area), Philadelphia, for our data set. Philadelphia was chosen because of its size (fourth largest city) and more common physical character than other very large cities (such as New York or Los Angeles). The survey contains 6,000 observations on units in Philadelphia. Of these 6,000 observations, only 900 are on rental units for which a full time series is coded from 1974 to 1977.

Of the 900 observations, 65 vacancies are coded. Forty-one of the 225 units experience a vacancy once in the four year period and 12 experience a vacancy twice. The mean duration of observed vacancies is 3.43 months (the median is 2 months). Table 5-1 provides mean rents for occupied and vacant units, overall and by year. With the exception of 1975, the mean rent for vacant units is higher than for occupied ones. The dynamic character of the data provides even more information about the relationship between vacancies and rents. The average rate of increase in rents from one year to the next for units which were occupied in both years is 8.95 percent, whereas if the unit was vacant in one year and occupied the next, the rate of increase was 2.65 percent. It appears that landlords of vacant units have set rents too high initially, but by experiencing vacancies, landlords realize that they have misestimated demand and compensate in the following period.

Several variables that describe the physical characteristics of the unit are available; vacancies appear to have no systematic pattern with each of these. Units built prior to 1939 comprise roughly 51 percent of the sample and 52

Table 5-1
Mean Rents for Occupied and Vacant Units

Mean Rent Overall	$161.20	
Mean Rent Vacant	$185.00	
Mean Rent Occupied	$159.31	

Year	Mean Rent Vacant	Mean Rent Occupied
1974	176.43	141.75
1975	143.08	157.77
1976	213.31	164.17
1977	204.94	173.22

percent of the vacancies. The mean rent for occupied units built prior to 1939 is $117, while for vacant units built prior to 1939, the average rent is approximately $155. It appears that units are not vacant because they are old but because their rent is too high. There is virtually no difference in the average number of rooms in vacant and occupied units. The number of units in the building does not appear to affect the overall vacancy rate. Location, as measured by whether or not a unit is in the central city, does not reveal a spatial bias for vacancies, since 41 percent of all units and 35 percent of vacancies are located in the central city. Table 5-2 provides, in detail, all this information.

Table 5-2
Vacancy Status by Age, Number of Units in Building, and Metropolitan Status

Vacancy Status by Age				
Age	*Number of Observations*	*Percent of Observations*	*Number of Vacancies*	*Percent of Vacancies*
Built prior to 1939	456	51%	34	52%
Built between 1940 and 1949	56	6%	1	2%
Built between 1950 and 1959	52	6%	3	5%
Built between 1960 and 1964	100	11%	9	14%
Built between 1965 and 1969	80	9%	6	9%
Built after 1969	156	17%	12	18%

Average Number of Rooms in Vacant and Occupied Units	
Average number of rooms in occupied units	3.81
Average number of rooms in vacant units	3.91

Vacancy Status by Number of Units in Building				
Number of Units in Building	*Number of Observations*	*Percent of Observations*	*Number of Vacancies*	*Percent of Vacancies*
One unit	164	18%	11	17%
Two units	176	20%	9	14%
Three to four units	176	20%	13	20%
Five to nine units	72	8%	7	11%
Ten to nineteen units	104	12%	9	14%
Twenty to twenty-nine units	120	13%	9	14%
Thirty or more units	88	10%	7	11%

Vacancy Status by Metropolitan Status		
Metropolitan Region, Observations	*Number of Observations*	*Percent of Observations*
Central city	372	41%
SMSA	528	59%
Central city vacancies	23	35%
SMSA vacancies	42	65%

Several quality variables are available, and for all these measures the percent of vacancies within a given quality type is close to the percentage of units in this type. Overall, there appears to be no systematic trend in the type of units which are vacant. Simple cross-tabulations indicate that the percent of units of a particular location, characteristic, or quality type approximate the percentage of vacancies within that type. Vacant units appear to be characterized only by higher asking-rents.

Table 5-3 provides a listing of variables and their corresponding codings which were used in the data analysis just presented and are to be used in the estimation section.

Preliminary Data Analysis

The empirical results are presented in three sections. First, two equations are estimated by ordinary least squares (OLS) to motivate questions posed earlier. Second, the asking-rent equation is estimated by an error-components method in which OLS is applied to transformed data. Third, a linear probability and probit model are estimated to determine the causes of vacancies. The economic interpretation of all results in discussed as estimates are presented.

Before plunging into more complicated estimation techniques, OLS estimates given in equations 5.4 and 5.5 are presented to provide insight into the determinants of asking-rents and the causes of vacancies.

$$\log R_{it}^a = Z_{it} \beta_1^a + \gamma V_{it} + \beta_2^a V_{it-1} + u_{it} \qquad (5.4)$$

$$V_{it} = X_{it} \delta_1 + \psi \log R_{it}^a + \delta_2 V_{it-1} + e_{it} \qquad (5.5)$$

The X_{it} data matrix consists of all variables in table 5-3 excluding vacancy status and rent but including age squared $(AGE)^2$ and room squared $(ROOM)^2$. Equation 5.4 is a hedonic that includes current and past vacancy status. Our previous discussion suggests the expectation that γ be positive and β_2^a negative. A positive γ reflects that landlords of vacant units have a higher asking-rent than landlords of comparable occupied units whereas a negative β_2^a indicates that landlords respond to vacancies of last period by lowering asking-rents this period. In equation 5.5, ψ is expected to be negative, again indicating that high asking-rents cause vacancies. The coefficient of V_{it-1} should be positive or insignificant in equation 5.5. If vacancies are random, V_{it-1} should explain nothing of V_{it}, but if they represent some kind of structural disequilibrium, the coefficient of V_{it-1} should be positive. Table 5-4 contains estimates of equations 5.4 and 5.5.

Table 5–3
Variables Used in Analysis of Annual Housing Survey

Variable Name		Coding
Rent (*R*)	In dollars per month	
Vacant (*V*)	0	Occupied
	1	Vacant
Year structure built (*AGE*)	30	Prior to 1939
	45	Between 1940 and 1949
	55	Between 1950 and 1959
	62	Between 1960 and 1964
	66	Between 1965 and 1968
	69	Between 1969 and 3/31/1970
	70–77	Between 1970 and 1977
Number of units in building, including vacant units (*NUNITS*)	1	One
	2	Two
	3	Three to four
	6	Five to nine
	12	Ten to nineteen
	25	Twenty to forty-nine
	60	Fifty or more
Number of rooms in unit (*ROOM*)	Coding equals number	
Metropolitan status (*METRO*)	0	In central city
	1	In SMSA but not in central city
Kitchen (*KITCH*)	0	None or not exclusive use
	1	Exclusive use
Air-conditioning (*AIR*)	0	No
	1	Yes
Electricity included in rent (*ELEC*)	0	No
	1	Yes
Oil included in rent (*OIL*)	0	No
	1	Yes
Street noise (*STR*)	0	Yes, condition exists
	1	No, condition does not exist
Rundown buildings in neighborhood (*RUN*)	0	Yes, condition exists
	1	No, condition does not exist
Schools, adequate (*SCH*)	0	No, not adequate
	1	Yes, adequate
Police protection, adequate (*POL*)	0	No, not adequate
	1	Yes, adequate
DUM 75	*0*	*If observation in 1976 or 1977*
	1	*If observation in 1975*
DUM 76	0	If observation in 1975 or 1977
	1	If observation in 1976

Table 5–4
Ordinary Least Squares Regressions

Independent Variable	Dependent Variables[a,b,c]	
	$Log\ R_{it}$	V_{it}
METRO	0.03810	−0.01640
	(1.42)	(0.68)
AGE	0.02740	−0.00358
	(3.72)	(0.54)
V_{it}	0.1140	
	(2.64)	
NUNITS	0.00475	0.00091
	(5.70)	(1.19)
ROOM	0.18400	0.02630
	(5.43)	(0.85)
KITCH	−0.00676	−0.14400
	(0.08)	(1.87)
AIR	0.07760	−0.08170
	(2.65)	(3.11)
$Log\ R_{it}$		0.09210
		(2.64)
ELEC	0.07800	−0.02090
	(2.33)	(0.69)
$(AGE)^2$	−0.00015	0.00004
	(2.12)	(0.57)
OIL	0.11400	0.00688
	(4.93)	(0.32)
STR	−0.05440	−0.00707
	(2.32)	(0.33)
RUN	0.26200	0.00139
	(6.86)	(0.04)
$(ROOM)^2$	−0.00981	−0.00409
	(2.74)	(1.26)
SCH	−0.01830	−0.07830
	(0.38)	(1.83)
POL	0.06780	−0.01280
	(1.62)	(0.34)
V_{it-1}	0.05690	0.04270
	(1.45)	(1.21)
DUM75	−0.12500	−0.03150
	(4.58)	(1.27)
DUM76	−0.02970	−0.03830
	(1.09)	(1.57)
CONSTANT	3.24000	−0.14400
	(16.69)	(0.69)
R^2	0.9969	0.1174
SEE	0.2858	0.2568
SSR	53.5934	43.2450

[a]Ratios of coefficients to OLS reported standard errors are in parentheses.
[b]$Log\ R_{it}$ as solved by equation 5.4.
[c]V_{it} as solved by equation 5.5.

All the estimated parameters of equation 5.4 have the expected sign except for lagged vacancies and two completely insignificant variables. Newer and larger units have higher asking-rents as do untis with air-conditioners and with electricity and oil included in the monthly rent bill. Those units in neighborhoods without rundown buildings also command higher asking-rents. The absence of street noise is negatively correlated with rent, but street noise may be a proxy for locations closer to the central business district. Most importantly, current vacancy status has a positive significant coefficient. The coefficient of lagged vacancy status is positive and insignificant, but this sign changes when the error-components structure of rent-ask equation is accounted for later.

The estimated parameters of equation 5.3 are all insignificant except for air-conditioning and rent. The absence of air-conditioners seems to contribute to higher vacancy rents. As expected higher asking-rents are positively correlated with the occurrence of vacancies.

It should be emphasized that these estimates are only suggestive since they have simultaneity bias, do not account for the possible error-components structure in the asking-rent equation (equation 5.4), and involve a binary dependent variable (equation 5.5).

Estimation of the Asking-Rent Distribution

The specification of the asking-rent equation postulated in equation 5.2 was:

$$\log R_{it}^a = X_{it}\beta_1^a + \beta_2^a V_{it-1} + \alpha_i + \varepsilon_{it}^a \qquad (5.6)$$

The error-components structure is a natural assumption when using panel data. To test for the presence of error components, we test:

$$H_0: \sigma_\alpha^2 = 0$$

Table 5-5
Maximizing the Likelihood Function

ρ	$(1 - \rho)/\hat{\sigma}^T$
0.0	42.2475
0.1	49.3230
0.4	80.7480
0.5	96.9180
0.6	114.6691
0.7	130.0600
0.75	133.4828
0.8	130.2300
0.85	117.4720
0.9	90.6618
0.95	50.2816

$$H_1 : \sigma_\alpha^2 \neq 0$$

Breusch and Pagan have suggested a Lagrange multiplier (LM) test[1] which involves the residuals from an OLS estimate of eqaution 5.6. The test statistic is

$$\xi = \frac{NT}{2(T-1)} \left[\frac{u'(I_N \otimes l_T l_T')u}{u'u} - 1 \right]^2 \sim \chi^2(1) \qquad (5.7)$$

under H_0, where N = number of units = 225
$\quad\quad\quad\quad\quad\quad$ T = number of time-series observations for each unit = 3
$\quad\quad\quad\quad\quad\quad$ l_T = vector of ones of length T
$\quad\quad\quad\quad\quad\quad$ u = vector of residuals from an OLS estimate of equation 5.6

The test statistic is approximately 345.0, which rejects the null hypothesis easily, and indicates the presence of error components that must be accounted for when estimating equation 5.2.

In developing maximum-likelihood estimates of the error-components model, OLS estimates of transformed-data sets are used where the optimal transformation is determined by a criterion derived from the likelihood function. The final parameter estimates are consequently consistent and asymptotically efficient (see Maddala).[2] The asking-rent equation is rewritten below such that V_{it-1} is included in the X_{it} matrix for simplicity of notation.

$$\log R_{it}^a = X_{it}\beta^a + u_{it} \qquad \text{where } u_{it} = \alpha_i + \varepsilon_{it}$$

$$Euu' = \Omega = \sigma_\varepsilon^2 I_{NT} + \sigma_\alpha^2(I_N \otimes l_T l_T')$$

The log-likelihood function is

$$\mathcal{L} = -\tfrac{1}{2} \log |\Omega| - \tfrac{1}{2}(\log R_{it}^a - X_{it}\beta^a)'\Omega^{-1}(\log R^a - X\beta^a) \qquad (5.8)$$

$$= -\tfrac{1}{2} \log |\Omega| - \tfrac{1}{2}u'\Omega^{-1}u$$

Now Ω^{-1} is positive definite and must have a factorization such that:

$$\theta^{-2}P'P = \Omega^{-1} \qquad \text{or} \qquad \theta^2 P^{-1}P'^{-1} = \Omega$$

Let

$$Pu = \tilde{u} \qquad P \log R_{it}^a = \tilde{R}_{it} \qquad PX = \tilde{X}$$

Then

$$\tilde{u}\tilde{u}' = PEuu'P$$
$$= P\Omega P'$$
$$= \theta^2 I$$

Therefore the regression of $\tilde{R}_{it}$ on $\tilde{X}$ will give maximum-likelihood estimates of β^a. The matrix P is of the form:

$$P = I_{NT} - \left(I_N \otimes \frac{\rho}{T} l_T l_T' \right)$$

As a preview to what follows, ρ will be estimated instead of σ_α^2 and σ_ε^2. New estimates of ρ will imply new transformations of X and log R_{it} and these, in turn, will yield new estimates of β^a. The factorization of Ω^{-1} will allow a transformation of the likelihood function, which will imply a criterion to judge the best ρ, β^a combination. Throughout, the only estimation technique used will be OLS on transformed data.

The form of P given above implies that:

$$\tilde{u}_{it} = u_{it} - \frac{\rho}{T} \sum_{j=1}^{T} u_{ij}$$

$$E(\tilde{u}_{it}^2) = \sigma_\alpha^2(1 - \rho) + \sigma_\varepsilon^2 \left(1 - \frac{\rho}{T} + \frac{\rho^2}{T} \right) = \theta^2$$

$$E(\tilde{u}_{it}\tilde{u}_{is} \mid t \neq s) = E \left(\varepsilon_{it} - \frac{\rho}{T} \sum_{j=1}^{T} \varepsilon_{ij} \right) \left(\varepsilon_{is} - \frac{\rho}{T} \sum_{j=1}^{T} \varepsilon_{ij} \right) + \sigma_\alpha^2(1 - \rho)$$

$$= \sigma_\varepsilon^2 \left(\frac{\rho^2}{T} - \frac{2\rho}{T} \right) + \sigma_\alpha^2(1 - \rho)^2$$

$$= \rho^2(\sigma_\alpha^2 + \sigma_\varepsilon^2/T - 2\rho(\sigma_\alpha^2 + \sigma_\varepsilon^2/T)) + \sigma_\alpha^2$$

Let

$$\phi = (\sigma_\alpha^2 + \sigma_\varepsilon^2/T)/\sigma_\alpha^2$$

Setting the covariance term equal to zero and solving for ρ implies:

$$0 = \rho^2\phi - 2\rho\phi + 1$$

$$\rho = 1 - \sqrt{1 - 1/\phi}$$

Therefore, $0 \leq \rho \leq 1$. Note that both OLS and fixed effects are special cases ($\rho = 0 \Rightarrow$ OLS; $\rho = 1 \Rightarrow$ fixed effects). Substituting $\Omega^{-1} = \theta^{-2} P'P$ into the log-likelihood function yields:

$$\mathcal{L} = -\frac{1}{2}\log \theta^{2NT} |P|^{-1} |P|^{-1} - \frac{1}{2\theta^2} u'P'Pu$$

$$= -\frac{NT}{2} \log \theta^2 + \log |P| - \frac{1}{2\theta^2} \tilde{u}'\tilde{u}$$

Now

$$|P| = (1 - \rho)^N$$

Therefore

$$\mathcal{L} = -\frac{NT}{2} \log \theta^2 + N \log (1 - \rho) - \frac{1}{2\theta^2} \tilde{u}'\tilde{u}$$

Since $\hat{\theta}^2 = \tilde{u}'\tilde{u}/NT$, the concentrated log-likelihood function can be rewritten as

$$\mathcal{L} = -\frac{NT}{2} \log \hat{\sigma}^2 + N \log (1 - \rho) - \frac{NT}{2}$$

$$= N \log \frac{1 - \rho}{\hat{\sigma}^T} - \frac{NT}{2}$$

The procedure then is to search over values of ρ between zero and one to find the ρ which maximizes $(1 - \rho)/\hat{\sigma}^T$ and therefore the likelihood function. The results are presented in table 5-5.

The maximum likelihood estimates of the rent-ask equation ($\rho = .75$) are presented in table 5-6. (Note that the t-statistics printed by a regression package for the β's are assymptotically correct since the information matrix is block diagonal between ρ and the β's.) Nearly all the significant coefficients have the expected signs. The coefficient of V_{it-1} has switched sign from the previous OLS estimates and is now negative. Landlords appear to be responding to the occurrence of vacancies by adjusting the asking-rents downward in the next period, suggesting that they view the vacancy not as a random occurrence but as a mistake on their part in estimating market conditions. This point cannot be pushed too hard since the coefficient is significant only at the 10% level (in a one-tail test against the alternative that is less than zero).

Table 5-6
Maximum-Likelihood Estimate of the Rent-Ask Equation Using Error Components

Independent Variable	Dependent Variable Log R_{it}
METRO	0.08700
	(1.99)
AGE	0.02540
	(2.41)
NUNIT	0.00640
	(5.15)
ROOM	0.19400
	(4.53)
KITCH	−0.16100
	(2.68)
AIR	−0.02740
	(1.18)
ELEC	−0.02830
	(0.95)
$(AGE)^2$	−0.00014
	(1.28)
OIL	0.02790
	(1.81)
STR	−0.00021
	(0.01)
RUN	0.04760
	(2.00)
$(ROOM)^2$	−0.01330
	(2.94)
SCH	0.00914
	(0.28)
POL	0.01670
	(0.66)
V_{it-1}	−0.02740
	(1.31)
DUM75	−0.16800
	(10.68)
DUM76	−0.06270
	(3.99)
CONSTANT	0.97100
	(14.89)
R^2	0.9908
SEE	0.1234
SSR	9.9824

Note: Asymptotic t ratios are in parentheses.

Estimation of the Vacancy Equation

In this chapter, two possible explanations for vacancies have been proposed. First, vacancies could just be random occurrences resulting from the stochastic nature of the search process. Second, vacancies may result from supply or demand shocks to which landlords adjust sluggishly. Landlords may value characteristics of their unit differently from the way tenants value these characteristics especially when market conditions are changing. In terms of the asking-rent and the offer-rent equations, the coefficients of the X_{it} in the asking-rent equation may diverge from the corresponding coefficients in the offer-rent equation. A divergence in the valuation of characteristics of a unit between landlords and tenants will affect the vacancy rate. For example, if landlords with air-conditioned units charge on average $10 more in rent than do landlords of comparable units without air-conditioners, but tenants on average feel air-conditioning is worth only $5 more, units with air-conditioners will have a higher vacancy rate than do comparable units without air-conditioners. This can be formalized in the hypothesis test below:

$$H^0: \beta_j^a - \beta_j^o = 0 \qquad\qquad \text{for all } j$$

where j represents characteristics of a unit

$$H^1: \beta_j^a - \beta_j^o \neq 0 \qquad \text{for some } j$$

If the null is rejected, then landlords do not correctly perceive tenants' valuation of some characteristics of their units. If the null cannot be rejected, landlords are correctly estimating the market valuation of the characteristics of their units and it would appear that vacancies are strictly random occurrences.

As a first approximation to determining the causes of vacancies, the linear probability model below is estimated by OLS:

$$V_{it} = \bar{X}_{it}\delta_1 + \delta_2 V_{it-1} + e_{it}$$

This equation is very similar to equation 5.5 except that current rent has been omitted. The estimates are in table 5-7. Only the coefficient of air-conditioning is significant, but the coefficients of number of units in building, exclusive use of kitchen, and adequacy of schools are close to being significant. The presence of air-conditioning and the exclusive use of kitchen lower the probability of a vacancy, whereas units in large buildings have higher vacancy rates. Units in neighborhoods with adequate schools also experience lower vacancy probabilities. Overall, these variables do not appear to be explaining much of current vacancy status. However, since the

Table 5–7
Linear Probability Model

Independent Variables	Dependent Variable V_{it}
METRO	−0.01310
	(0.54)
AGE	−0.00106
	(0.16)
NUNIT	0.00136
	(1.82)
ROOM	0.04370
	(1.43)
KITCH	−0.14600
	(1.89)
AIR	−0.07530
	(2.87)
ELEC	−0.01390
	(0.46)
$(AGE)^2$	0.00002
	(0.35)
OIL	0.01760
	(0.84)
STR	−0.01220
	(0.58)
RUN	0.02580
	(0.75)
$(ROOM)^2$	−0.00504
	(1.56)
SCH	−0.08080
	(1.88)
POL	−0.00667
	(0.18)
V_{it-1}	0.04840
	(1.37)
DUM75	−0.04340
	(1.77)
DUM76	−0.04140
(1.70)	(1.70)
CONSTANT	0.15600
	(0.89)
R^2	0.10810
SEE	0.25790
SSR	43.70494

Note: Ratios of coefficients to OLS standard errors are in parentheses.

dependent variable is binary, no formal statistical tests are performed on these estimates and the results in table 5-7 should be viewed as only suggestive. Definitive statements and inference can only be made from the results of probit estimation.

To test for a difference between the coefficients in the asking-rent and offer-rent equations, the statistical model posed earlier should be estimated. The model is restated below. The asking-rent and offer-rent equations are

$$\log R_{it}^a = X_{it}\beta_1^a + \beta_2^a V_{it-1} + \alpha_i + \varepsilon_{it}^a \qquad (5.6)$$

$$\log R_{it}^\circ = X_{it}\beta_1^\circ + \beta_2^\circ V_{it-1} + \alpha_i + \varepsilon_{it}^\circ \qquad (5.9)$$

As stated earlier, the probability of a vacancy is simply:

$$P(V_{it}) = P(R_{it}^a > R_{it}^\circ) = P\left(\varepsilon_{it}^\circ - \varepsilon_{it}^a < \frac{X_{it}^*(\beta^a - \beta^\circ)}{\sigma}\right)$$

$$= P(\varepsilon_{it}^\circ - \varepsilon_{it}^a < X_{it}^*\delta)$$

where X_{it}^* contains V_{it-1} for convenience and $\delta = (\beta^a - \beta^\circ)/\sigma$. To obtain estimates of the parameter δ, the following probit log-likelihood function is used:

$$\mathcal{L} = \sum_{i,t} [V_{it} \log \Phi(X_{it}^*\delta) + (1 - V_{it}) \log [1 - \Phi(X_{it}^*\delta)]\}$$

The probit estimates of the parameters are presented in table 5-8. No variable has a significant coefficient. However, the test of interest is the joint test of $\delta_j = 0$ for all j. To test if all coefficients are equal to zero, the following Wald test statistic has been computed.

$$\xi_\omega = \delta' \mathcal{I}_{\|}^{-2}\delta \sim \chi^2(K - 1)$$

where $\mathcal{I}_{\|}$ is the inverse of the Hessian, where the constant term elements have been eliminated. The value of the test statistic is 16.2 and therefore the null hypothesis that all $\delta_j = 0$ cannot be rejected even at the 25 percent level.

Surprisingly, the acceptance of the hypothesis that all coefficients are zero, has strong economic implications and is a positive result. This indicates that landlords and tenants value the characteristics of units identically and consequently the fact that a unit is vacant is simply due to unlucky draws from the offer distribution. There is no evidence that vacancies occur

Table 5–8
Maximum-Likelihood Estimate of the Probit Model

Independent Variable	Coefficient
METRO	−0.14650
	(0.585)
AGE	−0.00582
	(0.08)
NUNIT	0.00756
	(1.32)
ROOM	0.33710
	(0.55)
KITCH	−0.68320
	(1.72)
AIR	−0.84280
	(1.73)
ELEC	−0.18800
	(0.67)
$(AGE)^2$	0.00023
	(0.32)
OIL	0.12360
	(0.59)
STR	0.00563
	(0.03)
RUN	0.17090
	(0.58)
$(ROOM)^2$	−0.04552
	(0.62)
SCH	−0.63250
	(1.60)
POL	0.00117
	(0.01)
V_{it-1}	0.33230
	(1.06)
DUM75	−0.27590
	(1.18)
DUM76	−0.28510
	(1.18)
CONSTANT	−1.35000
	(0.78)

Note: Asymptotic t ratios are in parentheses.

primarily in low quality units as might be implied by filtering theory, or that they are largely in marginal neighborhoods.

Conclusion

There are three main conclusions which come out of this research. First, asking-rents are higher for vacant units than for comparable occupied units. Second, landlords respond only slightly to past vacancy experience in setting current asking-rents. Third, vacancies are uniformly distributed over the observable characteristics. There is no evidence that landlords systematically misperceive the preferences of renters, and thereby overprice or underprice the units. The outcome is just what one might expect from an equilibrium search model where all agents are well informed.

Notes

1. This test may not be strictly appropriate as V_{it-1} cannot be taken as a fixed regressor. However the distribution ought to be well approximated by chi squared.

2. Again V_{it-1} is taken as a fixed regressor which should have a small effect on the quality of the estimates. It is, of course, a zero for 95 percent of the observations.

References

Bradbury, K.; Engle, R.; Irvine, O.; Rothenberg, J. "Simultaneous Estimation of the Supply and Demand for Housing in a Multizoned Metropolitan Area." In *Residential Location and Urban Housing Markets*, edited by Gregory, K. Ingram. Cambridge, Mass: Ballinger, 1977, pp. 51–86.

Gordon, D., and Hynes, A. "On the Theory of Price Dynamics." In *Microeconomic Foundations of Employment and Inflation Theory*, edited by Edmund Phelps. New York: Norton, 1970.

Ingram, G.; Kain, J.; Ginn, J. *The Detroit Prototype of the NBER Urban Simulation Model*. NBER, 1972.

Kiefer, N., and Neumann, G. 1979a. "Estimation of Wage Offer Distributions and Reservation Wage." In *Studies in the Economics of Search*, edited by S. Lippman and J. McCall. Amsterdam: North Holland.

——— 1979b. "An Empirical Job Search Model with a Test of the Constant Reservation Wage Hypothesis." *JPE*, 87: 89–108.

Maddala, G. "The Use of Variance Components Models in Pooling Cross Section and Time Series Data." *EMA* 39, no. 2 (1971): 341–358.

Marshall, R. and Guasch, L. "Some Explanations of Vacancy Patterns in the Rental Housing Market." *UCSD Working Paper* 82-19(1982).

Rydell, Peter (1979). "Shortrun Response of Housing Markets to Demand Shifts." Rand Publication R-2453-HUD.

Simon, Herbert. "A Behavioral Model of Rational Choice." *QJE* 69, (1955): 99–108.

Stull, William. "The Landlord's Dilemma." *JUE* 5, no. 1 (1978): 101–115.

6

Estimates of a More General Model of Consumer Choice in the Housing Market

John M. Quigley

The multinominal logit model is an appealing representation of the choice processes of consumers in the housing market. Its appeal for empirical analysis of household behavior is based upon two salient features of the housing commodity: the dimensionality of the bundle of residential services, and the joint pricing of these residential attributes.

In any local market, most of the housing services consumed in a market run are provided by the existing stock. Since this stock is expensive to modify, the spatial pattern of prices in temporary equilibrium, such that suppliers earn identical normal profits and consumers of identical incomes enjoy equal satisfaction, is likely to include substantial positive or negative quasi rents to particular configurations of housing components at specific locations. Except in the longest of long runs, the temporary equilibrium pattern of housing prices is likely to be quite complex indeed.

Thus it is natural to view consumer choice as the selection of a single discrete dwelling unit out of a large number of alternatives indexed by their characteristics and prices. In selecting a particular dwelling unit, households jointly choose a vector of characteristics and a rental payment. In contrast to consumer choice in most markets, housing choices involve the joint selection of quantities and prices by demanders.

During the past few years, there have been a number of studies applying the multinomial logit model to observations on the choices made by housing consumers. This chapter begins by reviewing briefly the assumptions and maintained hypotheses of the housing market models estimated by Ellickson (1977, 1981), Case (1981), Kain and Apgar (1977), Lerman (1977, 1979), Quigley (1972, 1976), and Williams (1979) among others. We then consider several extensions of the basic theoretical model, extensions proposed by Domencich and McFadden (1975) and McFadden (1977). On the basis of these results, the parameters of a more general model of housing choice are estimated. The empirical analysis provides a comparison between the results of the more general model and those obtained from the class of so-called

This analysis benefited from discussions with Daniel McFadden about the general model and with William Apgar about the sources of data. Neither has any responsibility for errors or interpretations. Programming assistance was provided by Paul Pfleiderer and James Trask, and financial support by the National Science Foundation.

125

traditional models of housing choice. The specific comparison uses my own
paper, written in 1973, as the horrible example.

The Traditional Logit Model Applied to Housing Choice

Call the set of all dwellings D with J members $(j = 1, 2, \ldots, J)$. When a
consumer chooses a dwelling unit i out of D, he also selects a set of
neighborhood and public service amenities and a journey to work (X_i), as
well as a price, (that is, a monthly rent or purchase price R_i). Consumers of
income y have preferences over the set of public service-amenity packages,
housing characteristics, and other goods, $y - R_i$.

Assume the utility function for households consists of a systematic
component V and an additive stochastic component ε

$$U[X_i, y - R_i] = V(i) + \varepsilon(i) \qquad (6.1)$$

Assumptions (maintained hypotheses) about the form of the stochastic
component of the utility function permit probability statements about the
choice of any specific dwelling to be made. In particular, as is well known,
McFadden (1974) demonstrated that: if it is assumed that the stochastic
terms are independently and identically distributed according to the Weibull
distribution[1], then the form of the probability statement is

$$p(i) = \text{prob } [U(i) > U(j)] = \frac{e^{v(i)}}{\sum_j e^{v(j)}} \qquad \text{for all j, } j \neq i \qquad (6.2)$$

Equation 6.2 is a well-behaved probability statement with values bounded by
zero and one. The probability of choosing any dwelling unit depends upon the
characteristics of all dwellings in the choice set. Equation 6.2 is estimated by
maximizing a log-likelihood function of the form

$$\log L \propto \frac{1}{K} \sum_K \log \left(\frac{e^{v(i)}}{\sum_j e^{v(j)}} \right) \qquad (6.3)$$

for a sample size of K observations on choices i and on available alternatives
j.

Finally, if it can be assumed that the systematic component of the utility
function is linear in its parameters, McFadden has shown that the likelihood
function given in equation 6.3 is concave, and the parameters are unique up

to a factor of proportionality. For the problem of housing choice, a linear relationship (another maintained hypothesis),

$$v(i) = \alpha X_i + \beta(y - R_i) \qquad (6.4)$$

renders the parameters α and β of the model estimable. This maintained hypothesis is, of course, rather innocuous; any nonlinear function can be approximated by one linear in its parameters.

Under the maintained hypotheses of equations 6.1, 6.2, and 6.4, estimates of the discrete model of housing choice have been presented by a number of researchers.

It is worth pointing out two serious limitations shared by all these analyses of consumer behavior in the housing market—one conceptual limitation and one practical limitation, which comprises existing empirical work.

First, according to equation 6.2, the odds of choosing housing unit m relative to n are independent of the characteristics of all other alternatives available to consumers. This maintained hypothesis, the so-called independence of irrelevant alternatives (IIA), is simply not testable within the traditional model. The assumption is surely inappropriate in many situations involving the choice of housing and neighborhood characteristics.

Second, there is a real practical problem in maximizing the log-likelihood function in equation 6.3. Clearly, the theoretical problem solved by consumers in the marketplace is the selection of one *specific* dwelling unit out of the large number of alternative dwellings (D) actually available on the market. However, for an economist to maximize the likelihood function in equation 6.3 for any sample of consumers of size K, it is necessary to make the set of alternatives "small enough" somehow to render an iterative solution procedure computationally feasible. Note that this latter complication did not arise at all in the original applications of the mutinomial logistic model to model choice. Inherently, there are a relatively small number of available transport modes; in contrast, however, there are a large number of potential dwelling units available for occupancy by housing consumers.

Typically, analysts have "solved" this problem in an ad hoc way. They have represented the heterogeneity of the housing, neighborhood, and public services available to consumers by a small number of *types* of residential housing, for example, specified components of the bundle of housing services at particular values. Thus, in practical estimation, the choice problem has been defined as the selection of one *housing type* out of an arbitrarily defined set of alternatives.

Table 6-1 indicates the ad hoc definitions of the choice set employed by analysts in estimating the logit model of consumer choice in the housing market.[2]

Quigley (1972, 1976) formulated the consumer's problem as the choice of one specific type of housing out of a set of eighteen types of rental units, based upon dwelling units characteristics alone. Case (1981) considers the choice among nine types of housing. Kain and Apgar (1977) and Williams (1979) considered the problem of choosing one housing type out of fifty (based upon ten classifications of dwelling unit characteristics and five classifications of neighborhood). In contrast, Lerman's (1977, 1979) formulation investigates the household's choice of a census tract for residence, rather than the choice of a dwelling. In this formulation, alternatives are described by the average characteristics of housing in different tracts. The data consist of an observation on the census tract chosen by each household and observations on each rejected alternative in the urban area. Thus Lerman's analysis avoids the problem of defining arbitrary types of residential housing, but only by relying upon the average census characteristics of housing units (themselves a somewhat arbitrary aggregation of alternatives). Lerman's empirical work analyzes the choices made by 177 District of Columbia households. Thus the iterative procedure for maximizing the

Table 6–1
Definitions of Housing Alternatives Used in Multinomial Logit Analyses of Housing Choice

Author	Year of Study	Number of Housing Alternatives	Definition of Housing Alternatives
Kain and Apgar	1977	50 housing types	Single-family: two density classes by three size classes by five neighborhood categories.
			Multifamily: two density classes by five neighborhood classes.
Williams	1979	50 rental types	Ten combinations of lot size, structure type, and number of bedrooms, by five neighborhood classes.
Lerman	1977, 1979	145 census tracts	Average census characteristics of housing units in each tract.
Case	1981	9 housing types	Owner occupied: three size classes.
			Rental units: three size classes by three structure classes.
Quigley	1976	18 rental types	Three structure types by three size classes by two age classes.

likelihood function based upon a data set consisting of more than twenty-five thousand observations on consumer choices among available census tracts!

Applying the Extended Logit Model to Housing Choice

The bundle of services jointly consumed by the selection of a dwelling unit can be partitioned into at least two components: those that vary by dwellings within neighborhoods (or census tracts or towns), X_1; and those that are constant for dwellings within neighborhoods but vary across neighborhoods (or census tracts or towns), X_2. The size or condition of a dwelling unit or its price are examples of the first component; the quality of local schools or the racial composition of the neighborhood are examples of the second.[3]

From equation 6.2, under the usual assumptions, the probability of choice of neighborhood (n) and dwelling unit (i) is

$$p(i,n) = \frac{e^{\alpha_1 X_{1i} + \alpha_2 X_{2n}}}{\sum\limits_{j,k} e^{\alpha_1 X_{1j} + \alpha_2 X_{2k}}} \tag{6.5}$$

As with any joint probability statement, equation 6.5 can be decomposed into a marginal and a conditional probability statement. If $\sigma = 1$, then

$$p(i \mid n) = \frac{e^{\alpha_1 X_{1i}/(1-\sigma)}}{e^{I_n}} \tag{6.6a}$$

$$p(n) = \frac{e^{\alpha_1 X_{2n} + (1-\sigma)I_n}}{\sum\limits_{k} e^{\alpha_2 X_{2k} + (1-\sigma)I_k}} \tag{6.6b}$$

$$I_n = \log \sum\limits_{i \in n} \frac{e^{\alpha_1 X_{1i}}}{1 - \sigma} \tag{6.6c}$$

is arithmetically identical to equation 6.5. The parameters of the choice model can be estimated directly by using equation 6.5 or sequentially. The latter procedure involves estimating α_1, from equation 6.6a, using the parameters to calculate I_n for each neighborhood (or census tract or town) and then estimating α_2 from equation 6.6b. The sequential approach "involves some loss of efficiency relative to direct estimation of the joint choice model" (McFadden, 1977); it is, however, merely an alternative way of approaching the same problem.

The same sequential approach can of course be used to estimate the value of $(1 - \sigma)$, as well as α_1 and α_2 and thus to test whether σ is different from zero. McFadden and Domencich (1975) have shown that the joint probability function consistent with equation 6.6 is of the form

$$p(i,n) = \frac{e^{V(i,n)/(1-\sigma)}\left(\sum_{j \in n} e^{V(j,n)/(1-\sigma)}\right)^{-\sigma}}{\sum_{k}\sum_{j \in n} e^{V(j,k)/(1-\sigma)})^{1-\sigma}} \qquad (6.7)$$

This is a direct generalization of the traditional problem of joint choice. If σ is indeed equal to zero, then equation 6.7 reduces to equation 6.2, that is, to a choice model with the IIA property. If σ is equal to one, then from equation 6.6b the choice of neighborhood depends only upon neighborhood attributes, that is, all housing units within a neighborhood are viewed as identical. Thus sequential estimation of equation 6.6 provides a direct statistical test of the *degree* of independence of irrelevant alternatives.

Now consider the problem of estimating the theoretically correct choice model—the selection of one dwelling unit out of a large number of discrete alternatives. To estimate the choice model using as observations the entire set of metropolitan housing alternatives facing each consumer is clearly out of the question. If, however, for each consumer we select a subset of alternatives, d, and observe the consumer's choice among elements in this subset, then it may be possible to derive consistent estimates of the theoretically correct choice model. In particular, suppose $f(d|i)$ is the sampling rule for obtaining subset d, conditional upon the observed choice of dwelling unit i. McFadden (1977) has shown that if the sampling rule has certain weak properties, that is,

$$\text{if } f(d \mid i) > 0 \qquad \text{then } f(d \mid i) > 0 \qquad (6.8)$$

then maximization of the modified likelihood function

$$\log L \propto \frac{1}{K}\sum_{K} \log\left(\frac{e^{V(i) + \log f(d \mid i)}}{\sum_{j \in d} e^{V(j) + \log (d \mid j)}}\right) \qquad (6.9)$$

yields consistent estimates of the parameters of the choice function. Equation 6.8 specifies a sampling rule with the property that if rejected, alternative j is assigned to the subset d, then it is logically possible that j could have been the observed choice. Under these conditions, McFadden's result indicates that the likelihood function need only be modified to take into account the sampling rule for selecting d. Thus it is possible to estimate, consistently at least, the parameters of the model that views households as choosing one specific dwelling unit out of the entire set of available units in the metropolitan housing market.

Empirical Application

In a paper presented in 1973 and published in 1976, Quigley used the multinomial logistic model to investigate the housing choice decisions of households in the Pittsburgh metropolitan housing market. The basic data were drawn from a home-interview survey of 24,626 households conducted in 1967. Separately for thirty income and family-size classifications of white-renter households who had recently moved into their dwellings, the parameters of household choice among discrete types of residential housing were estimated according to the procedure described in equations 6.1 through 6.4. As noted in table 6-1, for each of these groups of households, the heterogeneity of housing alternatives was represented by eighteen types of residential housing: three structure types (single-family units, row-houses, or common-wall units, and apartments); three size classes (1, 2, and 3-or-more bedrooms); and two quality or age classes (units built before 1930 and those constructed after 1930). In addition, the average occupancy cost for each type of housing facing each consumer was estimated. For each housing type, the occupancy cost was computed for each household as the minimum of the sum of gross rental payments and the journey-to-work cost to the household's workplace in a set of 333 residence sites (zones) in the metropolitan area.[4]

Thus for maximization of the likelihood function, the X vector consists of variables representing structure type, age, interior size, and occupancy costs. The data consist of observations on the type of residential housing chosen and the seventeen rejected alternatives for each household in a given classification.

Table 6-2 is reproduced from that study. The table presents the coefficients of the choice model, estimated separately for middle-income households of 1, 2, 3, 4, and 5-or-more members. For any household class, ratios of the coefficients are interpreted as the marginal rates of substitution between housing characteristics; the bid-rents of consumers can be obtained by inverting the utility function.

Note the limitations of this approach. First, the IIA are a maintained hypothesis for this analysis. For example, the log odds of choice between new two-room–single-family units and old three-room–row-house units is assumed to be independent of the availability of new three-room–single-family units in the metropolitan housing market. Second, representation of the heterogeneity of housing by eighteen types is an extremely strong assumption. However, modelling a *realistic*-choice process by increasing the dimensionality of housing to include, say, neighborhood attributes would have increased the estimation cost more than proportionately.

The discussion in the section entitled "The Traditional Logit Model Applied to Housing Choice" indicates that a more general model which avoids these two assumptions can be estimated for reasonable cost.

Table 6-2
Estimated Coefficients of the Multinomial Logistic Model by Family Size for Income Class ($5,000–6,999)

$$\log \ (p_i/p_j) = b_1(CW_i - CW_j) + b_2(APT_i - APT_j) + b_3(BR_i - BR_j) + b_4(AG_i - AGE_j) + b_5(P_i^* - P_j^*) + P + b_6(ST_i - ST_j)$$

Family Size	Number of Observations	Common Wall (CW)	Apartment (APT)	Number of Bedrooms (BR)	Structure Age (AGE)	Relative PRICE (P*)	Stock (ST)
1	91	0.150	2.564	-1.222	-3.049	-1.888	0.009
		(0.31)	(5.50)	(3.21)	(4.26)	(1.20)	(6.54)
2	223	0.291	0.874	-0.223	-0.223	-2.906	0.003
		(1.65)	(4.29)	(5.13)	(1.25)	(3.98)	(7.79)
3	224	-1.500	-0.849	2.020	-2.383	-4.465	0.010
		(7.06)	(4.45)	(10.92)	(9.03)	(5.87)	(14.89)
4	194	-2.693	-0.903	3.823	-2.738	-4.140	0.014
		(10.12)	(4.23)	(13.54)	(8.86)	(4.91)	(14.16)
5+	223	-1.591	-2.013	3.170	-0.893	-6.116	0.008
		(7.53)	(7.32)	(13.46)	(3.98)	(6.61)	(12.16)

Source: Quigley (1976), table 6–1.

Note: Asymptotic t statistics are in parentheses.

Suppose that for each consumer who faces the choice of selecting one dwelling out of the metropolitan housing stock (D), we select a subset of dwellings d according to the following sample rule: include in the subset of alternatives d the observed choice and a number of rejected alternatives obtained by considering each element in D sequentially and including it with probability ρ. Under these conditions, the probability of d, $f(d\,|\,_i)$, depends only on the number of elements it contains according to the binomial formula. Obviously, if any rejected alternative j appears in the subset d, it has the logical possibility of being the observed choice i from that set. This particular sampling rule implies a somewhat stronger condition, however. Since d always contains the chosen alternative i and some number of rejected alternatives selected with equal probability, then the probability of any set d depends only upon its number of elements.

In this special case, termed the "uniform conditioning property" by McFadden (1977), the terms containing $\log f(d)$ in the numerator and denominator of equation 6.9 simply cancel out. Maximization of the simple likelihood function based upon a sample size K of observations on choices i out of subsets d yields consistent estimates of the parameters estimated by maximizing the likelihood function based on K observations on choices i out of D, the entire set of alternatives.

We now use this result to estimate the more general model of housing choice for one classification of consumers, a subset of the 224 observations on white-renter households with three members reported in table 6-2. The subset consists of those 131 households which had one full-time worker and which had moved into their present unit within the past year. From the survey data on the rental dwelling units in the metropolitan housing market (D), a subset (d) of alternatives was selected for each individual. For each household, the subset consists of its chosen dwelling unit and a number of rejected dwelling units obtained by including each other's rental unit in the sample with some probability ρ, chosen so that the subset of alternatives for each household would contain about five members. For each household, it was possible to estimate the journey-to-work time by auto and public transit for each dwelling unit in its subset. In addition, the average characteristics of the census tracts containing each sampled unit were obtained. Finally, it was possible to obtain information about the local spending of the jurisdiction servicing each dwelling unit.

Table 6-3 presents summary data on the alternatives chosen by these households and on the subset of rejected alternatives drawn for each household. The dwelling units chosen by these households are more likely to be single-family units and less likely to be apartments than those units not selected. On average, the 131 chosen units are slightly smaller, in slightly better condition, and slightly more expensive than those in the sample of 524 rejected alternatives.

Table 6-3
Sample Characteristics of Chosen Dwellings and a Sample of Rejected Units for 131 Renter Households

	Chosen Alternatives Located in			Sample of Rejected Alternatives Located in		
	Central City	Suburbs	Total	Central City	Suburbs	Total
Dwelling characteristics[a]						
Common-wall units	0.464	0.418	0.427	0.371	0.358	0.360
Apartment units	0.357	0.233	0.260	0.484	0.296	0.363
Number of bedrooms	1.821	1.961	1.931	1.774	2.148	2.015
Number of bathrooms	1.000	1.039	1.031	0.995	1.074	1.046
Condition (1 = bad)	0.036	0.010	0.017	0.054	0.056	0.055
Age (years)	42.04	37.77	38.68	42.55	38.27	39.79
Monthly rent	$82.11	$60.61	$65.21	$71.94	$60.70	$64.69
Auto journey to work (min)	27.36	24.46	25.08	38.13	51.05	46.46
Transit journey to work	40.71	56.17	52.87	73.31	86.96	82.11
Occupancy cost	$151.80	$122.90	$129.10	$169.00	$190.70	$176.20
Census-tract characteristics[b]						
Proportion vacant	0.036	0.030	0.032	0.084	0.039	0.055
Proportion homeowner	0.561	0.629	0.614	0.403	0.586	0.521
Proportion lacking plumbing	0.039	0.032	0.032	0.093	0.040	0.055
Median rent	$109.60	$101.80	$103.50	$111.50	$102.10	$105.50
Proportion black	0.018	0.029	0.027	0.191	0.053	0.102
Public-sector characteristics[c]						
Per capita spending	$3577.00	$3884.00	$3819.00	$3577.00	$4019.00	$3862.00
School spending per student	$795.70	$664.20	$692.30	$795.70	$641.60	$696.30
Student teacher ratio	19.46	19.87	19.78	19.46	19.47	19.46
Percent nonwhite in school	38.21	6.06	12.93	38.21	8.14	18.81
Number of cases	28	103	131	186	338	524

[a]Source: SPRPC Home Interview Survey. See Quigley (1976).
[b]Source: 1970 Census of Population and Housing.
[c]Source: See Quigley, Trask, and Trask (1977).

The dwelling units chosen by these households are considerably more accessible to their worksites than the sample of rejected alternatives. The average difference in accessibility is more than 20 minutes (one way) by auto and almost 30 minutes (one way) by public transit.

The differences in average-census-tract characteristics suggest that this group of households chooses housing in better neighborhoods—their chosen dwelling units tend to be in neighborhoods where ownership rates are higher (61 versus 52 percent), vacancy rates are lower (3.2 versus 5.5 percent), and minority population is smaller (2.7 black versus 10.2 percent) than in the neighborhoods containing the rejected units.

There are some differences in average-public-sector characteristics between the chosen and rejected units. The chosen units tend to be in jurisdictions with slightly lower per-capita spending and slightly lower school spending per pupil, but in jurisdictions where a larger fraction of public school students are white.

Twenty-eight of the 131 chosen dwelling units are located in the central city of Pittsburgh. Of the sample of 524 rejected units, 186 are located in the central city. Table 6-3 also compares the average characteristics of chosen and rejected units separately for central city and suburban locations. Conditional upon the choice of a central city unit, the size of the chosen dwelling is slightly larger; it is in better condition, more accessible, and more expensive than the average rejected unit. Conditional upon a suburban choice, the chosen unit is slightly smaller, but the other comparisons of dwelling characteristics are similar.

Table 6-4 presents estimates of the multinomial logit model based on this body of information describing the housing choices of recent movers. The first column of the table reports the results based only upon the housing market information used in the previous paper, that is, the structure type, size, and age class of the chosen and rejected alternatives. In addition, the occupancy cost or gross price of the units is included.[5] Despite the differences in the sample of households and in the choice set, the coefficients are qualitatively similar to those reported in table 6-2 for the same group of households.

Column 2 reports the results when the model is expanded to exploit the fact that it has been estimated from a sample of dwelling units, rather than from an exhaustive population of housing types.

The choice model is expanded to include the age and condition of the dwelling and the number of bathrooms. Column 3 expands the model to include measures of the characteristics of neighborhoods and the public services consumed jointly with housing attributes. When the analysis is conducted using a sample of actual dwellings as the alternatives, a major advantage is immediately apparent: it is now possible to include separately the monthly rent commanded by each dwelling and the accessibility of each dwelling to the workplace of specific consumers. When the occupancy-cost

Table 6–4
Alternative Specifications of Expanded Choice Model for 131 Pittsburgh Households

Variable	1	2	3	4
Structure type				
Common wall	−1.033	−0.056	−0.418	
	(2.10)	(0.17)	(1.14)	
Apartment	−0.637	−0.653	−0.408	
	(2.11)	(2.01)	(1.13)	
Size				
Number of bedrooms	0.830	0.360	0.381	
	(4.16)	(2.06)	(1.89)	
Number of bathrooms		1.621	1.742	
		(1.31)	(1.09)	
Condition				
Age class	−2.400			
	(3.10)			
Age (years) × 100		−0.410	0.257	
		(4.93)	(0.26)	
Condition (1 = bad)		−0.134	−0.054	
		(0.57)	(0.21)	
Cost				
Occupancy (gross price)	−2.631			
	(2.61)			
Rent × 10		−0.831	−0.995	
		(2.06)	(1.90)	
Commute time (hours per month)		−0.096	−0.106	
		(8.31)	(7.75)	
Neighborhood—Town			2.379	3.505
Home ownership rate				
			(2.63)	(1.53)
Proportion black			−2.742	−9.688
			(2.10)	(2.51)
School expenditure/student			0.170	−0.803
			(0.94)	(1.10)
Proportion black in			−0.029	−0.035
elementary school				
			(2.74)	(2.36)
$1 - \sigma$				1.034
				(3.67)
$-2 \log (L/L_o)$	86.2	166.1	208.0	121.7

Note: Asymptotic t ratios are in parentheses.

measure is replaced by monthly rent and the accessibility (auto commute time) of each dwelling to the worksites of consumers, both coefficients are significantly different from zero. Isolating the separate effects of rental expenditures and commuting times on utility levels permits a direct analysis of the bid-rents of consumers for housing attributes and permits an investigation of the tradeoff households make between the journey to work and the out-of-pocket costs of housing. For example, from column 2, households are willing to bid .0831 in additional rent to save .096 hours in monthly commuting times. The value of travel time estimated from the residential location decisions of consumers is thus $1.16 per hour on average, or about 39 percent of the hourly wage (that is, $6,000 annual income, 2000 hours of work). A similar comparison based upon the expanded model in column 3 yields a value of travel time equal to roughly 36 percent of the average pretax wage rate. These estimates of the value of commuting time are rather similar to those estimated in studies which have considered the implicit value of travel reflected in the modal choice decisions of commuters.

From column 2, the results indicate that this class of consumers is willing to bid $4.33 per month (or about 7 percent of their average rent) for an additional bedroom; they are willing to pay $7.86 more to enjoy the same housing services in a single detached rental unit rather than a higher density apartment. From column 3, the comparisons are $3.82 and $4.10, respectively. When the model is expanded to include the neighborhood and public services jointly consumed with housing services, the homeownership rate and the racial composition of the neighborhood are both significant. Interestingly, the variable measuring the age of the dwelling unit, highly significant in the models which do not include measures of the neighborhood environment, is totally insignificant. Apparently, given the historical pattern of development in the metropolitan area, the age of the dwelling itself is a good proxy for the condition of the neighborhood; given the characteristics of the neighborhood, however, the age of the structure itself is not associated with better or more desirable dwellings.

The fourth column of table 6-4 tests the IIA hypothesis in one particular form. For 116 out of the 131 renter households, the choice-based sample d selected by the binomial process included at least one dwelling in the central city and one in the suburban housing market. Thus we can analyze the marginal choice of central city or suburban neighborhood and the conditional choice of housing attributes, given central city or suburban neighborhood. In this analysis, the inclusive value is estimated from the conditional choice model reported in column 2.[6] The point estimate of $(1 - \sigma)$ is 1.034, and the t-ratio for the hypothesis that σ is significantly different from zero is 0.12. Thus the IIA hypothesis cannot be rejected for the choice of central city or suburban location and the marginal choice of housing attributes. The characteristics of dwelling units do affect the choice of central city or suburban location.[7]

Conclusion

This chapter presents some crude and preliminary estimates of a class of housing-choice models that are considerably more general statistically than those previously estimated. More important, however, the economic model is

considerably more faithful to the appealing theoretical notions: that households choose a single dwelling unit out of a large number of alternatives,
described by housing, neighborhood, public-service characteristics and
prices; and that, in considering the choice of particular dwelling-unit
characteristics, neighborhood characteristics, and public-service packages,
there may be a greater or lesser *degree* of indpendence among some of these
components, but the independence of irrelevant alternatives is an extreme
case.

Of particular interest to urban economists is the application of such
models to analyzing the housing-price–transportation-cost tradeoffs made by
households and their bid-rents for the attributes of housing services. On
theoretical grounds, these issues are central to understanding residential
location and urban spatial structure.

Notes

1. $(n - 1)$ prob $[\varepsilon(i) \le A] = \exp[-\exp(-A)]$ for all i
2. Ellickson's (1977, 1981) analysis is somewhat different from the
other studies noted in table 6-1. He estimates the parameters of consumers'
bid-rent functions directly rather than indirectly through utility parameters.
This reverse logit analysis estimates the conditional probability that a
dwelling will be occupied by a household of given characteristics.

This approach, however, does not avoid the problem of arbitrary definition of the discrete alternative. Ellickson defines households by eleven
discrete categories (race, income, and family-size groups) for his empirical
analysis.

3. For notational convenience only, consider the choices made by
households of the same income. Thus $(y - R_i)$ can be treated as one
component of the vector of characteristics X_{1i} that vary across dwelling units.

4. For housing type i, the occupancy cost for a household with workplace
j was computed as min $(P_{ik} + T_{jk}w)$ where P_{ik} is the rent for type i in zone k,
T_{jk} is (monthly) transport time from j to k, and w is the wage rate. This
occupany cost has subsequently been called the "gross price" of housing (see
Ingram, 1979).

5. This variable is constructed to be as close as possible to the
occupancy-cost measure used in the earlier analysis. For each dwelling unit
in the set, it is defined as the sum of the monthly rent and monthly commuting
costs. Commuting costs are computed from auto commute times using
assumed out of pocket costs are and assuming that commute time is valued at
the (average) wage rate. This procedure is described somewhat exhaustively
in Quigley (1972).

6. For each of the 116 households whose choice-based sample included
both central city and suburban dwellings, the inclusive value for the central

city (suburbs) is computed as $\log [(N/M) \Sigma_m e^{\alpha x_1}]$ where m is the number of elements in the assigned choice set in the central city (suburbs) and N is the number of rental units in the central city (suburbs).

7. Stated another way, the estimate of σ suggests that dwelling units are not viewed as identical within the central city or suburbs by consumers in their choice of residential location. A more useful test of this hypothesis would be: the choice of dwellings given neighborhood (census tract); the choice of neighborhood given town; and the marginal choice of town.

References

Case, Karl E. "A New Approach to Modeling the Effects of Demographic Change on the Housing Market." Wellesley: Wellesley College, Department of Economics, Working Paper #42, March 1981.

Domencich, Thomas A., and McFadden, Daniel. *Urban Travel Demand: A Behavioral Analysis.* Amsterdam: North Holland, 1975.

Ellickson, Bryan. "Economic Analysis of Urban Housing Markets: A New Approach." The Rand Corporation, R-2024-NSF, July 1977. Published as "An Alternative Test of the Hedonic Theory of Housing Markets." *Journal of Urban Economics* 9, no. 1 (January 1981): 56–79.

Ingram, Gregory K. "Simulation and Econometric Approaches to Modeling Urban Areas. In *Current Issues in Urban Economics*, edited by Peter Mieszkowski and Mahlon Straszheim. Baltimore: Johns Hopkins Press, 1979, pp. 130–164.

Kain, John F., Apgar, Jr., William C. "The Modeling of Neighborhood Change." Cambridge: Harvard University, Department of City and Regional Planning, Discussion Paper D77-22, October 1977.

Lerman, Stephen R. 1977. "Location, Housing, Automobile Ownership, and the Model to Work: A Joint Choice Model." *Transportation Research Board Record*, no. 610: 6–11.

_____. 1979. "Neighborhood Choice and Transportation Services." In *The Economics of Neighborhood*, edited by David Segal. Academic Press, pp. 83–118.

McFadden, Daniel. 1974. "Conditional Logit Analysis of Qualitative Choice Behavior." In *Frontiers in Econometrics*, edited by Paul Zarembka. Academic Press.

_____. 1977. "Modelling the Choice of Residential Location." New Haven: Yale University, Cowles Foundation Discussion Paper No. 477, December 1977.

Quigley, John M. "Residential Location with Multiple Workplaces and a Heterogeneous Housing Stock," Harvard University Program on Regional and Urban Economics, Discussion Paper No. 80, September 1972.

_____. "Housing Demand in the Short Run: An Analysis of Polytomous Choice." Paper prepared for the winter meetings of the Econometric Society, December 1963; *Explorations in Economic Research* 3, no. 1 (January 1976): 76–102.

Quigley, John M.; Trask, Gail M.; and Trask, James H. "Income and Product Accounts for the Local Public Sector." Institution for Social and Policy Studies Working Paper #795. New Haven: Yale University, September 1977.

Williams, Jr., Roberton C. "A Logit Model of Demand for Neighborhood." In *The Economics of Neighborhood*, edited by David Segal. Academic Press, 1979, pp. 17–42.

Part III
Externalities

7

Is a Local Public Good Different from Any Other?

Bryan Ellickson

"I see nobody on the road," said Alice.

"I only wish I had such eyes," the King remarked in a fretful tone. "To be able to see Nobody! And at that distance too! Why, it's as much as I can do to see real people, by this light!"
—Lewis Carroll

It is easy to understand why urban economists attach a great deal of importance to local public goods. The division of urban areas into separate political jurisdictions affects residential choice, and the location decisions of households, in turn, affect the nature of the services that local governments provide. It is the appreciation of the crucial role of this interaction that sets urban apart from traditional local public finance.

The significance of local public goods to urban economics does not stop there. The notion of a local public or, perhaps one should say, collective, good is very flexible, extending far beyond the province of those services that happen to be provided by local governments. Anything that is collectively consumed is a local public good. In particular, neighborhood attributes are local public goods, and, since characteristics of a neighborhood are the defining property of a slum or ghetto, the relevance of local public goods to urban economics is manifest.

What is less obvious is that local public goods are, or at least should be, of considerable interest to the pure theorist. The reasons for this have nothing to do with policy relevance but rather with the issue of what is meant by "perfect competition." It is a tribute to the subtlety of Adam Smith's vision that, two hundred years after *The Wealth of Nations*, there is still much to learn about what is, and what is not, competitive. In the last few years mathematical economics has begun to contribute to this learning process in a very significant way.

In the early going it was not all that obvious that the formal mathematical analysis of competitive equilibrium would prove particularly fruitful for the progress of economics. Convex sets, separating hyperplanes and fixed-point theorems, were harnessed to the task of establishing existence of equilibrium and the like, but the basic setting was just the standard neoclassical model and the conclusions were not very surprising.

I would like to thank Paul Samuelson for comments on an earlier version of this chapter.

143

The experience of economics is probably typical of the process of mathematizing a discipline. The first stages are more a matter of grammar than of substance. But as Reed and Simon observe in discussing the relationship between mathematics and physics:

> When a successful mathematical model is created for a physical phenomenon . . . , the mathematical structure of the model itself provides a new way of thinking about the phenomenon. Put slightly differently, when a model is successful it is natural to think of the physical quantities in terms of the mathematical objects which represent them and to interpret similar or secondary phenomena in terms of the same model. Because of this, an investigation of the internal mathematical structure of the model can alter and enlarge our understanding of the physical phenomenon.[1]

A similar process is happening in economics.

Pushing the definition of competition to its logical limit has led to a continuum of agents as the proper idealization of truly perfect competition, and in exploring such models, many of the assumptions thought to be important in competitive theory have turned out to be not intrinsic at all. Completeness and transitivity of preferences, convexity of production or preference sets, perfect divisibility of commodities, and finite dimensionality of commodity sets: none of these is necessary for competition. Analogues of the same conclusion hold even with a finite number of consumers, though sometimes only in an approximate sense. It seems clear that eventually these results will have a profound effect on the way that economists view the competitive process.

The reason why local public goods should be interesting to the mathematical economist is that they provide a natural, perhaps even canonical, illustration of the new way of looking at competition. In this chapter I will pursue that theme through a series of examples, simple enough to allow contact with the traditional literature on local public goods but described in terms sufficiently general to permit the problem to be viewed as an application of recent advances in mathematical economics.

The following section reviews the conclusions that are reached about local public goods when analyzed from a standard neoclassical point of view, highlighting the contradictions and generally puzzling features that such translations of the model of Tiebout typically produce.

The section "A Redefinition of Public Goods" introduces an alternative version of the Tiebout theory in which the representation of local public goods as perfectly divisible commodities is replaced by one in which they are regarded as indivisible commodities. Out of this emerges a competitive theory of local public goods that avoids the paradoxes of the standard approach, as best illustrated within the framework of a continuum of agents. However, the model does not fully capture all that is going on in the local public goods literature because, as I will indicate in the section discussing a continuum of public goods, even the simplest of such models tacitly employ an infinite-dimensional commodity space (while the analysis of the following section assumes finite dimensionality).

The section entitled "A Continuum of Public Goods" explores this issue, and the section after that demonstrates a sense in which the finite-dimensional models can be regarded as approximations to the infinite-dimensional case. The last section concludes the chapter with some comments on the implications of the abstract theory for the practical task of modeling the real world and with some suggestions for the direction of future research.

Competition and Local Public Goods:
The Conventional View

Pure Public Goods

To set the stage for the analysis of local public goods, we will begin with an economy with pure public goods. Let A denote the set of consumers in the economy, assumed finite for now. An allocation will be represented by a pair of functions, $x: A \rightarrow R_+^n$ for private goods and $z: A \rightarrow R_+$ for the single public good. $x(a)$ then gives the bundle of private goods allocated to consumer a, and $z(a)$ the public good that he receives. The distinguishing characteristic of private goods is that the commodity bundles $x(a)$, when summed over all $a \in A$, sum to the total amount provided in the economy. Pure public goods, on the other hand, exhibit a different property: the function z is constant on A.

The conditions for Pareto optimality in such an economy are given by the Samuelson conditions

$$\sum_{a \in A} MRS(a) = MRT \tag{7.1}$$

(one for each pairing of a private with the public good) plus the usual conditions asserting equality between marginal rates of substitution (MRS) and marginal rates of transformation (MRT) for all possible pairing of private goods. The Samuelson conditions are only necessary, not sufficient, for Pareto optimality, but when coupled with the usual convexity conditions on production and preferences, they, in fact, characterize the Pareto optimal allocations.

There is also a notion of Walrasian equilibrium for this economy, called Lindahl equilibrium, but it is not a genuine competitive equilibrium (as demonstrated, for example, by the failure of core equivalence as shown by Milleron or Muench).

Local Public Goods

Pure public goods are clearly a very special case, and it is natural that economists have devoted considerable attention to broader classes of collective consumption. Tiebout's suggestion that local public goods could permit the existence of competitive equilibrium (of the genuine sort, not the ersatz version of Lindahl) contributed to interest in the problem. The obvious way to proceed was to extend Samuelson's definition of a pure public good while modifying his methodology to the smallest extent possible.

A pure public good is shared equally by everyone in the economy, a local public good by a proper subset of A. An assignment of consumers that specifies a particular pattern of sharing will be denoted by $\Pi(A)$, where $\Pi(A)$ is a partition of the set of consumers into disjoint subsets. A particular subset $J \in \Pi(A)$ is a *jurisdiction*, and an allocation of local public goods is a function, $z: A \to R_+$, that is constant on the subsets J belonging to $\Pi(A)$. Thus, within a jurisdiction a local public good looks just like a pure public good, but the sharing does not go beyond the boundaries of the jurisdiction.

Provided that the partition $\Pi(A)$ is regarded as exogenous to the analysis, the methodology of Samuelson extends readily to the local public goods context. The Pareto optimality conditions given in equation 7.1 are replaced by conditions of the form

$$\sum_{a \in J} MRS(a) = MRT(J) \qquad \text{for all } J \in \Pi(A) \qquad (7.2)$$

where $MRT(J)$ denotes the marginal rate of transformation between public and private goods in jurisdiction J. While these conditions are only necessary and not sufficient, when coupled with the usual convexity conditions on production and preferences, they again characterize the Pareto optimal allocations. Lindahl equilibrium also extends in the obvious way, and it retains its ersatz character.

However, while fixing the partition is mathematically convenient, it is an endogenous partition that is the heart of the Tiebout story, and allowing consumers to choose among jurisdictions is what would seem to be the key to establishing the existence of a genuinely competitive allocation of public goods. But when the partition is allowed to vary, the analysis falls apart. Tiebout equilibrium emerges as a highly unlikely, almost absurd, construct requiring extremely stringent conditions if it is to exist. Any hope for a core equivalence theorem seems dashed by the fact that when the partition is endogenous, the core can be empty and the Lindahl construction disintegrates completely (Ellickson [1973]).

Furthermore, the generalized Samuelson conditions in equation 7.2 become essentially irrelevant to the determination of Pareto optimality. As indicated above, even under the best of circumstances these conditions are only necessary but not sufficient for Pareto optimality. That convexity of production and preferences coupled with the Samuelson conditions are also sufficient for Pareto optimality makes them useful when the assignment of consumers to jurisdictions is fixed. But if consumers are free to "vote with their feet," the Samuelson conditions no longer have any value. While they, of course, remain necessary for Pareto optimality, allocations which satisfy these conditions may not be Pareto optimal, even if production and preferences are convex. While this conclusion was tacit in Proposition 1 of Ellickson (1973), the fact that the Samuelson conditions continue to be employed in an irrelevant manner indicates that the point is still not well understood. For that reason a different example, more directly addressed to this issue, is presented in the appendix to this chapter.

The conclusions that emerge from these attempts to make Tiebout rigorous are probably rather different from what Tiebout had in mind. As the interpretations of Tiebout grow ever more sophisticated, it is easy to lose sight of the simple, in fact, rather naive, arguments that he employed. All that he said was that if consumers are faced with a wide variety of local public goods, then the situation looks very much like an ordinary competitive market with governments playing the role of firms. While it is, of course, true that there is no reason to assume that governments are trying to maximize profits, Tiebout cites Alchian's "survival" argument to support the view that this is irrelevant: "those local governments that attract the optimum number of residents may be viewed as being 'adopted by' the economic system."[2] Nowhere in Tiebout do we find a concern with conditions of "perfect homogeneity of jurisdictions" or "at least as many types of public goods as types of consumer," the conditions that play such an important role in latter-day interpretations of Tiebout. (See Bewley for a rigorous proof of the existence of "Tiebout equilibrium" under these conditions.)

What then are we to make of Tiebout equilibrium? The verdict after twenty-five years of study, as ably summarized by Bewley, is pretty clear: Tiebout was wrong. Competitive equilibrium with local public goods can exist, but the analogy to a private-good equilibrium is poor. Existence of Tiebout equilibrium requires conditions with no parallel in the corresponding private-good theory, conditions so stringent that they rob the concept of any conceptual, empirical, or normative value.

Before the jury is dismissed, however, I want to raise another possibility: perhaps it is the modern interpretations of Tiebout that are at fault. In the introduction I noted the radical changes which recent advances in mathematical economics have made in our way of thinking about competition. In the remaining sections of this chapter I shall explore what this means for Tiebout.

A Redefinition of Public Goods

A Theory of Tiebout Equilibrium

Suppose we were faced with the problem of modeling the market for neighborhoods or public schools without the benefit of the theory of local public goods accumulated over the last twenty-five years. Let K denote the set of possible types of neighborhood or school. Of course, the number of alternatives should be assumed infinite, but we know from experience that the best way to begin the construction of a competitive theory is to assume that commodity spaces are finite dimensional. (Private goods are also available in infinite variety, a fact which economists ignore with no evidence of embarrassment.)

Let z denote a typical element of K. In contrast to the preceding section, z has no interpretation as a "quantity" of the public good: it is simply a label. To emphasize this we can, for example, take $K = \{1, \ldots, m\}$ where m is the number of possible types of neighborhood or school.

When we pose the problem in this way, we are immediately faced with an apparently difficult situation: schools or neighborhoods are clearly indivisible commodities. A household sends its children to one school or to another and chooses to reside in one neighborhood or another. Partial membership makes no sense. Twenty-five years ago this would (and did) require the abandonment of this approach in favor of some alternative that treats public goods as though they were perfectly divisible commodities (for example, by interpreting z as a "flow" of services or a "quantity" of public good). But we now know that such a compromise is not necessary for the development of a competitive theory.

The description of the consumer choice process in the model we are going to present is the standard representation of competitive analysis: each consumer, acting as a price-taker, chooses that commodity bundle from his budget set which is a best element relative to a continuous preordering π_a. The key step in the analysis is to find an appropriate commodity space in which all this takes place.

Let $(x(a),\delta(a))$ denote the commodity bundle allocated to consumer a where, as before, $x(a)$ is an n-dimensional vector of private goods and $\delta(a)$ is a real-valued function on K. Specifically, $\delta(a) = \delta_z$ for some $z \in K$ where δ_z: $K \rightarrow \{0,1\}$ has the property that $\delta_z(z) = 1$ and $\delta_z(z') = 0$ *for* $z' \neq z$. The public-good choices available to each consumer are then given by the collection of these *delta functions*: $\Delta = \{\delta_z | z \in K\}$. Combining this representation of the public-good choices open to the consumer with the usual representation for the private goods, the consumption set for consumer a is given by $X(a) \times \Delta$ where $X(a)$ is a closed convex subset of R^n that is bounded from below.

The preferences of consumer a are described by a continuous preordering π_a defined on $X(a) \times \Delta$. In the examples used to illustrate this analysis, we employ a utility function $U_a: X(a) \times K \to R$ to represent preferences, where $U_a(x(a), z)$ is the utility enjoyed if the consumer chooses the bundle $x(a)$ of private commodities and a public good of type z. Let p denote the n-tuple of prices for the private commodites and the function $t: K \to R_+$, the tax prices of the pubic goods, where $t(z)$ is the tax required to consume a public good of type z. The budget set for consumer a is then given by

$$\beta(p,t,a): = \{(x(a),\delta(a)) \in X(a) \times \Delta \,|\, px(a) + \sum_{z \in K} t(z)\delta(a) \le pe(a)\}$$

where $e(a) \in R_+^n$ is the initial endowment of private commodities of consumer a (no public goods are initially owned). The demand set $\phi(p,t,a)$ of consumer a is then that set of elements of the budget set which is best relative to the preference relation π_a.

Turning now to the production side of the economy, to avoid inessential complications, we shall assume that no private commodities are produced and that public goods are produced using only private commodities as inputs. In the Tiebout literature, the average cost functions for public goods are usually assumed to be U-shaped. To simplify matters somewhat, we assume that average costs flatten out after some critical jurisdiction size $n_0(z)$, so that the average cost of producing public good z is given by function $c(z,n(z))$ where $n(z)$ is the size of the jurisdiction and $c(n,n(z)) = c(z,n_0(z))$ for $n(z) \ge n_0(z)$.

A competitive equilibrium for this economy is an allocation (x,δ): $A \to X \times \Delta$ (where $X = \cup_{a \in A} X(a)$) which takes $a \,|\to (x(a),\delta(a))$ and for which $(x(a),\delta(a)) \in \phi(p,t,a) \,\forall\, a \in A$ and the production plans are profit maximizing. This model is essentially equivalent to the theory of Tiebout equilibrium developed by Ellickson (1979), who showed that the main barriers to establishing the existence of a competitive equilibrium are both the nonconvexity introduced by the indivisibility of the public goods (which means that the demand sets $\phi(p,t,a)$ may not be convex-valued) and the presence of increasing returns in the production of the public goods (so that production sets are nonconvex).

The strategy employed in Ellickson (1979) as well as here, is to construct a *convexified* version $\mathscr{E}^*$ of the economy $\mathscr{E}$ described earlier. Specifically, each demand set $\phi(p,t,a)$ is replaced by its convex hull, $\phi^*(p,t,a): = \text{conv}\{\phi(p,t,a)\}$, where the convex hull of a set is the smallest convex set which contains it, and each production set is replaced by its convex hull. In terms of the cost functions we are using here, each average cost function $c(z,n(z))$ is replaced by the constant-returns-to-scale average cost function $c^*(z): = c(z,n_0(z))$ that coincides with the original cost function over its flat portion lying to the right of $n_0(z)$.

The only real difference between the model presented here and the one developed in Ellickson (1979) concerns the representation of the local public-good commodity bundles. In my earlier article, these commodity bundles were described in terms of the unit vectors $e_i \in R^m$ where m is the number of public-good types. Here the commodity bundles are represented by the delta functions δ_z (one for each $z \in K$), a construction that admittedly takes some getting used to. The reason for introducing the delta functions will only become apparent in the following two sections where they play a crucial role in making the transition to an infinite-dimensional commodity space. In the finite-dimensional context of this section, where m is the number of local public-good types, the main point to note is that the delta functions $\delta_z(z \in K)$ are in obvious one-to-one correspondence with the unit vectors e_i $(i = 1, \ldots, m)$ and that, in fact, the delta functions are unit vectors in an m-dimensional vector space isomorphic to R^m. The mathematics of Ellickson (1979) does not recognize any distinction between R^m and the vector space generated by the delta functions, and all of the conclusions of that paper carry over intact to the context considered here.

In particular, existence of a competitive equilibrium for the convexified economy $\mathscr{E}^*$ can be established in the usual way (subject, of course, to the standard qualifications concerning passage from quasi equilibrium to equilibrium and the like), and by investigating the relationship between $\mathscr{E}^*$ and the original economy $\mathscr{E}$, it is possible to capture most of the flavor of the applied literature on Tiebout equilibrium within this abstract setting. Rather than recapitulate all of the details of the discussion in Ellickson (1979), we instead illustrate the main conclusions in terms of a simple example.

Tiebout Equilibrium: An Example

Although we have been careful so far to emphasize that z is simply a label for a type of public good, in this example we revert to tradition and interpret z as the "quality" of the public good. We do this in order to stress the parallels between the theory presented here and the standard theory, and also to pave the way for discussion of the infinite-dimensional model of the following two sections. However, it is important to recognize the independence of the theory from any such interpretation. In particular, this example is easily modified to treat z as a label and nothing more, an exercise that is strongly recommended to the reader.

Assume that there are two divisible private goods in the economy and that all consumers have tastes described by a utility function of the form:

$$U(x(a),z) = x_1(a)x_2(a)z$$

where $z \in K$ and K is a finite set. Production of a public good of type z requires inputs of the two divisible commodities in equal proportion (a

Leontief fixed-coefficient technology) so that the convexified average-cost function is

$$c^*(z) = (p_1 + p_2)\, \gamma \sqrt{z}$$

where γ is a positive constant.[3] Because production of public goods in the convexified economy exhibits constant returns to scale, the price of any public good that is produced will equal its average cost:

$$t^*(z) = (p_1^* + p_2^*)\, \gamma \sqrt{z} \qquad (7.3)$$

where $p^* = (p_1^*, p_2^*)$ is the equilibrium vector of private-good prices.

For a consumer with income y (equal to the value $pe(a)$ of his endowment), the indirect utility function conditional on the choice of a public good of type z is given by

$$V(p, y - t(z), z) = \frac{(y - t(z))^2}{4\, p_1 p_2}\; z \qquad (7.4)$$

Assume for simplicity that there are only two types of public good: $K = \{z_1, z_2\}$ where z_1 and z_2 are real numbers with $z_1 < z_2$. (It is here that the interpretation of z as an index of quality comes into play.) As a consequence of the nonconvexity of the consumption sets and of all consumers having the same utility function, jurisdictions will exhibit stratification by income class in equilibrium. Consumers with income less than y_c will choose z_1, whereas those with income above y_c will choose z_2 where y_c is defined as the value of consumer income for which

$$V(p^*, y_c - t^*(z_1), z_1) = V(p^*, y_c - t^*(z_2), z_2) \qquad (7.5)$$

It is easy to see that this condition determines a unique value of income, so y_c is well defined.

If equation 7.4 is substituted into equation 7.5, we obtain the relationship

$$y_c = \frac{t^*(z_2)\sqrt{z_2} - t^*(z_1)\sqrt{z_1}}{\sqrt{z_2} - \sqrt{z_1}} \qquad (7.6)$$

Letting the first divisible commodity serve as *numéraire* with $p_1^* = 1$ and using equation 7.3 to determine the equilibrium tax prices, equation 7.6 reduces to

$$y_c = (1 + p_2^*)\, \gamma\, (\sqrt{z_1} + \sqrt{z_2}) \qquad (7.7)$$

To simplify the computation of equilibrium prices, assume that each consumer has equal endowments of the two divisible commodities. A consumer with endowment vector (b,b) will then have income

$$y = (p_1^* + p_2^*)b = (1 + p_2^*)b \qquad (7.8)$$

Letting b_c be the value of b corresponding to y_c, equation 7.7 becomes

$$(1 + p_2^*)b_c = (1 + p_2^*) \gamma (\sqrt{z_1} + \sqrt{z_2})$$

or

$$b_c = \gamma(\sqrt{z_1} + \sqrt{z_2}) \qquad (7.9)$$

Consumers with endowment parameter $b < b_c$ will choose the public good of type z_1; those with $b > b_c$ will choose z_2; and those with $b = b_c$ will be indifferent between the two public-good alternatives.

Because of the symmetry[4] inherent in this example, it is easy to guess what the equilibrium prices will be. $p^* = (1,1)$ and, therefore, $t^*(z) = 2\gamma\sqrt{z}$ for $z \in K$. In this example, the equilibrium prices for the economy $\mathscr{E}^*$ do not depend on the distribution of the endowment parameter b, although the amounts demanded and supplied of each commodity are, of course, dependent on that distribution.

The central issue for the competitive theory of local public goods involves the relationship between the competitive equilibrium for the convexified economy $\mathscr{E}^*$ and competitive equilibrium for the original economy $\mathscr{E}$. Whether an equilibrium for $\mathscr{E}^*$ is also an equilibrium for $\mathscr{E}$ depends on the distribution for the endowment parameter and the extent of increasing returns in the provision of the public goods. Letting $n^*(z)$ denote the number of those consumers in the competitive equilibrium for $\mathscr{E}^*$ who choose the public good of type z, we have a competitive equilibrium for $\mathscr{E}$ provided that

$$n^*(z) \geq n_0(z) \ \forall \ z \in K \qquad (7.10)$$

and

$$(x^*(a),\delta^*(a)) \in \phi(p^*,t^*,a) \ \forall \ a \in A \qquad (7.11)$$

To illustrate what these conditions mean, suppose that there are only two types of consumer: $A = A_1 \cup A_2$ where $A_1 \cap A_2 = \phi$ and

$$e(a) = \begin{cases} (b_1,b_1) & \text{for } a \in A_1 \\ (b_2,b_2) & \text{for } a \in A_2 \end{cases}$$

Let $z_1 = 4$, $z_2 = 9$, $b_1 = 3$, $b_2 = 7$, $\gamma = 1$, and $n_0(z_1) = n_0(z_2) = 10$.

From equation 7.9 we conclude that $b_c = 5$ and, as a result, consumers of type A_1 will choose z_1 and those of type A_2 will choose z_2. Provided that A_1 and A_2 have at least ten members, the condition in equation 7.10 will be satisified and it is easy to see that condition of equation 7.11 is met as well. Each jurisdiction is operating within the range of constant returns to scale, and a competitive equilibrium exists for the economy $\mathscr{E}$. If, on the other hand, either A_1 or A_2 has fewer than ten members, both conditions will fail, and the reason for the failure is classical: unexhausted economies to scale.

At this juncture, it is instructive to contrast these results with the conventional theory of Tiebout equilibrium (as formalized, for example, by Bewley). What the two approaches have in common is an emphasis on unexhausted scale economies as the primary reason why Tiebout equilibrium may fail to exist. The example given above also shares two other attributes with the conventional theory: the two public-good jurisdictions have perfectly homogeneous populations and the number of public-good types is at least equal to the number of consumer types. However, in contrast to the standard theory, neither of these attributes is essential to the theory presented here.

For instance, we can modify the example by replacing set A_1 by a group of consumers each with a distinct level of parameter b and doing the same for set A_2. Provided that endowment parameters b for consumers in A_1 are all less than 5 and that the parameters for consumers in A_2 are greater than 5, the conclusions we reached regarding this example are essentially unchanged. The equilibrium prices for the convexified economy $\mathscr{E}^*$ are the same, and if there are at least ten consumers in A_1 and at least ten in A_2, the competitive equilibrium for $\mathscr{E}^*$ will be a competitive equilibrium for $\mathscr{E}$.

While it is still true that the wealthier consumers choose the higher-quality public good and the less wealthy consumers, the lower-quality public good, that is the sort of relationship we normally expect to find in a competitive equilibrium. By allowing differences in tastes even this milder pattern of stratification by income can be broken (although, typically, consumers choosing high-quality public goods will have either a high income or a strong taste for public goods while those choosing low-quality public goods will have either a low income or a weak taste for public goods.) The main point is that stratification no longer appears as a necessary condition for the existence of equilibrium but only as one means of establishing that scale economies are exhausted.

At the same time, this modification of the earlier example shows that insisting that the number of public-good types be at least as great as the number of consumer types is also unnecessary for Tiebout equilibrium. In fact, in a broader sense, the opposite is true. A relatively small number of public-good types typically mean that markets are "thick," and it is thickness of markets that helps to *justify* the price-taking hypothesis.

Finally, we should note the absence of any role in the theory presented here for the generalized Samuelson conditions equating the sum of marginal

rates of substitution to the marginal rate of transformation within jurisdictions. To Bewley's credit, he does not fall prey to the tendency to use these
conditions, but the practice is common in the Tiebout literature (with the
important exception of Tiebout himself). To the extent that the concepts have
meaning within the context of indivisibility, there is a sense in which each
consumer equates his *MRS* to the *MRT*, but the summing of *MRS*s is
completely irrelevant.

Extension to a Continuum of Agents

In our discussion of the two conditions needed to pass from an equilibrium
for $\mathscr{E}^*$ to an equilibrium for $\mathscr{E}$, we have given greater stress to the condition in
equation 7.10 (exhaustion of scale economies) than to the condition in
equation 7.11, and there is a reason for this. In most practical applications of
the Tiebout model, the second condition can be regarded as a minor
technicality. As demonstrated in Ellickson (1979), the justification for this
assertion is provided by the Shapley-Folkman theorem. Corresponding to
any competitive equilibrium for $\mathscr{E}^*$, there is an approximate equilibrium for
$\mathscr{E}$ in which the cardinality of the set N of consumers for whom the second
condition fails is bounded by the dimension of the commodity space:
$\#N/\#A \leq (n + m)/\#A$. Thus, as the number of consumers in the economy
increases, the proportion for whom the condition of equation 7.11 fails
approaches zero as a limit. This suggests that with a continuum of consumers, the condition in equation 7.11 should no longer pose any difficulty
for existence, and that is the case. With a continuum of agents, exhaustion of
scale economies is the only requirement for passing from a competitive
equilibrium for $\mathscr{E}^*$ to an equilibrium for $\mathscr{E}$.

Although a full discussion of the extension of this theory to a continuum
of agents setting is beyond the scope of this chapter,[5] it is useful to describe
what happens to our simple example when the number of consumers is
infinite. As a preliminary, we consider first the calculation of total market
demand when A is finite. Recalling that $(x^*(a),\delta^*(a))$ represents an
equilibrium commodity bundle for consumer a, the total amount allocated in
equilibrium is found by summing the individual commodity bundles over A:

$$\sum_{a \in A} (x^*(a),\delta^*(a))$$

While the interpretation of the sum $\Sigma_{a \in A} x^*(a)$ is standard, $\Sigma_{a \in A} \delta^*(a)$
represents the summation of functions, and therefore the sum is itself a
function (over K). When the function defined by this sum is evaluated at $z \in$
K, the result is $n^*(z)$: the number of consumers who choose the public good of
type z.

Brushing aside measure-theoretic technicalities, essentially the only modification required for the extension of the theory to a continuum of agents is the replacement of sums by integrals. Instead of summing individual commodity bundles, we integrate over the set A of consumers to obtain $\int_A(x^*(a),\delta^*(a))d\mu$, or $\int_A(x^*,\delta^*)$ for short, where (A,α,μ) is the measure space of consumers. Adopting the convention that the measure of the set A is one, this integral should be interpreted as the *per capita* quantity of commodities allocated to consumers in equilibrium. In particular, $\int x^*$ represents the per-capita consumption of divisible commodities (an n-dimensional vector) while $\int\delta^*$ is again a function defined over K which, when evaluated at $z \in K$, yields $n^*(z)$. In keeping with the procedure of interpreting the results of integration in per-capita terms, $n^*(z)$ lies in the interval $[0,1]$ and it represents the fraction of consumers who demand the public good of type z.

To illustrate the ease with which the transition to a continuum of agents can be accomplished, consider the example discussed previously where $K = \{z_1, z_2\}$ with $z_1 = 4$ and $z_2 = 9$. The parameter $n_0(z)$ used in the definition of the average-cost function must now also be given a per-capita interpretation: for example, if $n_0(z_1) = n_0(z_2) = \frac{1}{4}$, then scale economies are exhausted for either of the two types of public good when the output is supplied to at least one quarter of the total population. As before, we let $\gamma = 1$, and we assume that each consumer has an endowment of the divisible commodities of the form (b,b) where b is a parameter that varies from consumer to consumer. In particular, we assume that the parameter b is uniformly distributed on the interval $[0,10]$.

To establish existence of a competitive equilibrium, a convexified version $\mathcal{E}^*$ of the economy is constructed in which each nonconvex technology set is replaced by its convex hull. But now with a continuum of agents, it is no longer necessary to replace the demand sets by their convext hulls. At this point the analysis of the example proceeds exactly as in the case of a finite number of consumers. Equation 7.9, derived in the same way, implies that $b_c = 5$ with consumers for whom $b < 5$ choosing z_1, those for whom $b > 5$ choosing z_2, and those for whom $b = 5$ being indifferent between the two public-good alternatives. Consumers who are indifferent constitute a set of measure zero and can therefore be ignored when integrating the demand functions. Equilibrium prices are given by $p^* = (1,1)$, $t^*(4) = 4$, and $t^*(9) = 6$. Computation of the equilibrium allocation of divisible commodities is left as an easy, but instructive, exercise for the reader.

Since half of the consumers choose z_1 and half choose z_2, scale economies are exhausted in the production of both public goods. Therefore, the equilibrium for $\mathcal{E}^*$ is also an equilibrium for $\mathcal{E}$. As this example illustrates, with a continuum of consumers, the existence of a Tiebout equilibrium is solely a matter of scale economies and nothing more. Indivisibilities no longer pose any problem at all.

A Continuum of Public Goods

The theory described above provides a powerful basis for the analysis of public goods. Experimentation with the choice of cost functions, endowment distributions, and preference indicators would quickly yield convincing evidence that this modeling strategy can satisfy the requirements of most, if not all, applications of the theory of local public goods that have been discussed in the literature. However, such a demonstration will be left for another occasion.

In this chapter, our primary concern is with the foundations of Tiebout equilibrium as a theory of competition, and our exploration is not yet complete. The theory we have developed lacks one feature which, were it present, would establish beyond doubt that we indeed have a rigorous representation of the Tiebout model. Recall that in the example used to illustrate the theory, the variable z was interpreted as an index of *quality*, an interpretation designed to invite comparison with conventional models of Tiebout equilibrium. Specifically, the set K was assumed to be a subset of R_+. However, in order to establish existence of equilibrium, we were forced to assume that K was finite. In the standard version of the Tiebout model, on the other hand, the *quantity* or *quality* of a public good can be any non-negative real number: that is, $K = R_+$.

This means that if we are to stick by the position that local public goods should be viewed as indivisible commodities, the representation of even the simplest of models of local public goods that have appeared in the literature requires an infinite-dimensional commodity space. Such a prospect seems disheartening, to say the least. However, as indicated in the introduction, recent developments in mathematical economics have begun to provide important new ways to look at competition, and in this case it is the model of equilibrium in an economy with differentiated commodities of Mas-Colell that comes to the rescue.

Theoretical Foundations

The key to a proper formulation of a competitive theory is again the selection of an appropriate commodity space, and the technique we will employ is, in fact, the primary motivation for the delta functions introduced in the preceding section of this chapter. Suppose now that K is a compact metric space. This rules out the case $K = R_+$, of course, but as we shall see, this is no real restriction so far as Tiebout equilibrium is concerned. We can, for example, take $K = [0,M] \subset R_+$ where M is a large positive constant. (For practical applications of the theory we are about to describe, letting K be a closed and bounded subset of R^m, $m > 1$, will usually be a better choice.)

To avoid the nuisance aspects of indivisibility, we will immediately move to the context of a continuum of consumers. A commodity bundle allocated to consumer $a \in A$ where A is the set of consumers, is denoted by $(x(a), \delta(a))$ where $x(a)$ is an n-dimensional vector of divisible commodities and $\delta(a)$ equals one of the *Dirac delta functions* $\delta_z (z \in K)$. Properly speaking, δ_z is not a function on K but rather an integer-valued measure that assigns mass one to any subset containing z and mass zero to all other measurable subsets of K. Letting Δ represent the collection of all Dirac delta functions on K, $\Delta = \{\delta_z | z \in K\}$, the commodity space of consumer a is then assumed to be $X(a) \times \Delta$ where $X(a)$ is a closed, convex subset of R^n that is bounded from below.

Let p denote the n-dimensional vector of divisible commodity prices and the function $t: K \to R_+$ the tax prices of the local public goods, where t is assumed to be a *continuous* function of z. The requirement that the function t be continuous is not innocuous: in a sense, it is the heart of the theory. Ordinarily when commodity spaces are infinite dimensional, we expect competition to fail as a consequence of the thinness of markets. What makes competition work in this context is the imposition of a certain uniformity on consumer preferences, an agreement among consumers that public goods with attributes z that are "close" in K (to use the terminology of hedonic theory) will be good substitutes. It is this property of preferences that Mas-Colell captures with the notion of a weak-* topology on preferences, and—as we will demonstrate through an example—the same assumption is implicit in the usual formulations of the theory of local public goods.

With these preliminaries, construction of the competitive model follows more or less standard procedure. Firms, acting as price-takers, select feasible production plans that maximize profits where production sets are convexified in order to establish the existence of equilibrium. Each consumer, acting as a price-taker, chooses that commodity bundle from his budget set which is best relative to a continuous preordering $\geq_a$ defined on $X(a) \times \Delta$ where the budget set is given by:

$$\beta(p,t,a) = \{(x(a), \delta(a)) \in X(a) \times \Delta \mid px(a) + \int_K t(z)\delta(a) \leq pe(a)\}$$

Comparison of the budget constraints in the finite and the continuum case is quite instructive. The only difference is that the sum $\Sigma_{z \in K} t(z)\delta(a)$ is replaced by the integral $\int_K t(z)\delta(a)$, precisely the change one would expect. If we restrict our attention to the choices available when the consumer selects a public good of type z (so that $\delta(a) = \delta_z$), then, in either case, the budget constraint reduces to

$$px + t(z) \leq pe(a)$$

a form that should be familiar to anyone who has read a little of the standard literature on local public goods (or hedonic theory, for that matter).

At this point the analysis becomes quite technical, and I will spare the reader the details. Instead I will again resort to an example which illustrates the main conclusions.

An Illustration of Tiebout Equilibrium

Suppose that $K = [0,M]$ where M is a large positive constant, say $M = 1000$. Production of each type of public good is described just as it was earlier in the first section, with average-cost functions precisely the same (as in the section on the continuum of consumers model), $n_0(a)$ should be interpreted as the proportion of consumers that must be provided the public good of type z for scale economies to be exhausted).[6] As a result, equilibrium tax prices are again given by equation 7.3:

$$t^*(z) = (p_1^* + p_2^*) \gamma \sqrt{z}$$

where, as before, nonconvex production sets have been replaced by their convex hulls. Note that t^* is a continuous function of z, as required by the theory. In fact, it is even continuously differentiable (except at $z = 0$, a technicality that raises no difficulty for the example). In this example, we will assume that $\gamma = 1$.

Preferences will be characterized by the utility function employed in the earlier example:

$$U(x(a),z) = x_1(a)x_2(a)z$$

Each consumer maximizes utility subject to the budget constraint

$$p^*x(a) + t^*(z) \leq p^*e(a) := y(a)$$

Conditional on the choice of a public good of type z, the solution to this constrained maximization problem is described by the indirect utility function given by equation 7.4:

$$V(p^*, y - t^*(z), z) = \frac{(y - t^*(z))^2 z}{4p_1 p_2}$$

where y is the income of the consumer.

Each consumer chooses the type of public good z that maximizes this indirect utility function. Setting $dV/dz = 0$, the first-order condition reduces to

$$y = 2(1 + p_2^*) \sqrt{z}$$

where we have let $p_1^* = 1$ for the *numéraire*. Consumers have endowment vectors of the form (b,b), and b is uniformly distributed on the interval $[0,10]$. The income of a consumer with endowment parameter b is then equal to $(1 + p_2^*)b$. Using this relationship, the first-order condition becomes

$$b = 2\sqrt{z} \qquad (7.12)$$

Solving for z in terms of b, we obtain $z = b^2/4$ which gives the choice of public good by a consumer with endowment parameter b.

Considerations of symmetry imply that the equilibrium price vector is $p^* = (1,1)$ and, as a result, $t^*(z) = 2\sqrt{z}$ is the equilibrium tax function. To describe the equilibrium commodity allocation, it is convenient to alter the notation somewhat by using the endowment parameter b to index consumers: we replace $A = [0,1]$ by $B = [0,10]$ where $b \in B$ is uniformly distributed with the measure of the set B equal to one. Consumer $b \in B$ has income $y(b) = 2b$ and demand functions for the two divisible commodities of the form

$$x_1(b) = \frac{y(b) - t(z(b))}{2p_1} \qquad \text{and} \qquad x_2(b) = \frac{y(b) - t(z(b))}{2p_2}$$

(the usual Cobb-Douglas demand functions) where $z(b)$ is the type of local public good chosen by consumer b. We observed above, as a consequence of equation 7.12, that a consumer with endowment parameter b will, in equilibrium, choose a public good of type $z^*(b) = b^2/4$. Since $t^*(z) = 2\sqrt{z}$, we conclude that the equilibrium allocation of the two divisible commodities is described by the pair of functions $x_1^*(b) = b/2$ and $x_2^*(b) = b/2$. Thus, the equilibrium consumption of each divisible commodity is unformly distributed over the interval $[0,5]$. Since $z^*(b) = b^2/4$, the equilibrium consumption and production of the public goods is concentrated on the interval $[0,25] \subset K$ with density $n^*(z) = (10 \sqrt{z})^{-1}$. Because the highest quality of public good produced is less than 1000, our initial choice of the constant M was large enough, and we are done.

As a check on these results, it is useful to verify that the equilibrium allocation is, in fact, feasible. Using the information given above, it is easy to see that the per-capita consumption of divisible commodities one and two is $\int_B x_1^* = 2.5$ and $\int_B x_2^* = 2.5$, respectively. The per-capita endowment of the first divisible commodity is $\int_B e_1 = 5$, while that of the second is $\int_B e_2 = 5$. If the allocation is to be feasible, the amounts of the divisible commodities left over after consumption must be sufficient to produce the public goods. The production technology implies that to produce one unit of public good of type z requires $\sqrt{z}$ units of each divisible commodity. Thus, the input requirements for either of the divisible commodities is given by

$$\int_B Z^*(b) = \int_B \frac{b}{2} = \int_0^{10} \left(\frac{b}{2}\right)(10)^{-1}db = 2.5$$

and so there is exactly enough input available to produce the public goods.

The equilibrium we have described is an equilibrium for the convexified economy $\mathscr{E}^*$. If this is also to be an equilibrium for the original economy $\mathscr{E}$, then economies to scale must be exhausted for each of the types of public good that is produced. But in this example, the subset of consumers choosing any particular type z is a set of measure zero, and therefore *jurisdictions* must also have measure zero.[7]

It is here that the approach we are advocating begins to produce some genuine insights into the nature of Tiebout equilibrium, in particular into the reasons for the peculiar conditions stressed in the literature: "perfect homogeneity of jurisdictions" and "at least as many types of public goods as types of people." In the conventional view, these conditions appear to be aspects of equilibrium somehow associated with the "publicness" of the local public goods, whatever that means. From the perspective offered here, on the other hand, the conditions are simply the natural consequence of the tacit assumption that the number of possible types of public good is infinite.

In the example we have been considering, no two consumers are, in effect, alike. With an absence of scale economies (the convexified economy $\mathscr{E}^*$), each consumer chooses a distinct type of public good. An infinite number of types of public good will be produced, each by a jurisdiction of infinitesimal size. An equilibrium of this sort cannot be a competitive equilibrium for the original economy if production of the public goods is subject to nonnegligible scale economies.

If the transition from an equilibrium for $\mathscr{E}^*$ to an equilibrium for $\mathscr{E}$ is to be made in the presence of nonnegligible scale economies, it seems obvious that there must be some form of redundancy among consumers. For example, suppose that the set A of consumers can be partitioned into a finite collection of disjoint subsets $\{A_i\}_{i=1}^r$ whose union equals A and where all members of a particular subset A_i have the same preferences and endowment. In a competitive equilibrium for the convexified economy, all consumers of the same type will choose the same type of public good, and only a finite number of different types of public good will be produced. If the proportion $n^*(z)$ of consumers selecting each of the public goods z that are produced exceeds the threshold $n_0(z)$ required for exhaustion of scale economies, then the equilibrium for $\mathscr{E}^*$ is also a competitive equilibrium for $\mathscr{E}$. This requires that there be as many types of public good as there are types of consumer (barring a fortuitous coincidence of tastes), and each jurisdiction will be populated by consumers all of the same type. This is, of course, just the standard model of Tiebout equilibrium in rigorous form.

When Is a Market Competitive?

We have seen that Tiebout equilibrium can be given a theoretical foundation as rigorous as any version of competition available. There is nothing special about Tiebout equilibrium: it is simply a well-disguised variant of a competitive equilibrium with indivisible commodities and an infinite-dimensional commodity space. However, the question remains whether Tiebout equilibrium has any value in analyzing the allocation of local public goods. Given the current stock of knowledge in the economics profession, there is no good answer to this question. It is more a matter of metaphysics than of science. Nevertheless, I think that making Tiebout rigorous helps to shed some light on this issue.

The advantage we have is that Tiebout equilibrium can now be evaluated in precisely the same terms that we judge the adequacy of any model of competitive equilibrium. To free ourselves from the bias accumulated from over two decades of thinking about local public goods as divisible commodities, it is useful to consider the market for some indivisible commodity that is not a local public good. Since most commodities are indivisible, examples are easy to find. My favorite choice would be the home computer, since the market for these devices seems to exhibit the virtues of competition in a particularly favorable light.

Suppose that we were to approach the task of modeling the home-computer market using the techniques of the traditional theory of local public goods. Although the variety of home computers available in the market is quite overwhelming, the number of types is, of course, finite. But the number of variations that could be produced with current technology is infinite. If I were to specify the characteristics of a computer to be tailor-made for me, the result would not match anything currently on the market (although some come close), and if that computer were produced at a scale comparable, say, to one of the Apple products (*convexification*), I would buy it.

To bring the computer market within range of the conventional theory, the local public good theorist would then have to introduce some notion of *quality* in order to represent the different types of computer on a comparable scale. For example, this index of quality could be called "computing power." If a competitive market for home computers is to exist, it must meet the two tests of the standard Tiebout theory:

1. The number of types of computer must be at least as large as the number of types of consumer
2. The consumers of any particular type of computer must be all alike

Both conditions fail for the home-computer market, and the same conclusion would be reached for any market for indivisible commodities that I can think of. Thus, the logic of the interpreters of Tiebout leads us to the conclusion that competitive theory in general has little value as a model of economic behavior.

At this juncture it is worth recalling the closing paragraph of Tiebout's article:

> Those who are tempted to compare this model with the competitive private model may be disappointed. Those who compare the reality described by this model with the reality of the competitive model—given the degree of monopoly, friction, and so forth—*may* find that local public government represents a sector where the allocation of public goods (as a reflection of the preferences of the population) need not take a back seat to the private sector.[8]

Of course, this is a two-edged sword: we *may* also conclude that competitive theory is worthless. (That is where metaphysics enters the picture.) It is safe to say that most economists would not accept that conclusion. Instead the profession tends to fashion models of competition that are appealing on their own terms, and then to argue that the resulting model is, in some sense, a reasonable approximation to reality.

The model that we discussed earlier, of local public goods with a continuum of public goods and an infinite variety of consumers, is not an appealing model on its own terms: jurisdictions are infinitesimal in size and each consumer selects his own brand of public good. The same could be said of the corresponding model of the home-computer market or virtually any other model of a market for indivisible commodities. The two obvious strategies for making the model more appealing are to assume that the number of commodities is finite (as it was earlier) or to assume that the number of types of consumer is finite (as the *type economy* was). Throughout its history, the economics profession has tended to opt for the first strategy. Local public-goods theory has chosen the second. The rationale for the first strategy is presumably that aggregation of supposedly similar commodities is a reasonable approximation technique, the rationale for the second that aggregating supposedly similar consumers is a good way to proceed. Provided that one does not misinterpret the consequences of the aggregation procedure (the major falling of the Tiebout literature), there may be little to choose between the two approaches. My own preference is for the former strategy because the models tend to be easier to construct and to manipulate.

Although there is no general proof that the aggregation employed by economics gives a good approximation to reality, a comparison of the models presented in earlier sections suggests that there may be some basis for this belief. Recall that in the continuum example, an infinite variety of public goods was produced, concentrated on the interval [0,25]. In the redefinition model, public goods were "aggregated" into two types: $z_1 = 4$ and $z_2 = 9$. We would not expect such a crude aggregation to give a very good approximation to the continuum model. However, suppose we were to add more points to the interval [0,25] while keeping the number of such points finite. As the number of public goods increases, the market for any one of them becomes increasingly thin, which weakens the case for competition. But, on the other hand, as we force more points into the interval [0,25], the average distance between adjacent points decreases (the fact that the interval is compact is crucial here). Thus, the producer of any particular public good faces competition from better and better substitutes for his product, and so his demand functions become more elastic. If the second effect compensates sufficiently for the first, then we expect competition to prevail in the limit (when the interval [0,25] has been all filled in), and we could hope that models with a sufficiently large number of public goods would provide a good approximation to the continuum model.

In fact, the preceding paragraph is a paraphrase of the technique employed by Mas-Colell in providing existence and core equivalence for a model with a continuum of indivisible commodities[9]—the result that we used in constructing the analogous public goods model earlier. We avoided giving details of the proof because it involves the use of functional-analysis techniques that are highly sophisticated. Fortunately, it is possible to illustrate the results, using the examples we presented earlier and a little calculus.

The redefinition example approximated the continuum with only two points, $z_1 = 4$ and $z_2 = 9$. Suppose now that we try to improve the approximation by letting $K = \{z_1, \ldots, z_r\} \subset [0,25]$ where $z_1 < z_2 < \ldots < z_r$. The indirect utility function for a consumer with income y conditional on choice of a public good of type $z \in K$ is still given by equation 7.4. For each adjacent pair of public goods z_i and z_{i+1} we set

$$V(p^*, y_c^i - t^*(z_i), z_i) = V(p^*, y_c^i - t^*(z_{i+1}), z_{i+1})$$

to determine the value of income y_c^i which makes a consumer just indifferent between choosing z_i or z_{i+1}. The solution of this equation yields

$$y_c^i = (1 + p_2^*) \gamma(\sqrt{z_i} + \sqrt{z_{i+1}})$$

as the generalization of equation 7.7 where we have again set $p_1^* = 1$. Noting that a consumer with income parameter b has income $(1 + p_2^*)b$, we obtain

$$b_c^i = \gamma(\sqrt{z_i} + \sqrt{z_{i+1}}) \qquad (7.13)$$

as the generalization of equation 7.9. The interpretation is the obvious extension of the result in the earlier section: consumers with income parameter $b < b_c^1$ choose the public good of type z_1, those for whom $b_c^1 < b < b_c^2$ choose z_2, and so forth. In the continuum model, the distribution of public goods in equilibrium is described by the continuous density function $n^*(z) = (10\sqrt{z})^{-1}$ on the interval $[0,25]$. In the model we are considering here, the equilibrium distribution is described by a discrete *probability measure* concentrated on $K = \{z_1, \ldots, z_r\}$. Let $F(z)$ and $F_d(z)$ denote the cumulative distribution functions corresponding to these two measures.

Consider a particular point $z \in K$ and suppose that we add more points to the set K in order to improve the approximation to the continuum. As the approximation improves, the public good z' just to the right of z will come arbitrarily close to z. Let $b_c(z) = \gamma(\sqrt{z} + \sqrt{z'})$ be the version of equation 7.13 corresponding to the pair z and z'. When we let z' converge to z in this way, equation 7.13 implies that $b_c(z)$ converges to $2\gamma\sqrt{z}$.[10] When $\gamma = 1$, the assumption employed in all of our examples, this limit becomes $2\sqrt{z}$. But $b = 2\sqrt{z}$ is precisely the result that we obtained for the continuum model (equation 7.12). Thus, as the approximation improves the discrete distribution functions, $F_d(z)$ will converge to the continuous limit $F(z)$ at every point $z \in [0,25]$. This is an illustration of the weak-* convergence demonstrated by Mas-Colell. It provides a precise sense in which the models with a finite number of public goods can be viewed as approximations to a model with a continuum of public goods.

Conclusion

For Tiebout it seemed obvious that the services provided by local government were no different from any other commodity that economists consider. But he offered no rigorous proof that local public goods could be competitively supplied, relying instead on a single analogy to ordinary competitive markets to support his claim. When public goods are viewed as perfectly divisible commodities, Tiebout's idea makes little sense: a competitive equilibrium for local public goods emerges as a caricature of the standard theory, a frail creature whose existence seems threatened by the slightest deviation from a set of extremely stringent sufficient conditions. However, if local public goods are thought of as indivisible commodities, then a Tiebout equilibrium becomes a straightforward application of competitive analysis.

Tiebout equilibrium provides a natural, perhaps even canonical, illustration of a powerful new way of looking at competition that has been developed in the mathematical economics literature. The new point of view involves a heightened appreciation of the sense in which competitive equilibrium should always be regarded as an idealization, a limiting case in which consumers have infinitesimal influence and there is enough substitutability among commodities to justify the price-taking hypothesis. Perfect divisibility of commodities and finite dimensionality of commodity spaces are only sufficient conditions and not at all essential to the attainment of the ideal.

The insight that mathematical economics has offered regarding the nature of competition is important to applied economics because, when venturing onto new terrain, it is all too easy to become confused about what competition means. Existing research on local public goods furnishes ample evidence on how readily one can go astray when competition is not well understood. Two obvious illustrations of this abuse of competitive theory, for example, are the suggestion that homogeneity of jurisdictions can be used as a criterion for testing the Tiebout hypothesis and the assertion that zoning can serve as a substitute for a properly functioning pricing mechanism. Any application of competitive theory involves approximation (if for no other reason than because the number of consumers is not infinite), and, as the theory I have presented should make clear, homogeneity of jurisdictions is not a characteristic of the Tiebout model short of the limiting ideal. Thus, homogeneity is not a test of the Tiebout hypothesis and, as a consequence of jurisdictional heterogeneity, zoning cannot substitute for the proper Tiebout prices.[11]

The main advantage of the reformulation of public goods theory presented here is that the connection to standard microeconomic theory is no longer obscure: what I have shown is that competition with local public goods is qualitatively indistinguishable from that for private goods. But this does not mean that there is no problem with allocating public goods, any more than the proof that a competitive equilibrium exists for a private-goods economy means that monopoly is not a problem. In either case, the relevance of the competitive model to the real world depends on the extent to which reality meets the requirements of the theory.

In some cases, markets for local public goods do appear to be reasonably competitive: the market for neighborhoods is one example. There are usually many good substitutes for any particular neighborhood, and scale economies do not seem particularly insignificant. The behavior of central cities and suburbs, on the other hand, appears to be far from competitive. The failure of competition probably is not due to the presence of scale economies, since the limited evidence we have suggests that jurisdictions exhaust the benefits of scale with populations well below the population size that we observe.

Why then does the provision of local public services fail to be competitive? The reason, I suspect, involves the peculiar role of one of the inputs to the production of local public services: land. The problem is not that land raises some intrinsic difficulty for the competitive theory of local public goods: the theory treats land as simply another input and, as an application to the market for neighborhoods would suggest, the presence of land inputs need not inhibit the workings of competition. What makes local governments different from neighborhoods is that governmental boundaries seldom change. In language more familiar to standard economic theory, an existing political jurisdiction monopolizes the use of the land that it occupies. A suburb can compete with the central city by offering an attractive public good alternative, but only the central city can supply public goods within its boundaries.[12] Thus, the provision of local public services is characterized by significant *barriers to entry*, and I think that this is the major reason why the Tiebout model fails to give an accurate picture of local governmental behavior. What we need is a theory of industrial organization for local government, a theory in which the Tiebout model will play only a part.

Finally, it should be noted that even if local public services could be competitively provided, Tiebout equilibrium may not be a suitable normative goal. In a federal system, local governments have a political as well as an economic function, and there is a danger that a naive application of Tiebout's theory could miss some of the most important issues that are involved. The competitive model can help to illuminate some of the strains that are imposed on our federal system as a consequence of urbanization. I doubt very much that it can provide all the answers on how that system can be improved.

Notes

1. Reed and Simon, p. ix.
2. Charles Tiebout, "A Pure Theory of Local Expenditures, *Journal of Political Economy* (1956): 420. All quotes reprinted with permission of the University of Chicago Press.
3. The reason for choosing $\sqrt{z}$ instead of assuming simply that average costs are linear in z is to discourage any tendency for the reader to conclude that linearity with respect to the "quantity" or "quality" z of the public good is necessary for existence of equilibrium. The true measure of the quantity of the public good is $n(z)$, the number of consumers to whom it is provided, and not z.
4. Consumers have equal endowments of the two divisible commodities and weigh them equally in the utility function. Inputs of the two divisible commodities are required in equal proportion to produce the public goods.
5. For some example of explicit continuum of agents' models in a closely related setting, see Ellickson (1981).

6. To be completely accurate, in this example $n^*(z)$ is the density for a nonatomic measure on K, and $n_0(z)$ must be interpreted the same way. To avoid a discussion of measure theory, I am going to be deliberately casual about this, relying instead on the reader's economic intuition when interpreting the results.

7. The allocation of local public goods is concentrated on the interval $[0,25] \subset K$ with density $n^*(z) = (10\sqrt{z})^{-1}$. As the reader will recall from statistics, such a density assigns mass (probability) zero to any single point. Thus, production also must exhibit constant returns to scale for any level of output that is nonnegligible. (Remember that the output of public goods is measured in terms of the number of consumers served.)

8. Tiebout, p. 424. Italics in original.

9. Since the models with a finite number of commodities have a continuum of consumers, I engaged in a little poetic license in talking about demand functions becoming increasingly elastic.

10. This argument glosses over some details needed for a completely rigorous mathematical proof. The reader interested in a more careful demonstration (in a different, but related, context) can look at Ellickson (1982).

11. With the advantage of hindsight, it is difficult to imagine that economists could ever have argued that a regulatory mechanism—zoning—could substitute for a pricing mechanism. Whenever such a conclusion is reached, there is *prima-facie* evidence that the underlying competitive process is not well understood.

12. I am not intentionally singling out the central city as the only local government with monopoly power. The same comments apply to suburbs as well.

References

Alchian, Armen. "Uncertainty, Evolution, and Economic Theory." *Journal of Political Economy* (1950): 211–221

Bewley, Truman. "A Critique of Tiebout's Theory of Local Public Expenditures." *Econometrica* (1981): 713–740.

Ellickson, Bryan. 1973. "A Generalization of the Pure Theory of Public Goods." *American Economic Review* 1973: 417–432.

_____. 1979. "Competitive Equilibrium with Local Public Goods." *Journal of Economic theory* 1979: 46–61.

_____. 1982. "Indivisibility, Housing Markets and Public Goods." To appear in *Research in Urban Economics*, edited by J.V. Henderson Vol. 3.

Mas-Colell, Andreu. "A Model of Equilibrium with Differentiated Commodities." *Journal of Mathematical Economics* (1975): 263–295.

Milleron, J.C. "Theory of Value with Public Goods: A Survey Article." *Journal of Economic Theory* (1972): 419–477.

Muench, Thomas. "The Core and the Lindahl Equilibrium of an Economy with Public Goods: An Example." *Journal of Economic Theory* (1972): 241–255.

Reed, Michael, and Simon, Barry. *Methods of Modern Mathematical Physics I: Functional Analysis*. New York: Academic Press.

Samuelson, Paul. "The Pure Theory of Public Expenditures." *Review of Economics and Statistics* (1954):387–389.

Tiebout, Charles. "A Pure Theory of Local Expenditures." *Journal of Political Economy* (1956): 416–424.

Appendix 7A: Pareto Optimal Allocation

When the assignment of consumers to jurisdictions is fixed, the derivation of the generalized conditions for Pareto optimality in equation 7.2 is a straightforward adaption of the method Samuelson used to arrive at the corresponding equation 7.1 for a pure public good. Once the optimal partition is known, the conditions in equation 7.2 will, therefore, be necessary for a Pareto optimum. However, with an endogenous partition, the partition that is optimal cannot, in general, be determined independently from the conditions for a Pareto optimum conditional on the choice of a partition. A momentary reflection should suggest why the gereralized Samuelson conditions in equations 7.2 are irrelevant to the Tiebout model. Their derivation takes no account of the allocations that are feasible under alternative partitions, and as a consequence it is impossible for them to be informative regarding the choice of partition. This raises no problem in the pure public goods model, precisely because the choice of partition is not at issue in that context.

To illustrate the irrelevance of the generalized Samuelson conditions to the Tiebout model, consider the following example. There are four consumers in the economy, each endowed with four units of a divisible private good (say, labor). Labor is used to produce a public good of quality z in a jurisdiction of size n subject to the technology:

$$nz = l$$

where l is the labor input. Utility functions are given by

$$U_a(x,z) = \begin{cases} xz & a = 1,2 \\ (x + 1)z & a = 3,4 \end{cases}$$

where a is the consumer index.

It is obvious in this example that Pareto optimality will require consumers one and two to form one jurisdiction and consumers three and four to form another.[1] Without loss of generality, we can assume that consumers one and two are treated equally (receiving utility u_b) and that consumers three and four are also treated equally (receiving utility u_c). A straightforward application of the generalized Samuelson conditions yields the utility frontier:

$$\sqrt{u_b} + \sqrt{u_c} = 4.5 \tag{7A.1}$$

for the partition $\{\{1,2\},\{3,4\}\}$.

Suppose now that we consider a partition that groups consumers of dissimilar types together, say, the partition {{1,3},{2,4}}. Again without loss of generality, we can assume that consumers one and two are treated equally (receiving utility u_b) and similarly that consumers three and four receive utility u_c. With this choice of partition, the generalized Samuelson conditions lead to the utility frontier:

$$u_b + u_c = 10.125 \qquad (7A.2)$$

If equations 7A.1 and 7A.2 are plotted on the (u_a, u_b) plane, it is readily seen that the graph of equation 7A.1 lies everywhere above[2] that of equation 7A.2. Thus, in spite of the fact that any allocation represented by a point on the utility frontier described by equation 7A.2 satisfies the generalized Samuelson conditions for the partition {{1,3},{2,4}}, it is Pareto-dominated by an allocation that can be achieved under the partition {{1,2},{3,4}}. This demonstrates that an allocation satisfying the generalized Samuelson conditions need not be Pareto optimal even though the relevant production and preference sets are convex (in the conventional setting where public goods are regarded as perfectly divisible commodities).

Notes

1. Actually it would be equally efficient to have each consumer form his own jurisdiction under these production conditions. We could avoid this possibility by assuming that there is no increase in the per-capita cost of producing public goods in moving from one- to two-person jurisdictions. I have chosen not to do so in order to highlight the insufficiency of the generalized Samuelson conditions even when production (as well as preference) sets are convex.

2. More precisely, at the point $(u_a, u_b) = (.0625, .0625)$, the graphs coincide. Otherwise the graph of equation 7A.1 lies everywhere above that of equation 7A.2.

8 Regulation May Be No Worse Than Its Alternatives

Ronald E. Grieson and
Donald A. Wittman

Economists look upon quantity regulation, in general, with disfavor, even though they acknowledge that in the presence of risk or different supply and demand elasticities, errors in taxes may be more or less harmful than quotas. Zoning, in particular, is abhorred. They also argue that zoning creates inefficient incentives: that even if it created the proper incentives, it would require too much information to be workable; that even if it were workable in the abstract, there would exist strong incentives for people such as developers or nonlandholding voters to redistribute wealth inefficiently towards themselves; and that even if the redistribution were efficient, zoning would generate random or unfair redistribution.[1] Sometimes implicitly, but often explicitly, zoning is contrasted with its major alternatives: the court system or an externality tax system. Here, the main thrust of the economic literature is the efficiency of the common law, in general, and liability rules, in particular.[2]

In this paper we demonstrate that (1) many of the arguments against quantity regulation are specious and (2) even if the arguments against quantity regulation were correct, the same logic would almost always argue against liability rules, pigovian taxes, property-right solutions, and restrictive covenants.

Minimizing Pollution Costs in the Short Run

In each section we will consider a different characterization of the issues. In this section, we assume that the government is trying to minimize the sum of short-run pollution and prevention costs. We assume that the government has all the relevant information. This simple characterization enables us to introduce the various concepts with minimum confusion. Later sections will consider other permutations, including long-run and allocation problems arising from imperfect information. Because this section is less controversial than the later sections, the reader may just look over the section long enough to get the notation.[3]

Part of this research was supported by NSF Grant 78—25721.

171

We will consider the classic example of factory smoke in a high-transaction-cost setting. The factory X can reduce smoke $s(x)$ by increasing expenditures on smoke prevention x. x is increased cost and represents not only the costs of smoke arresters but also any reduced-factor returns due to reduced output of the factory's product. Smoke causes damage to the pollutee(s) (Y). This damage can also be reduced by the pollutee if it engages in damage prevention (Y). For example, if the pollutee is a laundry, it may dry its clothes indoors. More formally, the sum of the pollution damage, $D(S(x),y)$, plus the cost of prevention is the following:

$$C = D(S(x),y) + x + y \qquad (8.1)$$

where $S'(x) < 0$; $D_s > 0$; $D_y < 0$. We also assume that D is convex in x and y.[4]

Society wishes to minimize total pollution-related costs. This is achieved where the marginal benefit of reduced damage due to one more dollar's worth of x is equal to one dollar and the marginal benefit of reduced damage due to one more dollar's worth of y is equal to one dollar. More formally:
First-order conditions for an interior minimum:

$$C_x = D_s S'(x) + 1 = 0 \qquad (8.2)$$

$$C_y = D_y + 1 = 0 \qquad (8.3)$$

We denote the optimal amount of smoke produced by X and the self-protection by Y as S^* and y^*, respectively.

Let's first consider zoning rules. While zoning rules are often characterized in the literature as being concerned only with general classifications (for example, factories, commercial establishments), there is no reason why they cannot be characterized in terms of output measures such as smoke. In fact, city zoning requirements are typically classified in this fashion.

A binding zoning requirement that the factory produce no more smoke than S^* will result in s^* being produced. The factory will not produce less than S^* as there are no economic incentives for it to do so. If $S^* > 0$, the factory will not move elsewhere, since, it can be assumed, the cost of moving is greater than the present discounted value of x^*. By definition x^* is the optimal amount of prevention. If it were optimal for the factory to move, S^* would equal zero.

Given that X has chosen S^*, Y will choose y^* since Y is fully liable for all damage. Y will minimize

$$C^Y = D(S^*(x^*),y) + Y \qquad (8.4)$$

This expression is minimized at $D_y + 1 = 0$. This is identical to the social-cost-minimization point for society: y^* (equation 8.3).

Zoning has results identical to those from a *negligence type* liability rule. Under this type of liability rule, X is only liable if he has not satisfied a certain standard. In this case, the standard is no more smoke than S^*.[5] More formally, X is liable for actual damage (LAD) according to the following:

$$LAD^N = D(x,y) \qquad \text{if } S > S^*$$
$$= 0 \qquad \text{if } S \leq S^* \qquad\qquad (8.5)$$

It can readily be shown that S^*, y^* is a Cournot equilibrium under this liability rule. When X is liable for damage, he minimizes the following expression:

$$C^X = x + D(x,y) \qquad\qquad (8.6)$$

This expression is minimized at $1 + D_x = 0$, which is identical to society's cost-minimization conditions. Thus under full liability, X will choose x^* (equivalently S^*). On the other hand, if X is not liable, he will have no incentive to reduce smoke. Therefore, X will choose the maximum amount of smoke consistent with no liability: S^*.

Given that X has chosen S^*, X is not liable. From Y's point of view, the situation is the same as if X were compelled to produce only S^* under zoning. As already shown, Y will choose S^*.

Thus, whether we have a zoning rule or a negligence-type liability rule, the outcome will be S^*, y^*. Furthermore, there will be no difference in wealth distribution, because in both situations X is not liable to Y.

Zoning and LAD^N also have identical effects if the most efficient outcome is for the factory to be located elsewhere. Zoning will not allow the factory to be located in location j (either because factories are outlawed explicitly or because the amount of smoke allowed creates excessive costs for the factory). Under LAD^N, the factory will not want to be located in location j as the cost of the liability and/or prevention costs (x) would be greater than the benefit of being in location j.

These results are just an example of the general economic result that prices and quantities are alternative means of allocation, each being the dual of the other.

Taxation is another alternative to zoning. It can readily be demonstrated that the tax on actual damage, TAD^N, will have an identical outcome to the analogous liability rule, LAD^N:

$$TAD^N = D(S(x),y) \qquad \text{if } S > S^*$$
$$= 0 \qquad \text{otherwise} \qquad\qquad (8.7)$$

Clearly, if X produces S^* and is not liable, it makes no difference whether factory is not liable to the government or not liable to Y; and if X is not liable, it makes no difference to Y to whom X is not liable.

Next we consider strict liability (SL). It can shown that strict liability for actual damage, LAD^{SL}, is not efficient because Y has no incentives to mitigate damages in such cases. Again this is readily demonstrated mathematically. Y will minimize the sum of his costs minus liability payments.

$$C^Y = D(S(x),y) + Y - D(S(x),y)$$

$$= y \qquad (8.8)$$

This expression is minimized at $y = 0$, which is not equal to y^* in general.

However, the analogous tax rule, TAD^{SL}, does produce an efficient outcome. We have already shown that X will choose x^* if X is fully liable. Since the tax payment goes to the government, Y is liable for damage and its own prevention costs, and therefore will choose y^* (as we have already demonstrated).

Another variant is to tax X a constant amount per unit of smoke. The amount being equivalent to the marginal cost of smoke at S^*.

$$TAM = S(x)D_S(S(x^*),y^*) \qquad (8.9)$$

x minimizes the sum of its prevention costs (x) and the tax (TAM). First-order conditions for X:

$$1 + S'D_S(S(x^*),y^*) = 0 \qquad (8.10)$$

These are equivalent to the first-order conditions for society as given in equation 8.2.

Because of the problem with LAD^{SL}, we consider an alternative liability rule: LOC^{SL}. This rule makes X liable to Y not for actual damage but for optimal damage and prevention costs given S^*. More formally:

$$LOC^{SL} = D(S(x),R(S)) + R(S) \qquad (8.11)$$

where $R(S) = \hat{y}$ or the optimal y *given* S. It is equation 8.3 with y as an explicit function of S.

Under this rule, all the costs of pollution are internalized by the polluter. Therefore the polluter will choose the optimal amount of smoke. Since payment to Y by the polluter is independent of what Y actually does, Y will also act optimally. This can be demonstrated more formally. X minimizes its costs:

$$C^X = x + D(S(x),R(S)) + R(S) \qquad (8.12)$$

First-order conditions for a minimum:

$$C_x^X = 1 + D_S S' + D_y R' S' + R' S' = 0 \qquad (8.13)$$

$$= 1 + D_S S' + R' S'[1 + D_y] = 0 \qquad (8.14)$$

By equations 8.2 and 8.3 the numbers $(1 + D_S S')$ and $(1 + D_y)$ equal zero at S^*, y^*. By the convexity assumption $C_x^X = 0$ at only one point. Therefore the cost-minimization point for X is equivalent to the cost-minimization point for society.

We now consider Y, which wants to minimize the following expression:

$$C^Y = y + D(S^*,y) - R(S^*) - D(S^*,R(S^*)) \qquad \text{where } R(S^*) = y^* \qquad (8.15)$$

First-order conditions for cost minimization:

$$C_y^Y = 1 + D_y = 0 \qquad (8.16)$$

This condition is equivalent to the social-cost-minimization condition for society (equation 8.3). Therefore Y will choose y^*. Thus this result will also be efficient.

It can readily be established that the tax counterpart, TOC^{SL}, to LOC^{SL}, as well as negligence versions of optimal cost in both liability form LOC^N and tax form TOC^N, also leads to an efficient outcome.

Long-Run Entry

A variety of techniques create an efficient outcome in the short run. In the long run, the possibility of too many polluters or pollutees arises. As a consequence, many simple liability rules do not provide the proper incentives for long-run efficiency. For example, if the pollutee is compensated for damages irrespective of whether it belongs in the location, the pollutee will not take into account the cost of damage in deciding where to locate. As a consequence, there will be too many pollutees in the area. We show that an explicit or implicit zoning restriction (on either the pollutee or the polluter) is required for long-run efficiency for virtually all the liability and tax rules.

If pollutees are compensated for damages, then potential pollutees will not take into account the cost of damage when they are deciding whether to locate in a polluted area. If polluters are not liable for the damage to the pollutee, then they will not take into account the damage to the pollutee when they are deciding whether to locate in an area composed of pollutees. Since both sides are inputs into the production of the damage, then both sides must take damage and their own prevention costs into account when they are making location and entry decisions in order for there to be long-run efficiency.[6] In the absence of other restrictions, this can only be the case when the side not damaged by the externality pays a tax equal to the damage imposed on the other side.

This can be demonstrated formally.

Let

$$B^x(N^x) - N^x x \qquad (8.17)$$

be the total benefit that N factories receive from being in the area minus the total dollar expenditure on smoke prevention:

$$B^{x''}(N^x) < 0$$

That is, the marginal benefit of an additional factory in the area increases at a decreasing rate (or possibly decreases at an increasing rate).

Let

$$B^y(N - N^x) - [N - N^x]D(y)N^x S(x) - [N - N^x]y \qquad (8.18)$$

be the total benefit of having $N - N^x$ pollutees in the area (we assume that there are only a total of N locations in the area available for either polluters or pollutees[7] minus the total damage from smoke minus the total prevention costs by all of the pollutees. Looking at the damage function more closely, we assume that $S(x)$, the amount of smoke emitted by each firm, is a decreasing function of x, the dollar amount of smoke prevention by each firm. For ease of exposition we assume that the technology of smoke prevention is identical for each polluter. We also assume that the technology of damage prevention is the same for each pollutee. $D(y)$ is a decreasing function of the dollar amount devoted to damage prevention by each firm. For expositional simplicity, we shall assume that a doubling of smoke will result in a doubling of damages, and shall point out how the results differ when this assumption is critical.

For efficiency, the net benefit to society from the polluters and pollutees (the sum of equations 8.17 and 8.18), denoted by $B^z(N^x,x,y)$, is maximized. With regard to the optimal number of polluters and pollutees, the first-order condition for maximizing B^z follows:[8]

$$B^{x'} - x - B^{y'} + D(y)N^x S(x) - (N - N^x)D(y)S(x) = 0$$
$$= B^{x'} - x - B^{y'} + 2D(y)N^x S(x) - ND(y)S(x) = 0 \qquad (8.19)$$

Equilibrium in the land market occurs when the marginal bid by the last polluter equals the marginal bid by the last pollutee. The bid by the pollutee is the partial derivative of equation 8.18 with respect to $N^y = N - N^x$. If each factory is taxed for its marginal contribution to damage, $(N - N^x)D(y)S(x)$, then the bid by the marginal polluter is the partial of equation 8.17 with respect to N^x minus the tax. Equivalently, the bid by the marginal polluter minus the bid by the marginal pollutee must equal zero:

$$B^{x'} - x - B^{y'} + D(y)N^xS(x) - (N - N^x)D(y)S(x) = 0 \qquad (8.20)$$

which is identical to equation 8.19.

Tax rules TAD^N and TAM will result in a long-run misallocation. Under TAD^N, the bid by the polluter will increase. Therefore we will have too many polluters and not enough pollutees.

If marginal damage from smoke is increasing, the total tax payment by the polluter under TAM is greater than the damage by the marginal polluter.[9] Therefore, the bid by the polluters would decrease and there would be too few polluters and too many pollutees.

It is now easy to see why liability rules (not conditioned on appropriate location) are not efficient.[10] Starting off with the efficient tax case: if part or all of the tax goes to the pollutee, then there will be too many pollutees and not enough polluters because the pollutee is not taking into account the additional damage and prevention costs when it is deciding whether or not to enter into a polluted location.

All these problems are solved by some kind of zoning. Under LAD^N, areas would have to be zoned so that not more than the optimal number of polluters would be allowed in any one area.[11] Under LAD^{SL}, the area would be zoned so that no more than the optimal number of pollutees would be allowed in any one area. In practice, the liability rule is conditioned on the pollutee being in the optimal spatial location. Thus pollutees can only collect liability if they are in an appropriate area for pollutees.[12]

Regulation itself has two levels. The long-run zoning regulation determines the optimal location of polluters and pollutees. The short-run regulation determines the amount of smoke.

Wealth Effects

In the previous section, we demonstrated that the outcome under a double zoning rule is equivalent to TAD^{SL} or to a long-run zoning requirement with any of the following: TAD^N, LAD^N, LOC^{SL}. But do these various rules create different patterns of wealth distribution among polluters and pollutees? The answer is no. The only wealth effect is on the original preregulation owners of the land. Contrast TAD^{SL} with double zoning. Under the tax rule, the bid by the marginal polluter will equal his marginal valuation of the land minus his tax payment. Under double zoning, we will have only a limited amount of land zoned for pollution activity. This amount of land is equivalent to the amont of land used for polluting activity under TAD^{SL}. Therefore the marginal polluter is the same marginal polluter as under a tax rule. This marginal polluter will bid his marginal valuation of the land. Although under zoning it is no longer bidding against pollutees, it is bidding against other polluters for a fixed supply of land available for pollution activity. Thus under zoning the polluter will pay more for its land than under the tax rule. The amount is exactly equal to the amount of taxes that it does not have to pay.[13]

Informational Requirements

Some authors would agree that under perfect information, zoning and liability rules are equally as good in achieving an efficient solution to spatial externalities; it has been claimed, however, that zoning requires more information (which is costly to obtain) than does a court system, and, as a consequence, is inferior to a system of liability rules. In this section, we show that zoning does not require that the zoning board obtain more information than the courts obtain.

We will compare three liability rules (LAD^{SL}, LAD^{N}, LOC^{SL}) and two tax rules (TAD^{SL}, TAM) with zoning in terms of the amount of information the government (zoning bodies or courts) is required to know.

Strict liability for the damage, LAD^{SL}, has already been shown to be inefficient in general. We consider it first, in order to highlight certain issues regarding information. This rule only requires the courts to know the damage to the pollutee. However it must assess this damage in all cases of damage.

Negligence liability, LAD^{N}, requires fewer court cases but more information when there is a court case. Recall that this rule has the following payoff structure:

$$LAD^{N} = D(S(x),y) \qquad \text{if } S > S^*$$
$$= 0 \qquad \text{if } S \leq S^*$$

There are two ways to interpret S^*. If every case is different, then S^*, y^* must be determined separately for each court case. The courts must know the cost curves of *both* the polluter and the pollutee in order to determine S^*.

If the court cases are members of a class, then S^*, y^* must be determined for the archetypal case. The cost curves of both the archetypal polluter and the pollutee must be known. For the particular polluter and pollutee, all that need be known is the actual damage and S. This method reduces the number of court cases as the polluter will not be brought to trial unless $S > S^*$. Thus compared to strict liability, the information requirements are high when there is a trial, but there are fewer trails under negligence.

LOC^{SL} has different informational requirements. The amount of liability is determined according to the pollutee's optimal response to the polluter's choice of S. The optimal behavior of the pollutee need not coincide with the pollutee's actual behavior, and therefore may not be as easily determined. However, under this rule, there are incentives for the pollutee to act optimally, so the optimal is likely to coincide with the actual. Recall that this rule has the following payoff structure:

$$LOC^{SL} = D(S(x),R(S)) + R(S)$$

If every court case is different, then the courts must know the pollutee's cost function and the level of S chosen by the polluter. However the courts need not know the pollutee's actual choice of y nor the polluter's cost function nor the actual damage.

If the court case is a member of a class, then the courts must know the archetypal pollutee's cost function. For the particular court case, only the level of S chosen by the polluter need be ascertained by the courts. However this rule involves the court in a great many cases. Whenever X imposes a cost on a pollutee, even if it is just a preventive cost and no damage results, a court case ensues.

Under all liability rules, there are incentives for both the polluter and the pollutees to present information, though possibly biased, to the courts.

We now consider zoning. If every polluter-pollutee pair is a special case, then the zoning authorities must know the relevant cost curves for both the polluter and the pollutee. On the other hand, if the polluter and pollutee are members of a class, then only the relevant cost curves for the archetypal polluter and pollutee must be known, as well as information regarding the amount of smoke. The zoning agency sets a general standard S^*. All that is measured is whether $S \le S^*$. If $S > S^*$, the establishment is not allowed in the zone. Zoning thus has identical information requirements to a system of negligence (LAD^N), except that the agency must consider all cases (although factories with potentially high S would not bother to see whether they could enter the zone). Note that if we have a class and $S > S^*$, the zoning agency does not determine damage $D(x,y)$ as it would in a court case. It would just not allow $S > S^*$. Thus zoning may even require less information than LAD^{SL} and LAD^N.

The relative costs of information requirements for zoning vis-à-vis LOC^{SL} can only be resolved empirically. Again there are incentives for both the polluter and pollutee to provide information (possibly biased).

Zoning is typically viewed as solving general-equilibrium issues of spatial development, while liability rules are typically viewed as solving partial-equilibrium issues. Clearly, general equilibrium requires more information than does partial equilibrium; however there is nothing special about quantity restrictions that require general-equilibrium solutions nor anything special about government-determined prices that require only partial equilibrium. Thus if liability rules are a substitute for zoning, and if zoning must be determined by a general-equilibrium framework, then so must liability rules be. On the other hand, if issues can be disaggregated and liability rules can solve spatial development using partial equilibrium, then so can zoning.

Now, in fact, courts tend to use a partial-equilibrium framework, since they are set up to handle two sides of one issue rather than a variety of sides in the intersection of numerous issues. If the courts were to use a partial-equilibrium framework in solving a problem requiring a general-equilibrium solution, the liability rule would give poor results and zoning is to be preferred.

Because of the historical development of courts, zoning boards are more capable of handling general-equilibrium problems than are courts. However, if general-equilibrium solutions cannot be practically solved, then zoning can always be practical and use partial-equilibrium analyses. Thus there is nothing special about zoning that requires more information than a liability rule.

Zoning is criticized because government requires more information about it than about a market. But the same criticism applies to a liability or tax system. For the government to set a proper price, the government needs the same information as it does to set up zoning. The only way in which the government need not have this information is for it to get out of the price- or quantity-setting business. But with high transactions costs, this is not feasible unless information costs are so high that they overwhelm allocative inefficiency. Thus, contrary to popular belief, zoning does not require more information than a liability or tax rule based on negligence.

Relative Welfare Loss When There Is Imperfect Information

Often the courts or zoning bodies have only imperfect information regarding the relevant cost and benefit of smoke curves. As a result, they may overestimate or underestimate the true costs of pollution and pollution control. In turn, the amount of liability or degree of regulation may cause the actors to behave in a suboptimal way. It has been argued that zoning is particularily susceptible to such problems. However, White and Wittman in "A Comparison of Taxes" have shown that the dead-weight loss from zoning is, in general, equivalent to the dead-weight loss from TAD^N and LAD^N, and depending on the circumstances, may be more or less than the dead-weight loss from tax rule TAM. The choice of one of these two methods over the other depends upon the relative elasticities of the marginal cost and benefit of smoke curves and the relative degree of measurement error of these two curves. Thus tax TAM is not in general superior or inferior to a system of zoning.[14]

One case where a tax appears to be superior to zoning is where there are many polluters and their contribution is to the ambient quality of the air (that is, the damage to the pollutees is just a function of the sum of the smoke emitted by all the polluters).[15] Because there are many polluters, the average of all the measurement errors associated with estimating the individual benefit (to the polluter) of smoke tends toward zero. Thus the tax will create the same total amount of smoke as a regulation. A tax will allow a variation in the amount of smoke emitted by each firm: those firms which gain a greater benefit from smoke will produce more smoke and pay greater taxes; those firms which gain less benefit from smoke will produce less smoke and pay lower pollution taxes. The same effect can be achieved if the area is zoned for a certain amount of smoke pollution but a uniform standard not applied to individual firms within the area. In practice this would be achieved by giving each unit of land a transferable property right to pollute. Firms would not be able to purchase the right to have more smoke from the pollutees (which would probably be impossible, even if legal, because of high transactions costs). This is a kind of regulation in that (1) only a certain amount of smoke is allowed even if firms are willing to pay more and (2) the firm may not pay for smoke damage in the short run. Of course, as we have already shown, the firm will pay in the long run for this right to pollute without being taxed. There is also the short-run opportunity cost from not selling the right.

Ostensible Deviations from the Efficient Outcome

While some authors have agreed that zoning works will in the abstract, they have argued that many of the actual practices have deviated from the ideal. In particular, they have pointed to the granting of variances for nonconforming uses as undermining the good qualities of zoning in the abstract. We will now show that this and other so-called deviations from the optimal can be explained on the grounds of achieving economic efficiency. Furthermore, these zoning practices have liability rule counterparts.

Zoning often grants variances for nonconforming land uses that existed before the zoning was enacted. For example, assume that a factory was initially located in an area that is now zoned residential. If the costs of moving the factory are greater than the benefits of the factory not being located in the area, the factory will be granted a nonconforming land-use variance. If the costs of moving the factory are less than the benefits of the factory not being in the zone, the factory will not be granted a variance. There are numerous liability rule counterparts. If it is most efficient for the factory to remain, the defense of "coming to the nuisance" will be upheld. The factory will not be held liable because it was there first and the neighboring land uses came to the nuisance. However, if it is more efficient for the factory to move, this defense of coming to the nuisance will not be accepted by the courts. Thus liability rules may also grant *variances* for previously existing nonconforming land uses.[16]

Just as some liability rules can be sequentially adjusted as courts obtain additional information, zoning can be sequentially adjusted as the zoning agency obtains new information. Thus sometimes we have rezoning as well as a redefinition of *standard of care* in liability cases.

Zones can be broad categories or narrowly defined, just as liability rules can be broadly defined or narrowly measured. A commercial establishment can be found not liable because it is located in a commercial area (a broad category interpretation) or found liable because it is a funeral home and not a grocery store (a specific type of commercial activity). Similarly, an area may be zoned for commercial use or it may be zoned for commercial use with the exception of funeral parlors. Thus spot zoning, special use districts, and similar practices all have liability-rule counterparts.

The Government May Have Goals Other than Efficiency Maximization

Numerous authors have argued that zoning agencies may act to achieve objectives besides the efficient solution to externalities. For example, it has been argued that local zoning boards succumb to various pressure groups who influence the zoning process in order to capture rents from unanticipated changes in the law. Depending upon the political persuasion of the author, zoning boards are either to be at the mercy of developers and land speculators whose concentrated money interest overcomes the wishes of a diffuse majority, or to be unduly influenced by the present majority who want to reduce their own tax load by excessively and inefficiently shifting their tax burden to the developers and future homeowners who have no vote.[17]

In this section we suggest that similar types of pressures exist or would exist on the courts or taxing agencies. There is *nothing* special about zoning that makes it susceptible to undesirable legal or illegal pressures such as corruption, yet makes courts or taxing agencies immune. In the last section we showed that often other goals can be achieved without a loss in spatial efficiency. In this section, we consider those circumstances whereby no other goals except an efficient solution to spatial externalities can be achieved.

We have demonstrated that zoning has identical long-run efficiency and distributive effects as do LAD^N, TAD^N, LOC^{SL}, all with a long-run zoning type restriction, and TAD^{SL}. Therefore even if one believed that polluters and/or pollutees entered the political arena in order to create nonoptimal decisions in their favor, one would have to have a special theory as to why zoning agencies, rather than taxing agencies and courts, responded differently to these political pressures. Polluters have as much incentive to bribe zoning officials to grant them a variance as they have incentive to bribe judges not to find them liable when efficiency dictates otherwise, or to pay for better lawyers. There are a lot of rents to be captured by unanticipatedly changing the zoning law in one's favor. However, the same holds true for changing the outcome of a court decision or a tax rule.

The zoning agency may have different goals than maximizing spatial efficiency. But courts and taxing agencies may also have different goals than maximizing efficiency.

While U.S. courts have generally left zoning up to local authorities, they have made legal decisions overruling zoning boards. This means that zoning is ultimately under the control of the courts. Thus in order to create a theory purporting that zoning boards act differently from courts, one would also have to have a theory explaining why the appellate courts allow inefficient behavior in one area and not in the other. While we do not want to claim that there are absolutely no differences between courts, taxing agencies, and zoning bodies in their response to outside pressures or internal goals, we feel that the differences have been greatly overemphasized and rely on very tenuous and ad hoc theories of political behavior.

Even with Other Goals the Outcome May Be Efficient

Even when a zoning agency has other goals besides spatial efficiency, if it has full property rights in zoning and there are low transactions costs, the outcome will still be spatially efficient. This is just the Coase theorem used in the public sector. Under low transaction costs it never pays to be inefficient. Thus we may see implicit trading in property rights. For example, the zoning agency may sell off its right to low-density zoning if the developer pays a high licensing fee. With regard to the issue of fiscal zoning, the agency will sell off rights to the land use which promises the highest fiscal surplus. This can never be spatially inefficient within the locality as inefficiency is a deadweight loss to the community and thereby reduces its fiscal surplus over what it would be otherwise. For example, an inefficient negative externality would decrease the value of surrounding homes—and the tax base—more than the increase in taxes accrued from the increased value of the polluter's land because it is allowed to pollute more than optimally.

If the property rights of the zoning agency are somewhat attenuated, then trades will involve some social cost (but less than the cost involved if no trades were allowed). Thus, for example, assume that the agency cannot change zoning for a monetary payment, but that it can only alter zoning in exchange for other actions by the developer (such as the donating of land for a park). This may not be efficient if the voters would rather have the money instead of one more park. Therefore, trades involve some social cost. The more attenuated the property rights, the more likely other goals may interfere with optimal spatial location. However recent court decisions have upheld the practice of money payments for zoning changes.

A second problem ostensibly arises because of the public bad nature of much of pollution. One polluter may affect many pollutees. Any single pollutee may not enter into the political system because the transactions costs are higher than the benefits. Courts partially overcome this problem via a class-action suit. Zoning agencies are also set up to partially mitigate this problem. Zoning agencies are elected or appointed by an elected official. The elected person maximizes probability of winning by creating efficient rather than inefficient platforms. In particular, this means efficient zoning policy. Elections are, thus, a means of partially overcoming the high transactions costs.

The less property rights are attenuated and the lower the transactions costs, the greater the likelihood that zoning creates efficient spatial location, even in the presence of other goals. Just as property rights and low transactions costs overcome possible inefficiencies in the private market, these Coasian assumptions can rescue zoning from being inefficient in the public market. Assignment of property rights in a private market with zero transactions costs has no effect on efficiency, thereby enabling the body which assigns property rights to achieve distributive goals without a loss of efficiency. Under similar assumptions, the same holds true for a zoning agency. While we do not argue that these assumptions necessarily hold to the extent that they do, zoning is more efficient than otherwise. Again, we must compare the ability of the zoning agency to achieve its own goals with a minimum loss of economic efficiency to the ability of the courts and taxing agencies to achieve their own goals with a minimum loss of economic efficiency. There is little evidence that transaction costs are higher for zoning agencies.

The Role of Competition

Even if the zoning authority has other goals besides efficient solutions to externalities and even if the attainment of these goals would result in a loss of economic efficiency, the zoning authority will be forced to be efficient if the community is in a competitive market and all land is homogeneous in use. In a competitive market supply and demand come into play and prevent inefficient solutions. For example, a community with low-income housing cannot get high-income housing because high-income housing will want to accrue as great a fiscal surplus for itself as possible. Therefore high-income housing will move to areas where there is high-income housing, and low-income housing will move to low-income areas (other things being equal). Zoning may prevent a decrease in the average tax surplus, but it cannot increase it. In general, to the extent that the market is competitive and there is unrestricted power to levy nonuniform taxes, the communities must zone efficiently, and the zoning agencies will have difficulty in achieving other goals at the expense of efficiency.

Once again, we must make a relative comparison. Does competition limit arbitrary behavior of the zoning commission more or less than competition limits arbitrary behavior of the courts and taxing bodies? While there have been numerous articles attempting to account for the invisible hand in the court system, the arguments have been quite weak (especially so when the pollutees are numerous).[18] The arguments for competition among local districts and competition for choosing members of the zoning boards within local districts maybe on firmer ground.[19]

Other Methods May Create Equal Inefficiencies

Several authors have argued that zoning has not been used to cure environmental externalities, but rather to keep poor people out and raise the tax base. (This is a different type of externality, as those who pay less than their share of property taxes have equal access to the services provided by the taxes.)[20]

It can be demonstrated that there can also be *fiscal taxation*. This fiscal taxation has basically the same efficiency properties as fiscal zoning. We first consider zoning and taxation only applied to new developments (selective) and then zoning and taxation applied to all property (general).

Selective Zoning or Taxation

When a developer wants to get a use permit, the authority can establish not only density but quality requirements so that the price of the home is implicitly raised. In other words, one can regulate for high-price homes.

Another approach is to charge a user fee that is the present discounted value of the difference between taxes collected and the desired rate of tax collection. Donations for parks and school-impact fees are examples. The user fee is probably superior, since it is possible, albeit unlikely, that lower-priced housing might pay the same amount of taxes per resident and house and effect an implicitly higher rate of taxes: that is, the user fee would result in a different allocation of quality housing.

General Taxes and Zoning

For ease of analysis, assume initially that everyone has the same income and wants to spend the same amount on housing ($100,000). There is no fiscal zoning or fiscal taxation. Everything is efficient. Now assume that there are poorer people who want to move into the area. Zoning for 1-acre lots with 2-car garages insures that demand for services per tax base remains lower than if half-acre zoning were allowed (unless there was absolutely no additional value from having more than one-half acre so that the one owner would pay less than one-half of what the two owners would have paid.) This means that zoning requires some people to inefficiently consume more land or more garages than desirable (although presumably the numbers coincide with the *average*, if not marginal, buyer's preferences).

As an alternative, the government might raise the tax rate to try to discourage the poor. Assume that it worked without distortion (contrary to the findings of Grieson (1975)). In spending the extra tax dollars above the previously determined optimal, we would again have inefficient consumption. This time, too much street cleaning as opposed to too much acreage to be consumed.[21]

Thus, if there can be fiscal zoning, there can be fiscal taxation. And if fiscal zoning results in inefficiencies, fiscal taxation probably does also.[22]

Property Rights as an Alternative Solution

Siegan has argued that zoning is unnecessary to accomplish the goal of reducing pollution because the market itself spatially separates incompatible land uses. A system of no zoning with no taxes on polluters and no liability rules giving rights to pollutees, in effect, confers a property right on polluters.[23]

In the absence of zoning or any other corrective system for nuisances, the unregulated market generally keeps pollutees out of areas already dominated by polluters when separation is the socially optimal solution. However, in the opposite case—keeping polluters out of areas already dominated by pollutees—the unregulated market does much more poorly. For example, polluters may move into an area already occupied by pollutees and may possibly force the pollutees to move, since polluters need not take into account the cost of pollution damage and abatement that they impose on pollutees.

Finally, spatial separation may not be optimal. Typically there are conglomeration effects which make it efficient for both polluters and pollutees to be located near each other (for example, cities have residents, factories, sewage disposal plants located in close proximity to save on transportation costs). In such cases, we want the polluter to abate pollution optimally by reducing the smoke level to S^*. Siegan's property-right solution will not accomplish this.[24]

Restrictive Covenants as an Alternative to Zoning

Ellickson (1973) has argued in favor of restrictive covenants. "When a developer drafts covenants that will bind people who move into his subdivision, market forces prompt him to draft efficient ones." Unfortunately, restrictive covenants require that ownership initially be in one large landholding. Clearly, public governments and zoning boards are substitutes for private "governments" when there are no large landholdings and the transaction costs of merger are prohibitive. Furthermore, situations change. Therefore to provide a flexibility, a covenant that can be changed by a majority (or two-thirds) of the landowners is required. This is virtually a zoning board, but with somewhat higher transactions costs.

The Possibility of Low Transaction Costs

Pollution typically involves very high transaction costs between the polluter and the pollutee. However, on those occasions when transactions costs are low, we would like our pollution control system to still deal effectively.

If zoning regulations are rigid, then there can be no transactions between the polluter and pollutee even when transaction costs would be low in the absence of zoning. In turn, this would prevent the polluter and pollutee from jointly correcting for any errors in the government regulation. However, the assumption of a rigid zoning regulation is somewhat unrealistic. If all parties to the externality prefer a different spatial pattern or level of smoke production than the present zoning regulations dictate, then they can petition the board for a change. The zoning board would almost certainly change the regulation when there is unanimous agreement. The present regulation may serve as a starting point for negotiations and bribes among the participants.

The inability to transact is certainly a drawback if the transaction would have improved the outcome. However, the main long-run alternative to zoning is TAD^{SL}. The effectiveness of this rule is undermined by low transaction costs. If there are low transaction costs, the polluter and the pollutee will choose to minimize the sum of damage, prevention costs, and *taxes*. The cost-minimization point of this sum is not x^*,y^*.[25]

Notes

1. Major critics of zoning include Siegan (1976), Goetz and Wofford (1979), and White (1975). Fischel (1979) argues that zoning is used mainly to redistribute wealth.

2. See, for example, Posner (1977).

3. The arguments in this section parallel the arguments of Lange (1938). The arguments in the later sections are in response to his many critics (see for example, Hayek (1945)) and consider issues which Lange did not address.

4. This assumption is standard.

5. *Negligence* is a legal term. Our use of it is more broad. Whenever the legal system does not hold a party liable if the party has performed up to a certain standard, we call that a *negligence rule*.

6. The conditions are even more severe if the relevant variables are discrete as opposed to continuous. Then both sides should also take into account the prevention costs by the other side. See White and Wittman (1982; 1983).

7. This simplifies the exposition, but does not alter the basic results. See Wittman (1981b) for further refinements of this model.

8. For our purposes it is not necessary to find the first-order conditions for x and y. When we discuss the various taxes and liability rules, we assume that these conditions are also met. This reduces unnecessary detail. For an an exposition of various short-run conditions, see the first section of this chapter.

9. For notational simplicity, we assumed constant marginal damage from smoke. Under this assumption, *TAM* would be efficient. See Carlton and Loury (1981) for a discussion of *TAM*.

10. If the *LOC* is based not on the optimal prevention costs by the existing pollutee, but rather is based on the optimal prevention costs of the optimal pollutee, then the liability rule will produce appropriate long-run incentives. See Wittman (1981a,b).

11. See White and Wittman (1981a) for a thorough discussion of zoning-based liability rules, including solutions to the problems involved when there are nonconvexities arising from different types of pollutees and polluters entering an area.

12. See Wittman (1981a) for a discussion of the law and further examples of the economic reasoning. See Grieson (1974), Grieson and White (1981), and Wittman (1981c) for the framework and development of this type of analysis.

13. This section thus shows that the argument that polluters prefer regulation over liability rules is fallacious. See, for example, Goetz and Wofford (1979) and Buchanan and Tullock (1975).

14. Of course, we are not arguing that pigovian taxes are not a perfectly

efficient source of revenue that could only be replaced by land taxes if quantity regulations are used instead.

15. It should be noted that ambient pollution does not characterize most of the externality problems with which zoning deals. For example, the damage from reduced sunlight and privacy that my neighbor creates by building next to the property line can be distinguished from the zero damage to me when someone two blocks away from me builds next to his property line. Even smoke may not be ambient. The smoke from U.S. Steel in Gary, Indiana, can readily be detected and affects people in Gary and South Chicago more than smoke from a power plant in the Northern suburbs of Chicago does.

16. For a fuller discussion of the role of being first, see D. Wittman (1980a).

17. For an example of the latter view, see Ellickson (1977).

18. See Rubin (1977), Priest (1977), Goodman (1978), Posner and Landes (1979), Cooter and Kornhauser (1980), and Terrebonne (1981).

19. See Tiebout (1956).

20. See for example, Ellickson (1977), White (1975), and Sagalyn and Sternlieb (1973).

21. Lump sum taxes could achieve fiscal taxation without distortion.

22. It could be argued that fiscal zoning is efficient in that it prevents poor people from moving into rich areas in order to get high-quality services at relatively low cost to the property poor owners.

23. We assume high transaction costs.

24. For a more thorough discussion, see White and Wittman (1982).

25. The double tax proposed by White and Wittman (1982) is immune from this problem. Tax TAD^{SL} is also immune, but it has undesirable long-run properties.

References

Buchanan, James, and Tullock, Gordon. "Polluter's Profits and Political Response: Direct Controls Versus Taxes." *American Economic Review* 65 (1975): 139.

Carlton, Dennis, and Loury, Glen. "The Limitations of Pigovian Taxes as a Long Run Remedy for Externalities." *Quarterly Journal of Economics* 95 (1980).

Cooter, Robert, and Kornhauser, Lewis. "Can Litigation Improve the Law without the Help of Judges?" *Journal of Legal Studies* 9 (1980): 139.

Ellickson, Robert. "Alternatives to Zoning: Covenants, Nuisance Rules, and Fines as Land Use Controls." *University of Chicago Law Review* 40 (1973): 661–781.

_____. "Suburban Growth Controls: An Economic and Legal Analysis." *Yale Law J.* 86, no. 3 (January 1977): 385–512.

Fischel, William A. "Externalities and Zoning." *Public Choice* 35, no. 1 (1980): 37–43.

Fischel, William A. "Equity and Efficiency Aspects of Zoning Reform." *Public Policy* 27, no. 3 (Summer 1979): 301–331.

Goetz, Michael L., and Wofford, Larry E. "The Motivation for Zoning: Efficiency or Wealth Distribution." *Land Economics* 55, no. 4 (November 1979): 472–485.

Goodman, John. "An Economic Theory of the Evolution of the Common Law." *Journal of Legal Studies* 7 (1978): 393.

Grieson, Ronald E. "The Economics of Property Taxes and Land Values: The Elasticity of Supply of Structures." *Journal of Urban Economics* 1 (October 1974): 367–381.

Grieson, Ronald E., and Murray, Michael. "On the Possibility and Optimality of Positive Rent Gradients." *Journal of Urban Economics* 9 (1981): 275–285.

Grieson, Ronald E, and White, James R. "The Effects of Zoning on Structure and Land Markets." *Journal of Urban Economics* 10 (1981): 271–285.

Hayek, F.A. "The Use of Knowledge in Society." *American Economic Review* 35 (1945): 519.

Hirsh, W.Z. "The Efficiency of Restrictive Land Use Instruments." *Land Economics*, 53 no. 2 (May 1977): 145–156.

Helpman, E., and Pines, D. "Land and Zoning in an Urban Economy: Further Results." *American Economic Review* 67, no. 5 (December 1977): 982–986.

Lange, Oscar, and Taylor, Fred. *On the Economic Theory of Socialism.* University of Minnesota Press, 1938.

Posner, Richard, and Landes, William. "Adjudication as a Private Good." *Journal of Legal Studies* 8 (1979): 235.

Priest, George. "The Common Law Process and the Selection of Efficient Rules." *Journal of Legal Studies* 6 (1977): 65.

Rubin, Paul. "Why Is the Common Law Efficient?" *Journal of Legal Studies* 6 (1977): 51.

Sagalyn, Lynne B., and Sternlieb, George *Zoning and Housing Costs.* Center for Urban Policy Research. New Brunswick: Rutgers University, State University of New Jersey, January 1973.

Seidel, Stephen R. *Housing Costs and Government Regulations: Confronting the Regulatory Maze.* Center for Urban Policy Research. New Brunswick: Rutgers University, State University of New Jersey, 1978.

Siegan, Bernard H. *Other People's Property.* Lexington, MA: Lexington Books, D.C. Heath and Company, 1976.

Terrebonne, Peter. "A Strictly Evolutionary Model of Common Law." *Journal of Legal Studies* 10 (1981): 397.

Tiebout, Charles. "A Pure Theory of Local Expenditures." *Journal of Political Economics* (1956): 416.

White, Michelle. "Fiscal Zoning in Fragmented Metropolitan Areas." In *Fiscal Zoning and Land Use Controls*, edited by E. Mills and W. Oates Lexington, MA: Lexington Books, D.C. Heath and Company, 1975.

White, Michelle, and Wittman, Donald. "Long-Run versus Short-Run Remedies for Spatial Externalities." In *Essay on the Law and Economics of Local Government*, edited by Daniel Rubinfeld, COUPE Papers on Public Economics, Washington, D.C.: The Urban Institute, 1979.

_____. "Optimal Spatial Rules under Pollution: Liability Rules and Zoning." *Journal of Legal Studies* 10, no. 2 (June 1981): 249–268.

_____. "Pigovian Taxes and Optimal Spatial Location." *Economica*. Forthcoming (1982).

_____. "A Comparison of Taxes, Regulation and Liability Rules under Imperfect Information." *Journal of Legal Studies*. Forthcoming (1983).

Wittman, Donald. "First Come, First Served: An Economic Analysis of Coming to the Nuisance." *Journal of Legal Studies*. 9, no. 3 (June 1980): 557–568.

_____. 1981a. "Optimal Pricing of Sequential Inputs." *Journal of Legal Studies* 10, no. 1: 39–64.

_____. 1981b. *Liability for Harm or Restitution for Benefit?* University of California. Santa Cruz.

_____. 1981c. *Pigovian Taxes, Liability Rules and Regulation of the Inputs*. University of California, Santa Cruz.

9 Optimal Tolls with High-peak Travel Demand

Ronald E. Grieson and *Richard J. Arnott*

Corresponding to any level of stationary-state traffic flow are two velocities. *Zero flow*, for instance, corresponds to travel both on an empty road and in a stationary-traffic jam. We refer to travel at the lower velocity associated with a given flow as *hypercongestion*, and periods during which hypercongestion is possible as being characterized by high-peak travel demand. Our aim is to determine optimal congestion tolls with high-peak demand. Our note builds on Vickrey's discussion of this problem.[1]

Before proceeding with the analysis, we must clarify our terminology. The technology of stationary-state travel is given by a function which relates stationary-state traffic flow to each vehicle's travel time. The seminal papers by Walters and Vickrey on optimal congestion tolls, framed the analysis in terms of average and marginal cost. To facilitate comparison between their analyses and ours, we treat travel cost as functionally related to travel time; the technology of stationary-state travel may then be characterized by a function relating stationary-state traffic flow to each driver's *time cost* of travel, which is termed either *average social cost* or *marginal private cost*. This relationship is shown in figure 9-1. We define the flat portion of this curve, on which travel is so light that a few extra cars on the road do not increase a driver's travel costs, as the region of *uncongested travel*;[2] the upward sloping portion as the region of *congested travel*; and the backward-sloping portion as the region of *hypercongested travel*. Stationary-state travel in the region of hypercongestion is demonstrably inefficient, since for each point in this region there is another point with the same flow and lower travel costs in either the congested or the uncongested region.

Previous published analyses of the determination of optimal congestion tolls have treated marginal private cost as a univalued function of flow. When, however, hypercongestion is possible, there are two marginal private costs associated with each level of flow, one corresponding to a point in the region of hypercongested travel and another to a point in one of the other two regions. To circumvent this difficulty, we treat flow as a function of marginal private cost,[3] and denote this function as $f = g(MPC)$.

We would like to thank David Pines for helpful comments on an earlier draft.

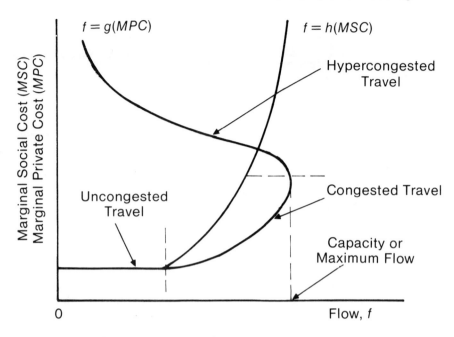

Figure 9-1. The Technology of Road Travel

In a stationary state, total travel costs per unit time equal each driver's travel costs multiplied by the flow. We define the increase in total travel costs from a unit increase in flow as its marginal social cost.[4] From $f = g(MPC)$, one can calculate the relationship between marginal social cost and flow, which is denoted $f = h(MSC)$. This function is plotted in figure 9.1 for congested and uncongested, but not for hypercongested, travel.[5]

We now characterize the demand side of the travel *market*. The number of cars entering the road per unit time depends on the cost to the driver of traveling on the road. This cost comprises the monetized value of travel time, MPC, plus the congestion toll τ. We denote the stationary demand for travel function as $d = d(MPC + \tau)$. We say that there is *high-peak demand* if the demand curve intersects the hypercongested region of $g(MPC)$, $d = d^2(MPC + \tau)$ in figure 9-2; *low-peak demand* if the demand curve intersects the congested, but not the hypercongested, region of $g(MPC)$, $d = d^1(MPC + \tau)$ in figure 9-2; and *off-peak demand* if the demand curve cuts neither the congested nor hypercongested regions of $g(MPC)$, $d = d^0(MPC + \tau)$ in figure 9-2. In our terminology, uncongested, congested, and hypercongested refer to the characteristic of traffic flow, while high-peak, low-peak, and off-peak refer to the characteristic of travel demand.

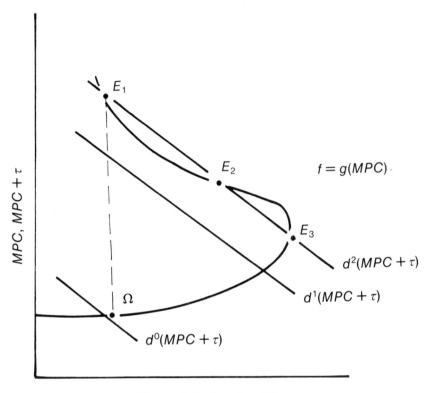

Figure 9–2. Levels of Demand

We define stationary-state equilibrium as being when a driver's travel costs inclusive of the toll are such that the flow of the road equals the number of cars wanting to enter the road per unit time. Thus, equilibria are characterized by the points of intersection of $g(MPC)$ and $d(MPC + \tau)$. Exploiting the analogy between market and traffic flow equilibrium, we see that $g(MPC)$ can be interpreted as a traffic supply curve.

Low-peak Demand

We now review the economics of optimal congestion tolls with low-peak demand, using our terminology.

Figure 9-3 depicts a low-peak demand situation. In the absence of a congestion toll, equilibrium occurs at J, the point of intersection of the supply and demand curves.

It is well known that, without a toll, equilibrium traffic flow in congested traffic is inefficient because there is an uninternalized congestion externality.

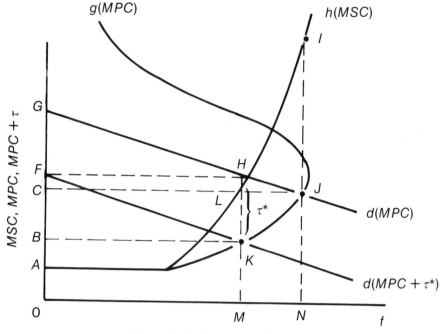

Figure 9–3. Low-peak Demand

In deciding whether or not to travel on the road, a drive considers only his own travel costs and ignores that his traveling on the road slows other drivers down.

There are two necessary conditions for efficient stationary-state utilization of the road. First, hypercongestion may not occur. Second, the social cost of increasing traffic flow by one unit must equal the social benefit; that is, the efficient flow level corresponds to the point of intersection of $h(MSC)$ and $d(MPC)$. These two conditions together imply that efficient travel occurs at the point K on $g(MPC)$ in figure 9-3.

We have already established that equilibrium occurs at the points of intersection of $g(MPC)$ and $d(MPC + \tau)$. In figure 9-3, for the equilibrium to coincide with the optimum, it is necessary to charge a toll of such a magnitude that $d(MPC + \tau)$ intersects $g(MPC)$ at K. The efficient size of the toll is therefore τ^*, the vertical distance between H and K, which equals marginal social cost minus marginal private cost at optimal flow.

In the absence of the congestion toll, social benefit from travel on the road equals $OGJN$, the area under $d(MPC)$ up to equilibrium flow, since the demand curve is also the marginal social benefit curve. Social cost can be measured as flow multiplied by time costs per driver, $OCJN$. Thus, social surplus equals CGJ. With the optimal congestion toll, social surplus is

BGHK. The excess burden from not imposing a congestion toll therefore equals $BGHK - CGJ = BCLK - HLJ$.[6] And the toll revenue collected is $BFHK$. Toll revenue less excess burden therefore equals $BFHK - (BCLK - HLJ) = FJHC > 0$. Thus, with low-peak demand if demand is less than infinitely elastic, toll revenue from an optimal toll always exceeds the excess burden from not imposing the toll.

High-peak Demand

The analysis of high-peak demand is similar to that for low-peak, but there are some complications. First, there may be multiple equilibria, as is shown in figure 9-2. Which of these equilibria are stable? To answer this question completely satisfactorily requires an explicit treatment of the dynamics of nonstationary-state traffic flow, which is beyond the scope of this chapter.[7] We can, however, provide a casual quasi-dynamic analysis using the tools employed in the chapter. We may reasonably assume that when demand either exceeds or falls short of supply, travel time increases or decreases, respectively. One may interpret *demand* out of stationary state as the flow rate onto the road and *supply* as the average flow along the road. The assumption is therefore that with increasing (decreasing) flow onto the road, travel time increases (decreases). It follows that in figure 9-2, E_1 and E_3 are stable equilibria, while E_2 is unstable.

Why, with equilibrium at E_1, is it not possible to have a sudden switch to Ω, with the same flow rate on the lower part of $g(MPC)$? A fundamental identity of traffic flow is flow $\equiv$ velocity x density. A sudden switch from E_1 to Ω, holding flow constant, requires a sudden fall in density, which is not possible. This line of argument establishes that whether E_1 or E_3 is the stationary-state equilibrium depends on the path of adjustment. If the demand curve were initially above d^2, intersected $g(MPC)$ only once above E_1, and then shifted down smoothly towards d^2, E_1 would be the stationary-state equilibrium; otherwise, there would have to be a discontinuous decrease in traffic density, which is not possible. Similarly if the demand curve were initially below d^2, intersected $g(MPC)$ only once below E_3, and then shifted smoothly upwards, E_3 would be the stationary-state equilibrium.

There are two high-peak demand configurations to treat. The first and the easier to analyze is shown in figure 9-4. The second, to be treated later, is shown in figure 9-5.

Following the procedure used to derive the optimal toll with low-peak demand, we find the optimal toll to be τ^*, the vertical distance between the point of intersection of $d(MPC)$ and $h(MSC)$, H, and the point with the same flow rate on the congested portion of $g(MPC)$, K.

If the initial equilibrium were at E_3 in figure 9-4, the social surplus from the road would be CGE_3. If it were at E_1, social surplus would be PGE_1.

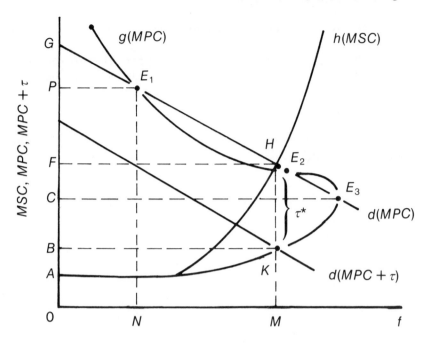

Figure 9–4. High-peak Demand—Simple Case

After the imposition of the optimal toll, social surplus is $BGHK$. The excess burden from not imposing an optimal congestion toll is therefore $BGHK - CGE_3$ with initial equilibrium E_3, and BPE_1HK with initial equilibrium E_1. Toll revenues are $BFHK$. Now,

$$BGHK - CGE_3 - BFHK = FGH - CGE_3 = -CFHE_3 < 0$$

while,

$$BPE_1HK - BFHK = FPE_1H > 0$$

Thus, with initial equilibrium E_3, toll revenues exceed the efficiency gain that results from imposing the optimal congestion toll. But with initial equilibrium E_1, toll revenues are less than the effeciency gain.

When demand is less than infinitely elastic, the relationship between toll revenues and the efficiency gain from imposing the optimal toll is as follows: *if imposition of the optimal congestion toll causes traffic flow to fall (rise),*

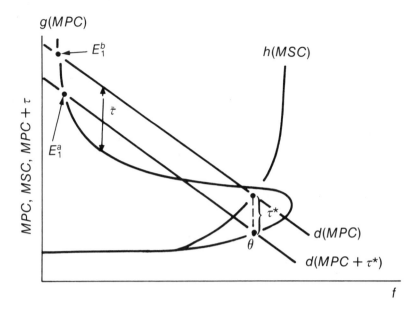

Figure 9–5. High-peak Demand—Complication

the excess burden associated with not imposing the toll is less than (is more than) toll revenue collected. When demand is infinitely elastic, toll revenues equal the efficiency gain. These proportions can be demonstrated by simple geometric argument and imply that *if the imposition of the optimal congestion toll causes traffic flow to increase,* or if demand is infinitely elastic, *then provided that toll revenues more than cover collection costs, the toll should be imposed* (according to the conventional cost-benefit criterion).

The above line of reasoning indicates that the excess burden from not imposing a congestion toll when travel is hypercongested may be very large and may even exceed the benefits from the use of the road in the absence of the toll.

The high-peak travel demand configuration in figure 9-5 illustrates an additional complication that has to be considered. The optimal stationary-state toll, computed as in the previous case, is τ^*. However, if the pretoll equilibrium is at E_1^b, then application of this toll during the period of adjustment to the new stationary state results in the posttoll equilibrium being E_1^a and not θ.[8] Imposition of a toll of magnitude at least $\bar{\tau}$ in the period of adjustment, so that $d(MPC + \bar{\tau})$ does not intersect the hypercongested portion of $g(MPC)$, circumvents this problem. After some period of time with the toll $\bar{\tau}$, hypercongestion ends, and the toll can then be reduced to τ^*.

Concluding Comments

The standard analysis in urban economics of traffic congestion is strictly correct only in stationary state and ignores hypercongestion. We have extended this analysis in examining the economics of congestion tolls, taking hypercongested travel into account.

Several interesting results have been obtained. First, under high-peak demand conditions, multiple stable hypercongested stationary-state equilibria are possible. Which of these possible equilibria occurs depends on the pattern of demand prior to establishment of the stationary state. Second, with high-peak demand, the efficiency gain from imposing the optimal toll may exceed both toll revenues and the benefits from road usage in the absence of the toll. Finally, in moving from an initial hypercongested equilibrium to efficient utilization of the road, it may be necessary to impose a temporarily larger toll to eliminate hypercongestion, after which the toll may be lowered to the efficient stationary-state level.

Actual traffic flow is inherently nonstationary-state. Over some sections of the road during some periods of the rush hour, there is hypercongestion; over other sections of the road and during other periods of the rush hour, there is not. The existing literature makes the assumption that, for most purposes, nothing essential is lost by treating traffic flow as uniform over the rush hour. On the basis of our analysis here we have doubts concerning the validity of this assumption. Whether our doubts are well founded will have to await an explicitly nonstationary-state analysis of the economics of traffic flow.

Notes

1. William Vickrey has presented several seminars on this topic. This chapter both commits to paper his important contribution and extends it.

2. Marginal private cost may actually decrease with flow at very low levels. For instance, a driver will be alerted to stop signs by cars ahead of him slowing down and stopping. Thus, he may safely travel at a slightly higher speed when there are a few rather than no other cars on the road. To simplify the discussion, however, we treat the region of uncongested travel as being horizontal.

3. That is, we work in terms of the inverse of the conventional function. Note that flow is a set-valued function of marginal private cost with uncongested travel. This is a notational inconvenience, but does not concern us, since we are interested in the other regions of the curve.

4. What happens if the hourly flow onto the entrance of the road exceeds capacity flow by one car per hour? If capacity flow on the road still occurs,

then a queue which increases in length by one car per hour develops. The cost of adding an extra car to the queue is the time taken to move up in the queue by one car, multiplied by the number of cars which enter the queue after the car in question. The cost is infinite with stationary demand. But this is an example of a nonstationary, not a stationary, state. Hence, marginal social cost is undefined at capacity flow.

5. We do not use that portion of the function $f = h(MSC)$ that corresponds to hypercongestion.

6. The more usual measure of the excess burden from not imposing a congestion toll is HIJ, the amount by which the social cost associated with the excess flow MN exceeds the private cost. We measure excess burden in a way that facilitates comparing it with toll revenues and hypercongestion.

7. Arnott, Lindsey, and Small are engaged in research on the economics of nonstationary-state traffic flow.

8. Otherwise, there would have to be a physically impossible discontinuous change in density.

References

Vickrey, W.S. "Pricing in Urban and Suburban Transport." *American Economic Review* 53 (1963): 452–465.

——. "Congestion Theory and Transport Investment." *American Economic Review* 59 (1969): 251–260.

Walters, A.A. "The Theory and Measurement of Private and Social Cost of Highway Congestion." *Econometrica* 29 (1961): 676–699.

10 On the Regional Labor-Supply Relation

George S. Tolley
and Ronald J. Krumm

A fundamental consideration in explaining the regional distribution of population and production is that for broadly defined geographic units, the location of population consumption and labor market activity are in the same area. A result is that a person, in comparing his well being between living in different locations, will have to consider not only the money wage he can earn but also locational differences in consumption opportunities. Only recently has serious attention focused on the conditions under which individuals would choose to live and work in one region relative to another, and the implications for the quantity of people that ultimately end up in an area.

One area of inquiry concerns the effects of market-good-price differences between regions on the nominal wage needed to induce persons to locate in a particular region. Tolley, for example, develops a model in which higher prices induce a higher labor-supply wage necessary to attract labor to the region and integrates this with the effect of wages on costs of production in the region. The relation between nominal wages in an area, city size, amenities, and local prices has been empirically examined by a number of authors, including Hoch, Getz and Huang, Izraeli, Rosen, and Henderson. The focus has often been on whether or not nominal wage differentials compensated by differences in price or amenity attributes result in the absence of real utility differences between areas and the implications for wage-differential–induced migration.

Several needs remain in the analysis of the regional labor-supply decision. Previous analyses have not considered how hours-worked decisions are influenced by choice of location and the resulting implications for regional–population-size differences or changes. A common conceptual approach is to assume that all people are the same whereas heterogeneity in characteristics of the population might lead to systematic location preferences and differences in regional labor-supply relations. A fuller recognition of these considerations leads to a more careful empirical specification including the distinction between hourly-wage and yearly-earning comparisons.

Department of Economics and Center for Urban Studies, University of Chicago. Partial financial support from the National Science Foundation, Grant SOC-78-25776 is gratefully acknowledged. A. Kelly and R.P. Bear provided most capable research assistance. The usual disclaimer applies.

The analysis presented here examines the region-location decision for individuals, building toward specification of a joint-region–labor-supply–residence-location–demand relation. In the following section of this chapter, an explicit model of individual location choice is developed and, in the context of population mobility, the implications for labor-market–supply wage in a region as well as for time spent in labor-market activity of market-good-price and amenity differences between regions are derived. Unlike previous work in this area, the decision of how much time to spend in labor-market activity is examined jointly with the decision of location of supply The role of amenities in determination of utility associated with location in a region is explicitly specified. A result is that substitution or complementarity between amenity levels in a region, market goods, and an individual's time may lead to systematic influences of those regional differences in prices and amenities on the labor-supply hourly wage that differ from the impacts on yearly earnings. An implication for analysis of regional growth and decline is that an equilibrium 10 percent growth in regional demand for labor services in each of two regions, for example, may not lead to growth of population in the two regions by the same amount.

The section on "The Region Labor Supply Relation" considers more fully the implications of population heterogeneity in analysis of regional differences in labor-market wages and time spent in labor-market activity. Implications of household-composition characteristics as well as labor-market–skill differences are brought out. Under somewhat restrictive but reasonable labor-demand assumptions, the labor-market wage that faces all persons in a region is set by persons who, on the margin, are just indifferent between alternative region locations. More variation in hours worked among individuals in the region, however, is a likely result of differences between individuals. Building on these results, an empirical model of hourly wages and hours worked is developed.

The section "Empirical Results" uses a sample from the Michigan Panel Survey on Income Dynamics to estimate the model. Systematic influences of human capital variables, household characteristics, location status, as well as unobserved, individual specific components are considered in the joint estimation of the hourly-wage profile, hours-worked relationship, and the yearly-earnings profile for an individual in each of 1976, 1977, and 1978. Region- and urban-location status variables are significant in explaining wage, hours-worked, as well as earnings differentials.

The empirical results suggest that the unobserved individual specific components are substantial in causing similarity over time in an individuals wage and yearly earnings but less so for hours worked. For any particular year, the unobserved factors influencing the wage or hours worked are positively correlated with earnings, but no relationship of this sort exists between the wage and hours worked.

Effects of variables on the hourly wage are, in general, more precisely estimated than on the hours-worked counterpart. Very often, however, the direction of the effects are opposite in sign, with yearly-earnings impacts closely related to the sum of these impacts. In particular, this is evident in the effects of region- and urban-location status, where the associated wage differentials differ sometimes substantially from the earnings differentials. These findings suggest the importance for regional analysis of considering the household-labor–supply decision to include the quantity of time spent in such activities, and the impropriety of using regional earnings differentials for inference concerning regional welfare differences.

The empirical results do not permit explicit distinction between equilibrium and disequilibrium characterization of regional labor markets. Some inferences from hourly-wage and hours-worked differences can be made about the nature of disequilibrium if it exists. For example, low nominal wages could be due entirely to high amenities or low costs of living in a region (the equilibrium hypothesis), or areas such as the South could be in disequilibrium relative to the rest of the nation. Under the latter condition, hours worked in the South may in part reflect labor-supply reaction to disequilibrium real regional wage differentials. If regional disequilibrium exists, the empirical findings in this study do not support the contention made in many migration studies that high nominal wages in areas reflect corresponding high real wages. Rather, the finding that nominal wages in the South are low while hours worked are high suggests that wages are still too high in the South, consistent with recent patterns of substantial migration and population growth in this region.

The Region-Location Decision

The analysis carried out in this section extends traditional economic modeling of household decision making to include the role of amenities and, more generally, to include the decision of location at which household consumption and labor-supply activity takes place. Amenities are viewed here as location-dependent public goods: Conditional upon location in a particular geographic area, the quantities of amenities are fixed and consumption by one individual in the area does not exclude consumption of the same amenities by others that locate in the area. Variation in amenities or market-good prices between regions could lead to real utility differences. In the presence of population mobility, however, the latter are limited. Regional differences in amenities and market-good prices lead to compensating wage differences so as to maintain equality of utility among regions and also lead to changes in the allocation of time between household and labor-market activities.

Amenities and Utility in a Region

Consider the allocation decision in a one-period setting in which the utility of an individual is a function of consumption of a vector of commodity services, $\underline{Z}$, over this period,

$$U = u(\underline{Z})\qquad\qquad(10.1)$$

Elements of $\underline{Z}$ might include such abstract services as climatic comfort and recreation. The ith element of $\underline{Z}$ is produced using market goods and services, $\underline{x}_i$, the individual's own time, t_i, and amenities in the area in which the individual chooses to live, $\underline{A}$,

$$Z_i = Z_i(\underline{x}_i, t_i, \underline{A})\qquad i = 1, \ldots, n\qquad(10.2)$$

Changes in elements of $\underline{A}$ serve to change the quantity of each Z_i that could be produced using the same quantities of $\underline{x}_i$ and t_i. More recreational services could be produced, for example, in a area with a warm, sunny climate compared to a cold, cloudy area for any given size swimming pool and time spent utilizing the services the pool provides. Amenities, however, may serve as compliments or substitutes with various market goods or time inputs. As such, for given market-good and time-input prices, a change in amenity levels may alter the proportions of inputs used. The production functions in equation 10.2 are assumed homogeneous of degree one for any set of $\underline{A}$, however. This means that regardless of climatic conditions, a 1-percent increase in both swimming pool services and time spent using them would result in a 1-percent increase in the associated Z_i if these were the only two inputs involved in its production. The level changes themselves, however, would be greater in areas where amenities were higher.

Substituting the production relations in equation 10.2 into equation 10.1, the individual's utility may be written as

$$U = U(\underline{x}, t, \underline{A})\qquad\qquad(10.3)$$

where each element of $\underline{x}$ is the sum of its uses in all Z_i, $\Sigma \underline{x}_i$, and t is total time spent in production, Σt_i.[1] The parameters of $U(\ )$ in equation 10.3 are functions of the parameters of the $Z_i(\ )$ and $u(\ )$ in equation 10.2 and 10.1. The structure of this reparameterization of utility from equation 10.1 to equation 10.3 is not explicitly addressed further in the current work.

The individual is assumed to have income only from labor-market earnings which are the product of the labor-market wage, W, and time spent in the labor market, t_w. It is also assumed that W is not affected by t_w. The income constraint for the individual is thus

$$I = Wt_w = W(T - t) = x'p \qquad (10.4)$$

where T is total time and p is the vector of market-goods prices corresponding to x.[2]

Conditional upon location in a particular region, amenity levels are given as are the prices of market goods and services. Further, the labor-market wage is fixed, set by aggregate regional labor demand and supply. Under these conditions, the individual maximizes equation 10.3 over x and t subject to equation 10.4 and given values of A, p, and W. The fixity of the amenity inputs used in production can be viewed as technological constraints on production, which is then still characterized by homogeneity of degree one in the choice variables. For an individual located in a particular region, the solution of the problem differs from that in Becker in that amenities are public goods in household production. Analysis of market-good demand and labor-market–supply differences between individuals, moreover, depends on their regional locations as these alter the conditions under which these decisions are made. In particular, for regions with the same nominal wage, relative price or amenity differences between regions might lead to variation in time supplied in labor-market activities. This would lead to divergence of regional wage and earnings differences. The structure of the solution to the utility maximization problem developed here is presented in the appendix of this chapter.

The between-region differences in market-good prices, amenity levels, or wages, however, may also lead to the situation where people are better off in terms of utility associated with location in one region rather than another and have an incentive to reside and work in the higher-utility region. The following section examines the implications of these regional differences in the context of population mobility between alternative locations.

Location Endogeneity

If people are mobile between regions, utility maximization involves comparison of the maximum utility associated with location in a particular region, outlined in the previous section, among all alternative locations. The implications for the decision to locate in a particular region as well as the nature of the labor-supply and market-good demands are developed in this section.

Consider location in the small region where maximization of equation 10.3 subject to equation 10.4 given $\underline{p}$, W, and A yields the indirect utility function

$$U = V(\underline{p},W,\underline{A}) \tag{10.5}$$

Let conditions in the aggregate of all alternative locations be characterized by $\tilde{p}$, $\tilde{W}$, and $\tilde{A}$. The maximum utility associated with locating outside the region is thus $\tilde{U} = V(\tilde{p},\tilde{W},\tilde{A})$. Only if

$$U = V(\underline{p},W,\underline{A}) \geq \tilde{U}$$
$$V(\tilde{p},\tilde{W},\tilde{A})$$

would the individual be better off or at least as well of living in the region relative to alternative locations in the economy. If this were true, decreases in $\underline{p}$ or increases in W or $\underline{A}$ would lead to the same sorts of impacts on behavior as a result of utility-maximizing behavior resulting from the framework developed in the preceding section, and utility would increase. In this case, and if all people were the same with $U = \tilde{U}$ to start with, all individuals would be willing to pay in order to locate in the small region to reap the associated utility gain. Decreases in $\underline{A}$ or W and increases in $\underline{p}$, on the other hand, would lead to a willingness to pay to not live in the region.

Consider a world where all people are the same; in such a world, $U = \tilde{U}$ would hold for all regions in order for them all to be populated. Further, let $\underline{p}$ be equal to the cost of producing goods and services in the region, taken exogenous to all residents or potential residents. The level of these prices depends on export- and import-good prices facing the region as these goods may be used in production of goods and services consumed by people in the region, as well as particular characteristics of the region that alter costs of producing elements of $\underline{x}$. The latter may include natural endowments and labor costs as well as amenities. The first is likely to lead to an upward-sloping supply curve for the $\underline{x}$, which means that size of the region in terms of a population demanding goods and services may affect $\underline{p}$. Differences between regions in amenities or labor costs serve to shift or rotate the cost curves. Given $\underline{p}$ and $\underline{A}$ in a region, conditions that would be necessary to induce people into the region so as to maintain equality of utility with residence in alternative locations is determined by finding that $\underline{x}$ and t which maximize utility in equation 10.3 at $\tilde{U}$ for the lowest W in equation 10.4.

The results for allocation of time and market-good demands differ from those that result from utility maximization given W in a region but are very much related to the latter result. The reason is that differences in elements of $\underline{p}$ or $\underline{A}$, for example, induce substitution effects between t and elements of $\underline{x}$ that are included in the utility maximizing response for a given W. The modification, however, is that W itself is also allowed to change in order that utility remains equal to that in other regions. This leads to (1) the absence of a real utility-change impact on demand for market goods and services and allocation of time and (2) an additional substitution effect as changes in W alter relative household-production input prices. The nature of the solution to this problem is presented in the appendix. The implications for analysis are highlighted below.

Labor-Supply Wage Impacts

A 1-percent increase in p_i in the region leads to a percent change in W equal to

$$\eta^*_{wp_i} = \frac{-u}{\lambda I} \, \eta_{u,p_i} \qquad (10.6)$$

where elasticities with asterisks represent the case where wage is endogenous and utility is constrained to equal that in the rest of the economy and elasticities without asterisks represent the case where W is given. In equation 10.6, however, η_{up_i} *is merely*

$$\frac{-\lambda x_i P_i}{u} \, .$$

Substituting

$$\frac{\lambda x_i P_i}{u}$$

in equation 10.6 results in a labor-supply wage impact of

$$\eta^*_{wp_i} = S_i \qquad (10.7)$$

where $S_i = x_i \, p_i \, / I$. As a result, a region with all market-good prices that are 1-percent higher than those in another region would have, all else the same, a 1-percent higher nominal wage. That effect on wages in two different regions which is due to a 1-percent higher p_i than that in the rest of the economy, however, may differ depending on other conditions in the region that alter the S_i.

   A 1-percent higher level of A_i leads to a percent change in w equal to

$$\eta^*_{wA_i} = \frac{-U}{\lambda I}\,\eta_{uA_i} \qquad\qquad (10.8)$$

Solution of the system in the previous section, however, gives η_{uA_i} equal to $A_i U_{A_i}/U$. Substituting $A_i U_{A_i}/U$ into equation 10.8 yields

$$\eta^*_{wA_i} = \frac{A_i U_{A_i}}{\lambda I} \qquad\qquad (10.9)$$

the negative of the ratio of the marginal utility of the amenity times its level to the marginal utility of income times its level. This term, in effect, translates a utility gain associated with a higher amenity level into its equivalent wage value.

A 1-percent increase in utility in the rest of the economy leads to a percent increase in the wage, η^*_{wu}, equal to $U/\lambda I$. Combining this with the results in eqautions 10.7 and 10.9 means that the labor-supply wage specification to a region can be written as

$$\dot{W} = k'_x\dot{\underline{p}} - k'_A\dot{\underline{A}} + \frac{U}{\lambda I}\,\dot{\tilde{U}} \qquad\qquad (10.10)$$

where dots over variables represent percent changes, k_x has elements S_i, and k'_A has elements $A_i U_{A_i}/\lambda I$. Increases in $\tilde{p}$ and decreases in $\tilde{A}$ or $\tilde{W}$ lead to decreases in $\tilde{U}$, which then translate into impacts on W. In particular, an increase in $\tilde{p}_i$ by 1 percent leads to a $\tilde{k}_i$ increase in W and an increase in $\tilde{A}_i$ by 1 percent leads to a reduction in W by $\tilde{k}_{A_i}$. A 1 percent increase in $\tilde{W}$ leads to an equal percent increase in W.

The expression in equation 10.10 can be used to examine changes in regional-wage differentials over time or between regions at any point in time. National inflation where all prices change by the same nominal amount in all regions leads to equal percent changes in wages in all regions. Relative regional-wage differentials are not affected. A region-specific price change leads to a change in the nominal wage by S_i. A uniform national increase in, for example, gasoline, would serve to change relative regional-wage differentials to the extent the S_is differ between regions. This is a likely case when substantial regional variation in nominal prices is present to start with. Implicit in the labor-supply–wage specification in equation 10.10 is the flow of population between regions in response to conditions that would otherwise cause for utility differentials between alternative locations. The direction of these flows, however, may depend on effects of the same conditions or their changes on demand for labor services. In the absence of such labor-demand impacts, decreases in p would lead to flows into the region as the associated lower wage increases the quantity of labor demanded along any labor-demand curve. Increases in amenities would lead to a similar inflow of individuals.

Shifts in demand for labor in production of an x_i that results from changes in costs of production or demand for x_i in the region that also affects p_i could exacerbate, mitigate, or even offset these flow responses. Increases in amenities are likely also to lower the region's costs of producing x_i, increasing demand for labor and thereby increasing the flow of people into the region. Region growth or decline associated with these considerations serves to shift the regional-labor-supply wage up or down as demand-induced movement along a cost curve of an x_i alters its price. The net impact on the wage is determined by the simultaneous solution of labor-wage–supply responses in equation 10.10 and market-good demand-and-cost impacts on prices.

Time-Allocation Impacts. From solution of the system when the wage in a region is given, a 1-percent increase in p_i leads to substitution and wealth impacts on t equal to η_{tp_i}. The wage change induced to maintain equality of utility in the region with that available elsewhere, S_i, from equation 10.7 leads to an additional change in t by η_{tw}. As discussed above, this term includes an income as well as a substitution effect. The total impact on t is substitution effect. The total impact on t is

$$\eta_{tp_i}^* = S_i\eta_{tw} + \eta_{tp_i} \qquad (10.11)$$

The wealth effects in η_{tp_i} and η_{tw} are offsetting, however, so that $\eta_{tp_i}^*$ includes only substitution impacts of the changing relative values of w and p_i. If all prices were higher by 1 percent and thus the wage were higher by 1 percent, no substitution would result as relative input prices have not changed. This is true even though the level of amenities, other inputs, have remained the same.

The effect of a 1-percent increase in A_i is made of similar components with

$$\eta_{tA_i}^* = \frac{U_{A_i}A_i}{\lambda I}\eta_{tw} + \eta_{tA_i} \qquad (10.12)$$

where $U_{A_i}A_i/\lambda I$ is the nominal wage-change resulting from the increase in A_i from equation 10.9. If amenities are, in general, complementary with time inputs in production (for example, sunbathing requires time to enjoy the sun), it is likely that η_{tA_i} is negative. Furher, if the reduced wage leads to net shifts out of use of market goods toward own-time goods (leisure or do-it-yourself), increases in amenities are likely to lead to fewer hours worked. To the extent that demand for such commodities are market-good intensive (such as boating is) hours worked could tend to increase.

An increase in utility in the rest of the economy by 1 percent leads to an increase in t by $U/\lambda I\ \eta_{tw}$ which is likely to be positive as the income elasticity of demand for nonworking time is likely to be higher than that for working time. As suggested by Becker, increased productivity of workers over time is likely to have reduced the hours worked.

The results presented above illustrate that effects on hours worked or differences between regions or changes over time in amenities or market good prices are not clearly signed a priori. Still, these impacts may be of sufficient magnitude to alter the quantity of labor services an individual will supply in a region. Although a reduction in a p_i or an increase in an A_i leads to a reduced wage at which labor is supplied and thus an increased quantity of labor demanded in a region, this does not necessarily mean that more labor would flow into the region if the impact of these also leads to a sufficient increase in t_w. An extreme example is that where the wage elasticity of labor demand in a region is very inelastic and not shifted by a particular A_i, which is a complement with market goods used in household production. A reduction in the A_i lowers the wage and leads to increases in t_w. The existing residents in the region may be willing to supply much of the small increase in quantity of labor services demanded because of the lower wage. A result would be less in-migration that would otherwise occur.

Regional Wage and Earnings Differentials. The impact on regional-earning differentials of amenity and market-good-price differences between regions depend on the combined impacts of these factors on the hourly wage and time spent in the labor market. These may be offsetting or augmenting influences and are likely to depend, in general, on whether it is an amenity or a market-good price difference and, in particular, on the specific amenity or market-good price involved. In the extreme, wage differentials may be offset by the associated hours-worked adjustments, so that earnings differentials are opposite in sign to their wage counterpart. In any case, it is unlikely that regional-earning differentials will be as closely related to indexes of regional cost-of-living differences such as those prepared by the Bureau of Labor Statistics and employed by Henderson in examination of regional-earning differentials.

Effects on Market-Good Demands. Similar to impacts on time allocation, effects of changes in elements of p and A induce only substitution impacts on the quantity of market goods demanded. The *own-* and *cross-price* elasticities of demand are

$$\eta_{ii}^* = S_i\eta_{iw} + \eta_{ii} \tag{10.13a}$$

$$\eta_{ij}^* = S_j\eta_{iw} + \eta_{ij} \tag{10.13b}$$

These represent compensated elasticities of market-good demands with respect to prices except as the wage compensation alters the price of the time input. If all prices increase by 1 percent and if the wage increases by 1 percent as compensation, no substitution occurs. Only relative price variation between areas, all else the same, would cause shifts in the market-good and time-input mix. A 1-percent increase in A_i leads to a percent change in x_j of

$$\eta_{jAi}^* = \frac{A_i U_{A_i}}{\lambda I} \, \eta_{iw} \qquad (10.14)$$

which is analogous to the relationships, which are characterized by compensation through wage changes, in equation 10.13.

Although the focus of the current work is on the implications of mobility for analysis of regional-labor-supply characteristics, there are also implications for specification and estimation of demands for market goods and services. In particular, comparison among regions of these demands by individuals with the same levels of human capital applicable in labor-market activities, not necessarily the same market wage or earnings, would be most appropriately specified without a wage or earnings variable. The resulting price or amenity elasticities, moreover, would represent estimates of the compensated elasticities on the left-hand sides of equations 10.13 and 10.14.

The Regional Labor-Supply Relation

Population Homogeneity

The relationship for allocation of time and labor supply in a region derived in the previous section are for an individual constrained so as to maintain equality of utility in alternative locations. If all individuals were the same, the labor-supply wage for a region would be that in equation 10.10. For example, a percent difference in p_i between regions would result in an S_i percent difference in the wage at which labor would supply itself between regions. No rents in terms of wages higher than that required to maintain utility equality among alternative locations would exist. Hours worked would differ systematically between regions as the allocation of time is altered through substitution effects of market-good prices and amenity differences, but would be the same for each worker in a particular region. In this situation all individuals would be indifferent as to their location of residence and supply of labor.

The restrictive, but not necessarily inappropriate, assumption that the hourly wage does not depend on hours worked is consistent with the equally restrictive assumption that demanders of labor services are indifferent between the number of workers hired and the hours worked per individual so long as the product of these two are the same. At extremes of these combinations, this is unlikely to be an appropriate characterization of the tradeoffs involved. For intermediate cases, however, this serves as a useful approximation.[3] One result is that that total quantity of labor services supplied in a region is the product of the number of workers and their hours worked. To obtain the same quantity of labor services, regions would differ in the number of individuals employed as the hours worked per individual differs depending on price and amenity differences as illustrated by equations 10.11 and 10.12. A 1-percent increase in quantity of services demanded in a region, for given p and $\underline{A}$, however, would induce a 1-percent increase in number of individuals in the region.

Implications of Population Heterogeneity

Population heterogeneity, for example, in terms of the parameterization of equation 10.3, affects the analysis in such a way that regional equilibrium would not require $U = \tilde{U}$ for all persons in all regions. Equilibrium would still require some individuals to be indifferent between at least two regions in a very diversified regional economy if this heterogeneity were characterized as a smooth, continuous distribution of parameter variation in equation 10.3. These marginal persons would, however, still determine the patterns of regional wage differentials as in equation 10.10. All individuals who did locate in a region would face the wage set by the behavior of these workers. For intermarginal individuals, the wage they receive in the region is greater than that which would be necessary to induce them to locate in the region. This does not mean, however, that their allocations of time and thus earnings would be the same. No systematic relationship between price and amenity differences between regions and hours worked by all individuals in a particular region need exist. Hours spent in labor-market activity may be lower or higher than those of workers on the margin.

  Identification of the characteristics of marginal workers is an issue in itself and a full treatment is beyond the scope of this analysis. An important consideration in this regard, however, is that the characteristics of regional demand for labor might play a major role. The set of individuals who would locate in a region may be ordered by that wage needed to equate equality of utility between location in the region and elsewhere. The equilibrium wage and number of laborers in the region would be determined by finding that marginal worker for whom the quantity of labor services demanded (at the marginal worker's wage) is equal to the total quantity of labor services supplied by him and those ordered above him. For even a small region, if it has amenity- and market-good-price characteristics very different from those available elsewhere, even slight changes in demand for labor in the region may cause not inconsequential changes in the wage, number of persons locating in the region, and their identity. Roy provides an example in a different context that illustrates the potential large magnitudes involved. For current purposes, the characteristics of the marginal worker are taken as given, avoiding such complications.

The approach taken here is to consider heterogeneity in workers as a result of individual specific differences in the production coefficients in equation 10.2 and/or variation in the values that may be attached to allocation of time in alternative uses. An example of the former is the role of formal education in altering the productivity of time spent in production of the Z_i. An example of the latter is the role of romal education in altering the labor-market wage. In addition, grouping of people of varying characteristics in a household means that effects of differences in individual-worker characteristics are not alone responsible for variation in time allocations. Other household-member characteristics also need to be taken into account.

The influences of heterogeneity may include preferences by some households for location in some regions rather than others as well as differences in the hourly wage or hours worked by individuals in a region. The same factors that might lead to variation in the market-wage and hours-worked behavior of individuals who choose to locate in a particular region, moreover, may also cause for differences among people in their location preferences.

In many cases, however, incentives based on regional differences in amenity and market-good prices are counteracted by the associated wage adjustment dictated by marginal workers. As an example, consider two regions differeing in amenity levels but having the same market-good prices and wage differentials determined by the relationship in equation 10.10 by marginal workers. A household with many members, say one adult who participates in the labor market and 10 children, would value the services of the amenities by more than a one-adult-only household because household value of amenity consumption is the sum of all individual-household-member valuations. All else the same, large-member households would gain relatively more by locating in a high-amenity area. On the other hand, the quantity of market goods demanded, which is the sum of all household member's quantities demanded, may be 1000 percent higher for this many-person household at equal per-capita income levels. The low relative wage in the high-amenity region makes it more difficult to obtain the income required to purchase these market goods. At the region wage, the workers in the ten-member household would have to have ten times the income of the single-member household were each member could consume market goods and services at the same rate. The tradeoff for a many-person household relative to a few-person household in this case is that the increased household utility associated with consumption of amenities in the high-amenity area is offset by a much-reduced capability to purchase market goods and services. If the large household did locate in the high-amenity region, it is expected, however, that more hours would be supplied in the labor market, possibly by multiple-household-member labor-force participation.

Consider alternatively, two regions that differ in market-good prices but not amenities with corresponding wage differentials set by some marginal workers. Regardless of where the large household locates, the same hours worked would result in the same ability to purchase the same quantities of market goods and services as well as the same amount of amenity services. No tradeoffs as in the previous example occurs, and no strong implications for hours worked under alternative-location assumptions arise.

The above discussion suggests that the role of population heterogeneity in providing incentives for location in particular regions is likely to be very closely associated with the resulting allocation of time-to-labor market activities. The impact of regional differences in amenity- or market-good-price characteristics on these location and/or allocation decisions will depend, moreover, on the type of regional difference involved. In a situation where many types of households are found to be located in a particular region, systematic influences of amenity- and market-good-price character-istics on allocation decisions described earlier are likely to be accompanied by possibly substantial household-specific differences.

A prominent sort of population heterogeneity is that associated with differences in the labor-market wage within a region. One cause may be differences between the level of skills that are valued in the market place, in which case wage variation within a region corresponds to wage differences. In a situation where the income elasticity of demand for all goods and services as well as amenities were unity, and people possessed only one type of skill, the same relative regional-wage differential would apply to all workers regardless of the amount of the skill they possessed.

Real-income effects on valuation of amenities or demands for market goods and services could cause regional sorting of people, however, even if all individuals had only one type of skill. If amenities were superior goods, high-skill individuals would tend to locate in high-amenity areas and low-skill individuals would tend to locate in low-amenity areas. In this case, the regional differential in returns to a unit of skill services would depend on the skill level of marginal workers. This would, in part, be determined by other factors that affect the regional distribution of demand for labor-skill services. Very high-skill workers and very low-skill workers would receive wages in excess of those needed to locate in their respective areas.[4]

In general, more than one type of skill is used in production, and people differ both with respect to type of skill possessed as well as quantities of each skill. Many types of workers who differ in quantity and type of skill might be found in a region. Wage variation within a region would reflect labor-market returns to different types of skill as well as differences in the quantities of each skill possessed by individuals. Substitutibility and complementarity of skill types in production may result in workers of any skill level receiving higher wages than those required to locate in the high-amenity region. Further, relative regional-wage differentials that are set by persons indifferent between alternative locations may differ by type of skill involved.

Heterogeneity in worker-skill attributes and/or diversity in household characteristics are likely to lead to a systematic choosing between regions of residence location for much of the population. Each household would still make comparisons between alternative locations as examined earlier, but its labor-supply characteristics may differ from those of marginal workers who determine regional-wage differentials. Below, the model developed earlier is integrated with population heterogeneity with the aim being toward measurement of regional wage, hours worked, and earnings differences.

Toward Empirical Analysis

Let the stock of human capital of the ith individual applicable in provision of labor-market services be Y_i. Such things as education and previous labor-market experience are likely to figure prominently in the determination of Y_i. The supply of labor-market service flowing from Y_i at any point in time is denoted as y_i. Transformation of Y_i into its flow-counterpart y_i depends on the intensity of utilization of the stock of applicable skills. Let α_i represent the percent of Y_i utilized per unit of time spent in the labor market. This does not mean that utilization of Y_i causes depreciation of the stock of skills, though for extremely high values of α_i this may be the case. The situation considered here does not explicitly treat Y_i as a depreciable asset through its utilization. The skill-service flow supplied by the ith individual per unit of time is thus $y_i = \alpha_i Y_i$.

In a particular labor market, w is the price per unit of skill services per hour, set by the marginal worker to the region as in equation 10.10. The labor-market wage for the ith individual in that labor market is

$$W_i = w\alpha_i Y_i \qquad (10.15)$$

The value of w is taken parametric to the individual and determined by aggregate labor-skill demand and supply conditions in the market. Under this restriction, wage differences in the labor market are determined solely by variation of the α_i or Y_i among individuals.

At this point, no attempt is made to define y_i by type of skill. An alternative approach would be to consider Y_{ij} the stock of human capital applicable in the jth labor-market task and α_{ij} the utilization of the jth stock. One restrictive but useful assumption would be that

$$\alpha_{ij} = 0 \qquad \text{for all but one } j.$$

Choice of type of skill supplied to the labor market could then be based on comparison of $w_j \alpha_{ij} Y_{ij}$ where w_j is the price per unit of skill services in the jth labor-market task. The individual might then choose that j for which W_{ij} is maximized. That limitation on the magnitude of wage differentials between individuals which is due to choice among alternative occupations as described above is that if substantial earnings differentials occurred between occupations, people would have incentives to gain the skills that yield relatively high returns. Although the costs of obtaining different skills may not be the same, the differential in market returns to these skills is limited by worker choice in investment in alternative forms of human capital. As a result, useful application of the specification in equation 10.15, which does not include differences in skill types, is not likely to be greatly hindered by such qualifications.

The quantity of hours spent in labor-market activity depends on returns in this activity, W_i, as well as on factors altering the value of an hour spent in nonlabor-market activities (the t_i in equation 10.2). As an example, the value of t_i is likely to be small relative to W_i for individuals with high Y_i in households where other members have low Y_i relative to their household-production human capital. This would lead to substitution toward time spent in labor-market activity of the individual with high Y_i. Let labor-market hours supplied by this individual be

$$H_i = H(W_i, C_i) \qquad (10.16)$$

where C_i represents shifts in the hours-worked relation for an individual due to household status.

Some factors affecting α_i and C_i are not likely to be distinct. Labor-market earnings, for example, could be increased by an increase in α_i or hours worked. Some conditions may cause one or both to change with the resulting changes in W_i and H_i depending on the magnitudes involved. A 10-percent increase in income, for example, could be induced by an increase in α_i of 10 percent or an increase in H_i of 10 percent. The former would be chosen to a greater extent than would the latter if the factor that caused the 10-percent increase in income also increased the value of time spent in household production.

For each individual facing a common w, log wage, and log hours-worked relations resulting from the specifications in equations 10.15 and 10.16 are

$$\ln W_i = \ln w + \ln \alpha_i + \ln Y_i \qquad (10.17)$$

$$\ln H_i = \xi_w[\ln w + \ln \alpha_i + \ln Y_i] + \xi_c \ln C_i \qquad (10.18)$$

when ξ_w and ξ_c are the partial derivatives of H with respect to W_i and C_i. A sample of individuals in this labor market, where w is assumed constant, could be used to estimate the parameters of equations 10.17 and 10.18, even though no variation in w exists. The presence of labor unions could throw light on effects of variation in w in a particular area, although labor-union status could also structually alter the higher-wage impact on H_i through accompanying restrictions on hours worked.

The specifications in equations 10.17 and 10.18 are for an individual supplying labor in a particular region where p and A are given. Variation in W among individuals facing common $\underline{p}$ and $\underline{A}$ represents a real-wage effect, possibly leading to hours-worked responses. Variation in w between regions facing different p and $\underline{A}$, however, need not represent a real-wage effect, since this is partially compensation set by the marginal individuals' region-labor-supply response. The assumption maintained here is that nominal regional-wage differentials are compensations for amenity- and market-good-price differences. Differences between regions in w thus do not represent real-wage impacts on hours worked in equation 10.18. Rather, based on the result in equation 10.10, at any point in time

$$\ln w - \Sigma k_i \ln p_i + \Sigma k_{A_i} A_i \qquad (10.19)$$

is the appropriate real-wage term to be used instead of $\ln w$ in equation 10.18. This expression more adequately reflects potential effects of returns to labor-market activity on time spent in the labor market. For all individuals in a region, this takes on the same value. In equilibrium, for individuals in different regions, this term will also be the same because that higher value of $\ln w$ in one region relative to another which results from either higher prices or lower amenity levels is exactly offset by the second two sets of terms in equation 10.19. In disequilibrium, however, this term could differ between regions, resulting in a systematic regional difference on hours worked.

Regional differences in $\ln w$ affect $\ln W_i$ in equation 10.17 directly and influence $\ln H_i$ indirectly through substitution of the expression in equation 10.19 for $\ln w$ in equation 10.18. These represent the effects on the nominal hourly wage and hours worked of an individual through compensation for price and amenity differences on the nominal value of the price per unit of skill services. In addition, these same differences may alter the α_i or C_i terms in equations 10.17 and 10.18. As discussed earlier, these would represent substitution or complementarity effects of $\underline{x}$ and $\underline{A}$ with time spent in the labor market or intensity of work. Region-specific shifts in the nominal-wage or hours-worked specifications would result. Building on this framework, the next part specifies and estimates an econometric model of the regional-labor-supply relation.

Empirical Results

The empirical analysis presented here is based on a sample of 1,831-male-headed households from the Michigan Survey on Income Dynamics. The sample was chosen on the basis of the presence of observations for hourly wage, yearly-hours worked, and yearly-earnings data for the household head in 1976, 1977, and 1978. The variables used in the analysis are defined in table 10-1, where summary sample statistics over the three years is presented. The variables *EDUCATION* and *DEGREE* are intended to reflect the formal education characteristics of the household head. Following along the lines of Mincer, the head's age and years of experience at the present job are intended to capture life-cycle as well as on-the-job training aspects of the household head. In the empirical analysis which follows, both of these variables are included in a quadratic fashion. *UNION* reflects whether or not the head is in a labor union, which, in turn, reflects either a higher real hourly wage or skills associated with acceptance in a union. *VETERAN* reflects either differential hiring policies afforded veterans or their systematic skill variation. *MARITAL* reflects the impact of household status on labor-supply responses. *RACE* is included here only to capture the systematic influence of racial status on labor-market participation patterns and wages.

All of the above variables are intended to capture household-head differences in the α_i, Y_i, or C_i components of hourly-wage and hours-worked determination. No *a priori* exclusion of any of the variables from affecting any of these components is imposed.

Location status is broken down into four broad regions in the United States—Central, East, South, and West—and within these categories, urban- and rural-location differences. These broad classifications are only meant to be suggestive and admittedly do not capture the potentially substantial variation in amenity- or market-good-price characteristics included within these geographic boundaries. One approach would be to include measures of amenities and prices of market goods explicitly into the analysis, even for the broad geographic units used here. This would allow for decomposition of amenity and price effects on labor-supply characteristics. A shortcoming of this approach is that there are likely to be many amenities that figure prominently in altering the wage and hours-worked relationships, possibly in complicated ways. Even after control for many of these effects, location-dummy variables might still be needed. An additional shortcoming is that

Table 10–1
Variable Definitions and Sample Means (1976 through 1978)

Variable	Definition	Sample Mean
EDUCATION	Number of years of schooling	11.94
DEGREE	College degree = 1	0.17
AGE	Age of household head	38.2
YEARS	Number of years worked full time	15.8
HOURS	Annual hours of work	2136.7
MARITAL	Married = 1	0.74
UNION	Belong to labor union = 1	−0.30
RACE	White = 1	0.32
VETERAN	Veteran = 1	0.41
RURNE	Lived in rural northeast in 1977	0.009
URBCEN	Lived in urban central in 1977	0.203
RURCEN	Lived in rural central in 1977	0.048
URBSTH	Lived in urban south in 1977	0.298
RURSTH	Lived in rural south in 1977	0.131
URBWST	Lived in urban west in 1977	0.136
RURWST	Lived in rural west in 1977	0.024

even if market-good-price data were available by these geographic units, the effect of, for example, variation in energy prices would depend on the levels of other prices and amenities as the associated shares of energy expenditures differ. This would mean that the effect of the regional price of energy on the wage, for example, would itself be region-specific.[5] The approach taken here is to use location-dummy variables alone, sacrificing information regarding specific amenity or price effects, but avoiding misspecification of the manner in which regional differences occur.

The data on the hourly wage are for the household head's primary occupation. The data for hours worked, however, include hours spent in all types of labor-market activities. As indicated by the average of yearly-hours worked in table 10-1, a substantial portion of the sample participated in the labor market over an average of 40 hours per week (2,080 hours per year). This may reflect overtime in the primary occupation or second jobs. If this were not the case, yearly earnings would be the product of W_i and H_i, $E_i = W_i H_i$. Assuming all individuals with $H_i > 2080$ worked full time in their main occupation, yearly earnings would be

$$E_i = \begin{cases} W_i H_i & \text{for } H_i \leq 2080 \\ W_i(2080) + 1.5 W_i(H_i - 2080) & \text{for overtime workers} \\ W_i(2080) + g(W_i)(H_i - 2080) & \text{for multiple-job holders} \end{cases} \quad (10.20)$$

where $g(W_i)$ represents the relationship between the wage earned in the primary occupation and that in the other labor-market activities. For hours worked greater than full-time employment in the primary occupation, overtime pay is assumed equal to one and one-half times the regular wage. If the excess time spent in the labor market is on another job, $g(W_i)$ is intended to capture any systematic relation between the human capital of the individual and/or intensity of work in the primary occupation on the wage received in the second job. A likely case is that $g(W_i) < W_i$ where perhaps a standardized work week in many places of employment becomes a restriction on the desired hours of work that the individual would be willing to supply in that occupation.

The specification in equation 10.20 illustrates that a simple relationship between W_i, H_i, and E_i is not realistic if the manner in which hours worked in excess of 2,080 hours is not observed. The decisions to work overtime or hold more than one job are partly choice variables themselves, however, just as are decisions to supply less than 2,080 hours to labor-market activity. Even though E_i may be either understated by the product of W_i and H_i for individuals working overtime or overstated by the same measure for individuals with jobs in addition to their primary occupation, its relation to the same variables that affect W_i and H_i may be empirically examined. In particular, the same variables as those in table 10-1 may be used to analyze yearly earnings together with W_i and H_i.

Estimation Approach

Let the value of the set of independent variables in table 10-1 for each individual in year t be denoted by the vector v_{it}. The estimated relation for W_{it}, H_{it}, and E_{it} are

$$W_{it} = \alpha'_t v_{it} + \varepsilon_{it}$$

$$H_{it} = \beta'_t v_{it} + \mu_{it}$$

$$E_{it} = \delta'_t v_{it} + \gamma_{it} \qquad (10.21)$$

where the α_t, β_t, and δ_t are vectors of parameters that measure effects of elements of v_{it} on the hourly wage, hours worked, and yearly earnings, and the ε_{it}, μ_{it}, and γ_{it} are error terms. The error terms are made up of an individual specific component—ε_i, μ_i, and γ_i—and a transitory component—v_{it}^ε, v_{it}^μ, and v_{it}^γ—with

$$\varepsilon_{it} = \varepsilon_i + v_{it}^\varepsilon$$

$$\mu_{it} = \mu_i + v_{it}^\mu$$

$$\gamma_{it} = \gamma_i + v_{it}^\gamma \qquad (10.22)$$

where the ν_{it} terms are serially independent variables with zero mean and variances σ_ε^2, σ_μ^2, and σ_γ^2 and independent of the ε_i, μ_i, and γ_i terms, which are random variables with zero means and variances ρ_ε^2, ρ_μ^2, and ρ_γ^2. The presence of the individual-specific, unobserved components in equation 10.22 allows for individuals that are homogeneous in their measured attributes to be heterogeneous in their labor-market wage, hours worked, or yearly earnings. This represents a systematic influence on an individual's labor-supply characteristics that persists over time. The correlation coefficient between the ε_{it} in any two years, for example, is $\tau = \rho_\varepsilon^2/(\rho_\varepsilon^2 + \sigma_\varepsilon^2)$. Contemporaneous correlation between, for example, ε_{it} and μ_{it} represents the correlation between unobserved factors affecting both the individual's wage and hours worked.

Empirical Findings

Estimation of the parameters in equation 10.21 were obtained taking into account the error-component structures in equation 10.22 through joint estimation of all relationships in equation 10.21. Table 10-2 presents the estimated correlation matrix[6] of the ε_{it}, μ_{it}, and λ_{it}. The highest values are for the ε_{it} and λ_{it} between years. The results indicate that the substantial presence of individual-specific, unobserved characteristics influence both hourly wage and yearly earnings and that these are positively correlated. The results for μ_{it} suggest a relatively smaller, yet positive correlation over time. The μ_{it} and ε_{it} appear uncorrelated, while the μ_{it} and λ_{it} show positive correlation. These results suggest that those unobserved factors influencing earnings come about because of factors influencing the wage or hours worked. For all significant correlations in table 10-2, there is a tendency for the same-, or contiguous-year values to be higher than those between 1976 and 1978. This is suggestive of a declining relationship between the individual specific components in equation 10.22 as time span increases.

The parameter estimates of the α_t, β_t, and γ_t in equation 10.21 are presented separately in tables 10-3, 10-4, and 10-5. Effects of rural/urban location status differences are jointly significant for all wage, hours, and earnings specifications taken together at the 99-percent confidence level. They are significant at the 99-percent confidence level for each of the wage and earnings specifications taken separately and significant at the 90-percent confidence level for hours taken alone. Estimates for the other parameters were not sensitive to the exclusion of these region/urban status variables, however. An implication is that the individual-specific characteristics that are modeled to figure prominently in explanation of labor-market behavior are not systematically correlated with region/urban location status. Heterogeneity in the population that might cause for such a spatial sorting, discussed earlier, is thus not indicated by these results. Below, the parameter estimates are briefly discussed and their implications analyzed.

Table 10-2
Estimated Correlation Matrix of the ε_{it}, μ_{it}, and γ_{it}

	LWAGE 76	LWAGE 77	LWAGE 78	LHOURS 76	LHOURS 77	LHOURS 78	LEARN 76	LEARN 77	LEARN 78
LWAGE 76	1.00	.78	.66	.004	.006	-.002	.66	.61	.50
LWAGE 77		1.00	.72	-.008	.032	-.009	.65	.68	.52
LWAGE 78			1.00	.027	.076	-.009	.63	.72	.57
LHOURS 76				1.00	.46	.30	.35	.20	.12
LHOURS 77					1.00	.42	.20	.36	.19
LHOURS 78						1.00	.11	.17	.34
LEARN 76							1.00	.76	.60
LEARN 77								1.00	.67
LEARN 78									1.00

Table 10–3
Hourly Wage Profile Estimates

Independent Variable	Dependent Variable		
	LWAGE 76	LWAGE 77	LWAGE 78
INTERCEPT	4.81	4.93	5.13
	(30.08)	(31.34)	(24.55)
EDUCATION	0.050	0.050	0.056
	(14.09)	(14.86)	(13.21)
DEGREE	0.076	0.071	0.126
	(2.77)	(2.74)	(3.88)
AGE	0.0283	0.0282	0.0146
	(2.96)	(3.08)	(1.24)
AGE^2	−0.00036	−0.00036	−0.00020
	(3.13)	(3.34)	(1.45)
EXP	0.0200	0.0146	0.0243
	(3.86)	(3.02)	(3.96)
EXP^2	−0.00025	−0.00016	−0.00034
	(2.20)	(1.52)	(2.58)
UNION	0.068	0.086	0.026
	(5.72)	(8.01)	(1.83)
VETERAN	0.021	0.021	0.020
	(1.67)	(2.07)	(1.97)
MARITAL	0.023	0.018	0.019
	(1.25)	(1.11)	(0.92)
RACE	0.158	0.163	0.191
	(8.78)	(9.55)	(8.85)
URBCEN	0.052	0.042	0.044
	(2.22)	(1.89)	(1.59)
URBSTH	−0.070	−0.070	−0.064
	(3.06)	(3.27)	(2.33)
URBWST	0.034	0.064	0.070
	(1.31)	(2.60)	(2.25)
RURNE	−0.037	−0.014	0.075
	(0.58)	(0.24)	(1.03)
RURCEN	−0.090	−0.083	−0.144
	(2.74)	(2.69)	(3.65)
RURSTH	−0.176	−0.147	−0.167
	(6.77)	(6.01)	(5.35)
RURWST	−0.030	0.006	−0.029
	(0.71)	(0.16)	(0.57)

Note: *t* statistics in parentheses.

Nonlocation Variables

Wage Profiles. Effects on the hourly wage of *EDUCATION* and *DEGREE* are positive and precisely estimated. The magnitude of the former is consistently smaller than that of the latter over the three-year period: an increase in years of education increases the hourly wage by approximately 5 percent and a college degree increases the wage by over 7 percent. The rather

Table 10–4
Hours Worked Profile Estimates

Independent Variable	Dependent Variable		
	LHOURS 76	*LHOURS 77*	*LHOURS 78*
INTERCEPT	7.56	7.35	7.32
	(54.62)	(55.23)	(43.69)
EDUCATION	0.0079	0.0049	0.0012
	(2.73)	(1.82)	(0.38)
DEGREE	0.002	0.026	0.039
	(0.08)	(1.25)	(1.58)
AGE	−0.0049	−0.0080	−0.0038
	(0.59)	(1.03)	(0.04)
AGE^2	−0.00002	−0.00021	−0.00005
	(0.23)	(2.24)	(0.47)
EXP	0.0086	−0.0007	0.0022
	(1.94)	(0.17)	(0.46)
EXP^2	−0.00007	0.00017	0.00004
	(0.77)	(2.00)	(0.34)
UNION	−0.057	−0.057	−0.038
	(4.52)	(4.98)	(2.72)
VETERAN	0.087	0.156	0.199
	(6.78)	(14.93)	(20.53)
MARITAL	0.070	0.005	0.045
	(3.70)	(0.29)	(2.17)
RACE	0.013	0.008	0.004
	(0.87)	(0.56)	(0.21)
URBCEN	0.40	0.009	0.003
	(2.00)	(0.47)	(0.15)
URBSTH	0.025	0.037	0.035
	(1.25)	(2.03)	(1.57)
URBWST	0.008	−0.005	−0.007
	(0.34)	(0.24)	(0.28)
RURNE	0.082	0.110	0.106
	(1.30)	(1.95)	(1.57)
RURCEN	0.011	0.024	0.008
	(0.38)	(0.89)	(0.24)
RURSTH	0.025	−0.009	0.029
	(1.09)	(0.43)	(1.18)
RURWST	0.117	0.037	0.015
	(2.96)	(1.02)	(0.35)

Note: t statistics in parentheses.

substantial impact of a college degree is consistent with its role as a signal to employers of an individual's capabilities, a real human capital effect, or a sorting effect where higher-skill persons are more likely to obtain a college degree.

The effect of an increase in *AGE* on the wage is characterized by a positive, but diminishing, impact until *AGE* is between 35 and 40, when it yields negative effect. A similar qualitative relation characterizes increases in experience, although the peak cumulative impact on the wage is sensitive to

Table 10–5
Yearly Earning Profile Estimates

	Dependent Variable		
Independent Variable	LEARN 76	LEARN 77	LEARN 78
INTERCEPT	7.85	7.95	7.62
	(35.56)	(37.10)	(28.18)
EDUCATION	0.063	0.062	0.063
	(12.88)	(13.06)	(11.61)
DEGREE	0.121	0.106	0.101
	(3.21)	(3.02)	(2.44)
AGE	0.0127	0.0136	0.0230
	(0.97)	(1.09)	(1.51)
AGE^2	−0.00022	−0.00025	−0.00036
	(1.40)	(1.66)	(2.02)
EXP	0.0352	0.0277	0.0192
	(4.94)	(4.19)	(2.42)
EXP^2	−0.00048	−0.00035	−0.00020
	(3.11)	(2.41)	(1.18)
UNION	0.074	0.062	0.075
	(4.48)	(4.23)	(3.76)
VETERAN	0.104	0.143	0.205
	(6.01)	(10.41)	(14.63)
MARITAL	0.123	0.074	0.073
	(4.88)	(3.37)	(2.47)
RACE	0.175	0.171	0.178
	(7.05)	(7.39)	(6.48)
URBCEN	0.077	0.058	0.053
	(2.40)	(1.93)	(1.46)
URBSTH	−0.057	−0.045	−0.040
	(1.80)	(1.53)	(1.11)
URBWST	0.042	0.040	0.051
	(1.17)	(1.17)	(1.26)
RURNE	0.021	0.043	0.080
	(0.24)	(0.08)	(0.80)
RURCEN	−0.149	−0.152	−0.168
	(3.29)	(3.63)	(3.24)
RURSTH	−0.157	−0.184	−0.127
	(4.39)	(5.53)	(3.10)
RURWST	−0.002	−0.036	0.013
	(0.03)	(0.64)	(0.20)

Note: t statistics in parentheses.

the year estimates used. The results suggest that this peak to be between 35 and 45 years of experience. For most workers, this point is reached late in the life cycle, if at all.

The impact of union membership is positive, relatively large in magnitude and precisely estimated for 1976 and 1977 and less so for 1978, and are consistent with the estimates in Lazaer. These results do not necessarily indicate that union membership is associated with a higher value of w as persons choosing union-membership status may also have higher levels of Y_i

Table 10–6
Regional Wages, Hours Worked, and Earnings Differentials

	Urban/Rural Status[a]					
	Urban			Rural		
Region	Wage	Hours	Earnings[b]	Wage	Hours	Earnings
Central	5	1	6 (6)	−9	−10	−19 (−19)
South	−7	3	−5 (−4)	−15	−9	−20 (−24)
West	6	0	4 (6)	2	−11	−6 (−9)

[a]Percent differences from location in the Northeast.
[b]The numbers in parentheses for earnings differentials are the differentials implied by the individual wage and hours-worked differentials.

or α_i not controlled by the other variables in table 10-1. The effect of veteran status is positive and consistent in magnitude across all three years but not very precisely estimated in any year. Similar to the results for *UNION*, veteran status may reflect a selectivity of higher-skill persons in the process of obtaining acceptance into a military position. Health standards and even minimal reading skills required for induction into military service serve as examples. Recent work by De Tray finds support for the screening role of veteran status. The results indicate that being a veteran increases the wage by approximately 2 percent. A similar value is associated with being married, although the estimates have low precision. Racial status impacts are very precisely estimated. The results indicate that white racial status is associated with a wage higher by between 15 and 20 percent.

Hours Worked. In general, effects of the impacts on hours worked are less precisely estimated than are those for the wage. The effect of an increase in years of education is estimated to be positive but less than 1 percent for an additional year of schooling. The impact of a college degree is very small in

Table 10–7
Urban-Rural Wages, Hours Worked, and Earnings Differentials

	Category Differentials[a]		
Region	Wage	Hours	Earnings[b]
Northeast	02	−11	−4 (−9)
Central	16	00	21 (11)
South	10	01	11 (11)
West	06	00	06 (06)

[a]In percent differences between location in an urban versus rural area.
[b]The numbers in parentheses for earnings differentials are the differentials implied by the sum of the individual wage and hours worked differentials.

1976 but very unprecisely estimated. The precision increases for 1977 and 1978 and the results suggest a positive impact of between 2 and 4 percent on hours worked.

The quadratic specification for age does not yield precise estimates for the influence of age on hours worked. In all years, however, it suggests that hours worked decline with age. An increase in age from 40 to 41 years, for example, is predicted to result in a decline in hours worked by between 0.6 and 0.9 percent. A similar imprecision is associated with the estimated impact of years of experience. For reasonable values of *EXP*, however, an additional year of experience leads to an increase in hours worked. For example, an increase in years of experience from 20 to 21 years results in an increase in hours worked by between 0.4 and 0.6 percent.

Union membership leads to a precisely estimated decline in hours worked by approximately 5 percent. Veteran status, on the other hand, leads to rather substantial increases in hours worked. The point-estimates in Table 10-3 indicate this effect to be between 9 and 20 percent. Marital status leads to an increase in hours worked. The relatively more precise estimates for 1976 and 1977 suggest that this to be between 4 and 8 percent. The effects of RACE are very small and not significant in any year, suggesting no influence of race on hours worked.

Yearly Earnings. An increase in education by one year and the attainment of a college degree are estimated to increase yearly earnings by approximately 6 percent and over 10 percent. These estimates compare roughly to the sum of the effects of these variables on the wage and hours worked. Age- and experience-earning profiles are characterized at first by increasing functions, which level off at approximately age 30 and 40 years of experience. These are consistent with the age- and experience-wage profiles and the negative effect of age on hours worked and the small positive impact of years of experience on hours worked.

The magnitude of the union effect is approximately the same as that for its effect on wage. The associated negative and relatively substantial impact on hours worked suggests that union members' hours restrictions in outside work are offset by the gains in overtime-wage payments. Veteran status increases earnings by between 10 and 20 percent. The results in tables 10-3 and 10-4 suggest this is mainly due to increased hours worked. Marital status increases earnings by between 7 and 12 percent. Higher wages are in part responsible for this, but the effect of the increase in hours worked is of larger magnitude in explaining this increase. Racial status earnings differentials, on the other hand, appear due to wage differentials and not due to systematic differences in hours worked.

Location Influences. Based on the point-estimates of equation 10.2 under the constraint that all rural/urban and regional differentials are equal over the three-year period, table 10-6 shows the estimated percent differences by region for both urban and rural residences.[7] For individuals in urban locations, nominal wages are highest in the West and lowest in the South. On the other hand, hours worked are greatest in the South and lowest in the West and East. Yearly earnings are highest in the Central region and lowest in the South. The divergence between predictions for earnings based on the point-estimates for wages and hours worked in tables 10-3 and 10-4 and those for actual yearly earnings is not substantial. For residents in rural areas, wages are lowest in the South and highest in the West. Hours worked are lower in the Central, South, and West regions by approximately 10 percent compared to that for the Northeast. Yearly earnings are highest in the Northeast and lowest in the South and Central regions. Again, earnings differentials based on the point estimates for wages and hours worked in tables 10-3 and 10-4 show no substantial divergence from those based on the actual earnings results in table 10-5.

The results in table 10-6 suggest often substantial regional differentials, in wages, hours worked, and yearly earnings. These differences, however, show dissimilarities depending on urban/rural status. This distinction appears most noticeable for locations in the Central region, where earnings are highest for residents in urban areas and very close to lowest for rural residents compared to their regional counterparts. Similarly, hours worked are greatest in the urban South and very close to lowest in the rural South compared to their regional counterparts. On the other hand, wages are lowest in the South, regardless of urban/rural status compared to their regional counterparts.

Table 10-7 shows urban/rural differentials in wages, hours worked, and yearly earnings by region. The wage differential is highest in the Central region and lowest in the Northeast. Hours worked differentials are very small for residences of the Central, South, and West regions, while substantially large in magnitude and negative in the Northeast. Earnings differentials due to urban/rural status show consistent ordering by region regardless of point estimates used. They are highest in the Central region (dominated by the wage differential) and lowest (negative) in the Northeast, apparently dominated by the hours-worked differential.

Implications for Regional Labor Supplies. Regional differences in real-wage inducements to the quantity of time spent in labor-market activity are most appropriately based on nominal wage differences after compensation for market-good price or amenity differences between regions. The specification in equation 10.18 together with that in equation 10.19 suggests that nominal-wage differentials alone are not sufficient for such an analysis. If nominal-wage differentials themselves did indeed reflect real-wage differentials in a straightforward manner, it is likely that in areas where nominal wages are high, individuals would spend more time in labor-market activity, reaping the rewards (possibly only temporarily until migration-flows brought back equality of utility among alternative locations) in terms of higher real wages.[8]

The results in table 10-6 do not support such a notion on a regional basis.[9] While urban and rural wages are highest in the West, the hours worked are lowest. Similarly, urban and rural wages are lowest in the South, yet hours worked in urban areas in the South are greatest. This does not mean that regional disequilibrium is not present and that the wage and hours-worked differentials are solely due to regional differences in amenities or market-good prices. Disequilibrium could also be associated with excess labor supply in some regions which would otherwise be high-nominal-wage areas, and with excess demand in other regions which, in equilibrium, would be low-nominal-wage areas. If interpreted in this way, the results in table 10-6 suggest excess labor demand a likely characterization of the urban South.

With respect to labor-market disequilibrium, within region urban/rural wage and hours-worked differentials can be viewed in a similar fashion as the interregional differentials described above. In many cases, moreover, some amenity levels may be the same between urban and rural areas in the same region, lessening the role of amenity influences on relative wage or hours-worked differentials. Climatic conditions serve as a useful example. The results in table 10-7 might then be suggestive of the substantial decline of urban areas relative to rural areas in the Northeast and the possible growth of urban areas relative to rural areas in the South.

Comparison of interregional or urban/rural wage, hours-worked, or earnings differentials for the purpose of analysis of potential labor-market disequilibrium, however, can only be suggestive. Especially on a region wide basis, amenity differentials may very well serve as the reason for the wage or hours-worked differences implied by the empirical results. To distinguish between these two potentially offsetting influences, analysis of people's behavior by a more refined geographic unit over a longer time horizon is required.

Summary and Conclusions

A conceptual framework is developed that explicitly incorporates decisions about where to supply labor, the labor-supply wage, and the time to be spent in the labor market. Regional wage variation for workers of the same skill is a result of compensation required to induce workers into a region because of market-good-price and amenity differences between regions. At the same time, systematic regional differences in hours worked may result in response to these same price or amenity differences. A result is that regional wage and earnings differentials may not be of the same magnitude or sign.

Heterogeneity between people may lead to the situation where in regional labor-market equilibrium many people are better off locating and working in one region relative to another. Under reasonable assumptions, all workers with the same labor-market skills located in a region will face a common wage. Conditional upon this wage, population heterogeneity may lead to substantial variation within the region in their hours worked.

The empirical results strongly support the presence of systematic nominal wage and hours worked differences between regions. Where these are offsetting, regional-earnings comparisons understate the magnitude of amenity- and price-differential impacts of the cost of labor services in a region. With either offsetting or augmenting wage and hours-worked impacts on earnings, regional differences in the quantity of labor services demanded will not necessarily closely correspond to differences in the number of laborers employed. A need that remains is to incorporate this regional-labor-supply relation with regional labor demand to explain more fully the nature of regional population and production dispersion and its change.

Appendix 10A:
Utility Maximization

The problem facing an individual already located in a region given a labor-market wage, W, amenities, $\underline{A}$, and market-good prices, $\underline{p}$, is to maximize utility,

$$U(\underline{x}, t, \underline{A}) \qquad (10A.1)$$

subject to the full-income constraint,

$$I = Wt_w = \underline{p}'\underline{x} \qquad (10A.2)$$

The first-order conditions for utility maximization are

$$\underline{U}_i = \underline{\lambda} p_i \quad \text{and} \quad U_t = \lambda w \qquad (10A.3)$$

where the U_i is the vector of derivatives of $U(.)$ with respect to each element of x and where U_t is the partial derivative of $U(.)$ with respect to t. Subject to the conditions in equation 10A.3 and the budget constraint in equation 10A.2, the relationship between changes in conditions imposed on the individual, dp, dA, and dW, the resulting changes in market-good consumption, time spent in household production, and utility, $d\underline{X}$, dt, and dU, are given by

$$
\begin{bmatrix}
\{U_{ij}\} & \underline{U}_{it} & -\underline{p} & \underline{o} \\
\underline{U}'_{it} & U_{tt} & -w & 0 \\
-\underline{p}' & -w & 0 & 0 \\
-\underline{U}'_i & -U_t & 0 & 1
\end{bmatrix}
\begin{bmatrix}
d\underline{x} \\
dt \\
d \\
dU
\end{bmatrix}
=
\begin{bmatrix}
\{\lambda I\} & \underline{0} & \{U_{iA}\} \\
\underline{0}' & 0 & -U'_{tA} \\
\underline{x}' & -t_w & \underline{0}' \\
\underline{0}' & 0 & \underline{U}'_A
\end{bmatrix}
\begin{bmatrix}
dp \\
dW \\
dA
\end{bmatrix}
$$

$$(10A.4)$$

where $\{U_{ij}\}$ is the matrix of second-order partial derivatives of $U(\ )$ with respect to the i, j elements of $\underline{x}$, $\underline{U}_{it}$ is the vector of derivatives of $\underline{U}_i$ with respect to t, I is the identity matrix, $\{U_{iA}\}$ is the matrix of derivatives of $\underline{U}_i$ with respect to elements of $\underline{A}$, and $\underline{U}_{tA}$ is the vector of derivatives of U_t with respect to elements of $\underline{A}$.

The system in equation 10A.4 consists of a set of n (number of market goods) $+ 3$ equations in as many unknowns. Solution of the system results in expressions of $d\underline{x}$, dt, $d\lambda$, and dU as linear functions of dp, dW, and $d\underline{A}$. In elasticity form, this solution is written as

$$
\begin{bmatrix} \dot{x} \\ \dot{t} \\ \dot{\lambda} \\ \dot{U} \end{bmatrix} =
\begin{bmatrix}
\{\eta ij\} & \underline{\eta}_{iw} & \{\eta_{i\underline{A}}\} \\
\underline{\eta}'_{tp} & \eta_{tw} & \eta'_{t\underline{A}} \\
\underline{\eta}'_{\lambda p} & \eta_{\lambda w} & \underline{\eta}'_{\lambda\underline{A}} \\
\underline{\eta}'_{Up} & \eta_{Uw} & \eta'_{U\underline{A}}
\end{bmatrix}
\begin{bmatrix} \dot{p} \\ \dot{W} \\ \dot{A} \end{bmatrix}
\qquad (10A.5)
$$

where dots over variables represent percent change. Each η term is an often complicated function of the parameters in the matrices on the right- and left-hand sides of equation 10A.4. Effects on $\underline{x}$ and t of changes in elements in $\underline{p}$ or W, as captured by the appropriate η term, include substitution effects (between elements of $\underline{x}$ and t) as well as income effects. Decreases in $\underline{p}$ and increases in W or $\underline{A}$ lead to increases in utility, with elements of $\underline{\eta}_{Up}$ negative and elements of $\underline{\eta}_{U\underline{A}}$ and η_{UW} positive in sign.

For an individual determining the labor-supply wage as well as quantities of x and t for a given level of utility if located in the region, the problem is to find those values of $\underline{x}$, t, and W that result in utility, $\bar{U}$, in equation 10A.1 subject to the income constraint in equation 10A.2 for given levels of A and p. The first-order conditions in equation 10A.3 for attaining maximum utility still apply. Changes in $\underline{x}$, t, λ, and W are determined by solution of

$$
\begin{bmatrix}
\{U_{ij}\} & U_{it} & -\underline{p} & \underline{o} \\
\underline{U}'_{it} & U_{tt} & -w & -\lambda \\
-\underline{p}' & -w & o & t_w \\
-\underline{U}'_i & -U_t & o & o
\end{bmatrix}
\begin{bmatrix} d\underline{x} \\ dt \\ d\lambda \\ dW \end{bmatrix} =
\begin{bmatrix}
\{\lambda I\} & \underline{o} & \{U_{i\underline{A}}\} \\
\underline{o}' & o & -\underline{U}'_{t\underline{A}} \\
\underline{x}' & o & \underline{o}' \\
\underline{o}' & 1 & \underline{U}_A
\end{bmatrix}
\begin{bmatrix} d\underline{p} \\ d\hat{U} \\ d\underline{A} \end{bmatrix}
\qquad (10A.6)
$$

This differs from the system in equation 10A.4, as W is endogenous while $\bar{U}$ is exogenous, set by conditions in the rest of the economy. In elasticity form, the solution to equation 10A.6 is written as

$$
\begin{bmatrix} \dot{x} \\ \dot{t} \\ \dot{\lambda} \\ \dot{W} \end{bmatrix} =
\begin{bmatrix}
\{\eta^*_{ij}\} & \eta^*_{iu} & \{\eta^*_{i\underline{A}}\} \\
\underline{\eta}^{*'}_{t\,p} & \eta^*_{tu} & \underline{\eta}^{*'}_{t\,\underline{A}} \\
\underline{\eta}^{*}_{\lambda p} & \eta^*_{\lambda u} & \underline{\eta}^{*}_{\lambda\underline{A}} \\
\underline{\eta}^{*'}_{wf} & \eta^*_{wu} & \underline{\eta}^{*'}_{w\underline{A}}
\end{bmatrix}
\begin{bmatrix} \dot{p} \\ \dot{U} \\ \dot{A} \end{bmatrix}
\qquad (10A.7)
$$

The η^* terms in equation 10A.7 differ from the η terms in equation 10A.5 but are functions of the same underlying parameters. The effects of those changes in elements of $\underline{p}$ or $\underline{A}$ in equation 10A.5 that alter utility are not allowed in equation 10A.7. Rather, these effects are compensated by changes in W that are not considered in equation 10A.5. In particular, an η^* term is made up of the associated η term and wage-compensation term related to the η terms in the last row of the matrix on the right-hand side of equation 10A.5.

Notes

1. In principal, t is equal to total time T. In this situation some of the Z_i may be viewed as consumption services rendered at work. Amenities, for example, may serve to shift the "disutility" associated with labor-market participation and alter the incentives for allocation of time and market goods used in that activity. For current purposes, t is taken as time spent in household production only, with the time spent at work, $t_w = (T - t)$. This does not affect the analysis dramatically, because a change in t corresponds to a change in t_w equal in magnitude but opposite in direction. Changes in allocation of time between household-production and labor-market activities, induced, for example, by a change in amenities, would then be a result of offsetting or augmenting effects of household- and work-related Z_i impacts.

2. Nonlabor market income could be included in specification of the income constraint in equation 10.4 but begs the question of where it comes from. In a similar manner, saving could be introduced as an alternative to purchase of market goods and services in the time period under consideration, which begs the question of its purpose. Appropriate analysis of these issues would require an intertemporal model of consumption and labor-market activity in a multiregion setting, which is beyond the scope of the current effort. Such an analysis would have to allow for divergence of the region of labor supply and region of consumption opportunities. A prominent consideration would be the choice of locating in a high nominal wage (high cost-of-living, low-amenity) region, supplying labor there, saving some of it, and later on locating in a low cost-of-living area (possible low-nominal-wage area) where savings associated with the previous high-nominal-wage earnings increase consumption opportunities relative to what they would have been in the high cost-of-living region.

3. Lewis (1957) presents the classic treatment of the hourly wage-hours relationship. Both labor-service demand and supply characteristics are likely to play important roles in altering the relationship employed here.

4. This type of skill-level regional-location incentive relationship would mean that policy-induced wage restrictions on labor-market activity might lead to changes in regional wage differentials as the marginal worker's characteristics are affected. Such influences might alter the otherwise regional neutral effects on wage differentials associated with national minimum-wage legislation as presented in Krumm (1981).

5. Location-specific price indexes may be useful for analysis of market-good-price–induced portions of wage differentials, but not necessarily

appropriate for hour-worked differentials. Two regions may have the same price-index levels, but their composition may differ substantially. Time spent in household production may be more of a substitute or compliment with some market goods than others, with differences in the composition of the price index resulting in differences in hours worked.

6. These numbers correspond to the correlation matrix of residuals used in the second stage of the estimation of equation 10.21 as in Zellner.

7. All comparisons made in this section are based on estimates of equation 10.21 under the constraints that region/urban status effects are the same in each year. Estimates for variables not reported here were not sensitive to this restriction.

8. A permanent increase in the real wage need not lead to increased hours worked by individuals already working: the income effect of the higher real wage may outweigh the substitution effect. For real-wage gains not expected to be of long duration, however, an additional substitution effect toward work now and away from work when the real wage declines reinforces the previous substitution effect. The assumption made here is that these two substitution effects are dominant in relating potential real-regional-wage differentials to hours worked.

9. A similar inducement to increased labor-market activity associated with upturns in labor demand related to business cycles may also cause regional differences in hours worked not related to other wise persistent real-regional-wage differentials. The former type of influences will mask patterns of hours worked and regional-wage differentials associated with the latter phenomenon. These two effects may be disentangled, however, by joint analysis of migration patterns which would not be as likely under business-cycle-related, transitory, wage differentials compared to those that would persist in the absence of migration. Krumm (1982) finds both types of phenomena present in analysis of regional-wage differentials in the 1960s and 1970s.

References

Becker, G.S. "A Theory of the Allocation of Time." *Economic Journal* 75, no. 299 (September 1965).

De Tray, D. "Veteran Status as a Screening Device." *American Economic Review* 72, no. 1 (March 1982).

Getz, M., and Huang, Y. "Consumer Revealed Preference for Environmental Goods." *Review of Economics and Statistics* (1978).

Henderson, J.V. "Evaluating Consumer Amenities and Interregional Welfare Differences." *Journal of Urban Economics* 11 (1982).

Hoch, I. "Climates, Wages and Quality of Life." In *Public Economics and the Quality of Life* edited by L. Wingo and A. Evans. Baltimore: Johns Hopkins Press, 1977.

Izraeli, O. "Differentials in Nominal Wages and Prices Between Cities." *Urban Studies* 14 (1977).

Krumm, R.J. *The Impact of the Minimum Wage on Regional Labor Markets.* Washington: American Enterprise Institute, 1981.

    "Regional Wage Differentials, Fluctuations in Labor Demand and Migration." Forthcoming in the *International Regional Science Review*, 1982.

Lazaer, E. "Age, Experience, and Wage Growth." *American Economic Review* 66, no. 4 (September 1976).

Lewis, H.G. "Hours of Work and Hours of Leisure." *Proceedings of the Ninth Annual Meeting of the IRRA.* Madison, Wisconsin: industrial Relations Research Institute, 1957.

Mincer, J. *Schooling, Experience and Earnings.* New York: Columbia University Press for the National Bureau of Economic Research 1974.

Rosen, S. "Wage Based Indexes of Urban Quality of Life." In *Current Issues in Urban Economics*, edited by P. Mieszkowski and M. Straszheim. Baltimore: Johns Hopkins Press, 1979.

Roy, A.D. "Some Thoughts on the Distribution of Earnings." *Oxford Economic Papers* 3 (1951).

Tolley, G.S. "The Welfare Economics of City Bigness." *Journal of Urban Economics* 1 (1974).

Zellner, A. "An Efficient Method of Estimating Seemingly Unrelated Regressions and Tests for Aggregation Bias." *Journal of the American Statistical Association* 57 (1962).

About the Contributors

Richard J. Arnott is associate professor of economics at Queen's University in Kingston, Canada. He received his undergraduate training at Massachusetts Institute of Technology, and his graduate training at the University of Toronto and Yale University. His dominant research interest has been urban economic theory, especially local public finance, transportation, housing, and spatial economic theory, and he has published widely on these topics. He is currently on the editorial boards of the *Journal of Urban Economics, Regional Science and Urban Economics*, and the *Journal of Regional Science*, and is the regional and urban economics editor for the *Encyclopedia of Economics*.

Phoebus J. Dhrymes is professor of economics at Columbia University. He received the B.A. from the University of Texas in 1954, and the Ph.D. from Massachusetts Institute of Technology in 1961. His previous appointments include professorships at the University of Pennsylvania and University of California, Los Angles, and a visiting professorship at Stanford University. He has published articles in many of the leading journals and is author of several books.

Bryan Ellickson received the B.A. in physics from the University of Oregon and the Ph.D. in economics from Massachusetts Institute of Technology. A member of the economics department of the University of California, Los Angeles, since 1968, his research interests combine mathematical economics and urban economics with a particular focus on indivisible commodities. He is currently writing a book on general equilibrium theory which includes the application of models with a continuum of agents and infinite dimensional commodity spaces to urban-housing markets and public goods.

Robert F. Engle is professor of economics at the University of California, San Diego, a fellow of the Econometric Society, and associate editor of the *Journal of Regional Science*. He has published and lectured extensively in econometrics and in urban and regional economics.

Ronald J. Krumm received the Ph.D. from the University of Chicago, where he is now assistant professor of public policy.

Robert C. Marshall is a Ph.D. candidate in the economics department at the University of California, San Diego. His research is primarily in the areas of applied econometrics and housing.

239

Richard F. Muth is professor of economics at Stanford University. He received the A.B. from Washington University in 1949 and the Ph.D. from the University of Chicago in 1958. His previous professorship was at Washington University. His prolific research and publications include some of the earliest and most fundamental in urban economics, especially housing. He is author of *Cities and Housing*.

John M. Quigley is professor of economics and professor of public policy at the University of California, Berkeley; he is also an associate of Berkeley's Center for Real Estate and Urban Economics. He has authored numerous books and articles on urban housing and labor markets, transport, and local public finance, and has served as consultant to many federal agencies.

Jerome Rothenberg is professor of economics at Massachusetts Institute of Technology. He received the B.A. in 1945 and the Ph.D. in 1954 from Columbia University. He previously served as professor at Northwestern University and visiting Fellow at Oxford University. He has also taught at the University of Chicago and Amherst College. His main interests are housing, intrametropolitan location, and social-welfare measurement. He is the author of *The Measurement of Social Welfare*.

George S. Tolley is professor of economics at the University of Chicago. He received the B.A. from American University in 1947 and the Ph.D. from the University of Chicago in 1955. He is director of the Center for Urban Studies at the University of Chicago and has served as deputy assistant secretary and director of the Office of Tax Analysis of the U.S. Department of the Treasury. His publications are numerous.

Donald A. Wittman received the Ph.D. in economics from Berkeley in 1970. He taught political science at the University of Chicago and is currently a professor of economics at the University of California, Santa Cruz. He has published articles in the *American Economic Review, American Political Science Review, Journal of Economic Theory,* and *Journal of Legal Studies*. Recently his research has focused on the economic analysis of law and the problems of externalities.

About the Editor

Ronald E. Grieson is professor of economics at the University of California, Santa Cruz. He received the Ph.D. from the University of Rochester. Previously he was professor of economics at Massachusetts Institute of Technology and Columbia University, and visiting professor at Princeton University. His works appear in the *American Economic Review, National Tax Journal, Journal of Urban Economics, Journal of Public Economics*, and various other journals and collections of essays. His two previous books were *Urban Economics: Readings and Analysis* and *Public and Urban Economics*. He has lectured widely at universities and other institutions, and has been active in policymaking.